SEEING GHOSTS

SEEING GHOSTS

A Memoir

KAT CHOW

GRAND CENTRAL
PUBLISHING

New York Boston

Grand Central Publishing
Hachette Book Group
1290 Avenue of the Americas, New York, NY 10104
grandcentralpublishing.com
twitter.com/grandcentralpub

First Edition: August 2021

Grand Central Publishing is a division of Hachette Book Group, Inc. The Grand
Central Publishing name and logo is a trademark of Hachette Book Group, Inc.

The publisher is not responsible for websites (or their content) that are not owned
by the publisher.

The Hachette Speakers Bureau provides a wide range of authors for speaking
events. To find out more, go to www.hachettespeakersbureau.com or call (866)
376-6591.

All photos were provided courtesy of the author. Used with permission.

"The Exodus" and "A Bird in Chile, and Elsewhere" are from *Ghost Of* © 2018 by
Diana Khoi Nguyen. The poems appear with the permission of Omnidawn
Publishing. All rights reserved.

LCCN: 2021939238

ISBNs: 978-1-5387-1632-8 (hardcover), 978-1-5387-1630-4 (ebook)

Printed in the United States of America

LSC-C

Printing 1, 2021

For my mother, who guides everything that I do.

After, I feel a tingling in my body that does not yet register as catastrophe. A small leak has sprung, but still I feel buoyant enough, and continue to let life push me along like a bruised catamaran, pelted by rain.

—Anelise Chen, *So Many Olympic Exertions*

it's the greening of the trees
that really gets to me.... Patient, plodding, a green skin
growing over whatever winter did to us, a return
to the strange idea of continuous living despite
the mess of us, the hurt, the empty. Fine then,
I'll take it, the trees seem to say, a new slick leaf
unfurling like a fist to an open palm, I'll take it all.

—Ada Limón, "Instructions on Not Giving Up"

PART ONE

1.

Like many of the ghost stories I've grown up with, this one needs to start with a death.

So let me begin with this: The first time you faced a dead body, you were a little girl. You told me this when I was eight. I perched on your lap. We were at the kitchen table on a weekend afternoon with plates of mostly eaten cheung fun and bowls lined with the sticky residue of juk clustered in front of us. Caroline and Steph started to clear the table, chattering about whatever concerned high schoolers. Daddy retreated to the family room. I don't know how you settled on this topic.

As you spoke, I imagined you in a village somewhere in southern China. Gray, boxy buildings worn from decades of rain and sun; sheets of green and beige beneath the fog: rice paddies and farms, overgrown grass reaching toward the pale sky. I know now that this specific image from my childhood is wrong. I probably lifted it from a story Daddy told me about his childhood. Or maybe I saw it in a movie, some vague landscape with a pi-pa playing in the background. Kids, so impressionable, always picking up the most subtle things, like the way you slurped your soup or sighed when stressed. I swear to God or the gods or goddesses or whomever that eighty-five percent of my personality traits are yours that I saw and held on to as a kid, the remaining fifteen percent a result of the fallout of your death.

Now that I'm old enough to ask questions, I know that day when you found the dead body, you were likely living in Hong Kong.

In my vision of you, your hair was cut short but long enough for your older sister, my yi ma, to pull into pigtails before you went to school. I've pictured your child self this way ever since I saw a photo of you on a beach with Yi Ma and a cousin. The water is a gray slant that stretches behind you. You are maybe four, and Yi Ma clutches your hand as if to keep you still. There is something mischievous on your face, your gaze distant like you're lost in thought.

That day you saw the dead body, mist rose off of the grass and dew collected on your shoes.

You were all alone on the path to school, which you'd ventured down many times before. It was eerie in my imagination. You were on the precipice of danger, though I don't know if, in your reality, you felt threatened. The sun was higher than normal because you were late, and it reminded you to walk faster.

I passed by this bush, you told me, *and I saw this hand on the ground.*

I pictured, emerging from an overgrown hedge, a set of fingers attached to a forearm attached to an elbow attached to a real human.

There was a person, you said.

I can't recall whom you found, if they were old or young, if their eyes were open wide or shut tight, if there was blood or just gray skin. I wish that I remembered these details, if you shared them with me in the first place. I do recall, though, that you said you knew immediately that the person was dead.

You ran.

Your voice split into a scream as you pumped your legs and raced toward your school, the morning quiet around you.

When I think of this younger version of you, I see with dread what will surface in your life: the strains of immigration, motherhood, money, and then cancer.

But let me correct your memory now, Mommy. Or maybe, let me correct mine: That is not the first time you saw a dead body. The first time you saw a dead body, you were only four years old. It was your own mother.

You lived most of your life not knowing the woman who created you, and I wonder if that terrified you the way just the thought of it terrifies me. I don't even know what your mother looked like. When I try to conjure an image of her, I only see an absence.

X

There is a memory I summon to recall how you look: You stood nearly naked by your bedroom closet. Your underwear was giant and saggy around your ass and speckled with little holes. You rolled pantyhose over your calves, careful not to tear them with your fingernails, which you'd grown long and filed at the ends so they were round. Your stretch marks were little white veins that ran all over your body. You were not self-conscious. I understood as I looked at you that our bodies were similar, that I was an extension of you, that I came from you, that I could one day become like you.

I watched as you tugged the nylons up and up and up your legs and over your thighs and then your hips until they were taut. I'd witnessed this morning ritual as you readied yourself for work so many times from my seat on the floor, you towering above, a little shy of five feet. You leaned back and asked me to zip your dress or fasten a clasp, and eagerly I obliged, wanting any chance to help you.

Your hair was cropped and wavy. You always told us how unusual your hair was in a way that makes me uncertain today whether you liked being unique or resented it. *People like us don't have hair like this*, you said as your waves fell through your fingers. These days, when I see Sandra Oh on TV, this glamorous version of you with her glossy hair and rounded face, something in me seizes.

Careful, you said as I eased the zipper away from your skin so it wouldn't catch. I smelled a whiff of the strawberry shampoo and conditioner you bought from Walmart, knocking a half-dozen bottles into your cart whenever there was a sale.

I'm being careful, I promised. Your hair framed a large mole on your forehead.

I did not know the mole was uncommon, or that someone might think you were anything but beautiful. As I sat watching you by your closet, you looked at once radiant and exhausted. You were plump and a train track of scars from your many surgeries stretched down your stomach. I understood then that your body was not meant to be permanent.

I wonder now if you ever felt betrayed by it, if you ever raged that the form that was meant to protect you instead failed before you were ready to expire. Inside, a cyst ballooned your belly, though we wouldn't know that for some time. You collected excuses to explain away what was happening: You had irritable bowel syndrome, or maybe it was that you were getting older and this was what happened with age. Our family could not see it then, but you were dying.

X

When I was nine years old, you plucked a sunflower seed from a plastic bag and popped it into your mouth. You sat on the copper carpet of our family room, surrounded by a spread of newspapers. From my spot in front of the TV, I could hear you sucking on each shell for a few seconds, *thckthckthck*, the roof of your mouth smacking with salt and saliva. You positioned the seed between your teeth and split the shell, chewing before spitting the rest onto a grocery store flyer.

My eyes were glued to the TV, watching a rerun of *Dragon Ball Z*. But without looking, I knew exactly what teeth you used. You taught me a few years back.

Like this, you said. You made a big show of pulling your lips back so I could see your gums. You placed the seed at the back of your mouth so that each end met a molar.

And then you bite down, gently.

You bit down, gently. I followed your lead. I showed you my gums. I nudged the seed between my molars. I bit down, gently.

On this afternoon, you sorted through the newspapers that had multiplied over the past week and muttered under your breath about my father, your husband of two decades, who had left the mess there earlier.

He can't throw these out himself? Why's he need all this anyway?

You leaned over to scrape a handful of shells into the trash. We rarely had sunflower seeds in the house, especially not the salted kind. In Daddy's mind, salted snacks—nuts, seeds, chips, french fries—were part of a conspiracy to rob us of our money. *They add all the salt so it taste so good,* he'd say, *but also so that you get thirsty and have to buy sodas and spend more money on their product.*

You sat up slowly and fixed your gaze on me. You spread your lips wide into a grin and jutted out your top front teeth, like you were a curly-haired, round-faced Dracula. This was our family's special face, the one you slipped on suddenly and presented to me, Steph, and Caroline. You dug your top teeth into your bottom lip and widened your eyes, huge, until we mirrored your expression, all of us laughing until we approached tears. Sometimes you gave a long blink, which was your way of winking, since you had trouble closing only one eye. You made the face at random: standing by the boxes of Frosted Flakes in the cereal aisle, or when you walked into the house after a long day at work, or when you were in the driver's seat of your van and ferrying us to an appointment.

When I die, you said as you made that face, *I want you to get me stuffed so I can sit in your apartment and always watch you.* This was the first—and would be the only—time that you would address your death with me.

You raised your eyebrows. I was nine, and nowhere near having my own apartment. I still shared my bed with you. Each night, I fell asleep with my head nestled into your armpit with a leg thrown over your waist while you flew through one of the romance novels you borrowed from the library in bagfuls and called "kissing books," making smooching noises gleefully whenever you said those words. I always assumed you slept in my room because you loved me so much. I never considered any other reasons.

Now you bared your teeth like you were wild, like the stuffed grizzly bear we saw at the L.L.Bean store when we took a vacation to Maine earlier that year. I wailed immediately upon seeing the bear's face molded into a grimace, and I continued to howl each time we stumbled upon a fawn or moose or goat scattered throughout the store. The sight of their faces, locked in the same position for eternity, shot a prickly sensation into my feet. *It's OK*, you had said. You stepped closer to the bear, its body hulking over us, its paws the size of dinner plates.

OK? you asked. You reached across the couch to hold my hand.
Would you like that?
Would I like for you to be stuffed*?*
You studied me expectantly as though you wanted me to make the face. I snatched my hand back and let out a yip.

As a kid, I pictured future dead you sitting with future alive me in my apartment. I could not tell if I was peering into a dream or night-mare: It was a small rental, though inside it looked exactly like our family's kitchen. My entire apartment was just our kitchen. There was the red Formica counter that you and Daddy picked because you insisted a bright vermilion like that meant good fortune. Piles of newspapers coated nearly every surface. A bundle of jade plants sat in a corner, their rounded leaves hanging limp on the ceramic tile floor, which had been stained a tired, spotted beige. A ceiling fan whirred gently above, and a rhythmic clunk from the motor filled the room.

You hadn't aged one bit, though I'd grown into adulthood. You perched at my table, which was set fancy, a soup bowl stacked neatly on top of a dish that rested on top of a slightly larger plate, a collection of polished forks and spoons and chopsticks and knives lined up next to them. There was no soup. There was no food on the table. Just orange juice in each of the glasses, and plenty of it, with extra pulp. I sat next to you, and we gulped glass after glass. It was silent, except for the glugs down our throats. You were not rationing how much we drank or insisting that we add water to make it last longer, worried like Daddy that it was expensive. *Four dollars a gallon? Wah, gum gwai!*

In my imagination, I had not quite escaped our house, but I had some luxuries: a bounty of orange juice, and an inexplicable excess of plates and cutlery. Your arms were stiffly posed, and you loomed over a sheet of newspaper and scanned the morning's headlines. Never mind that you hardly had time to read the newspaper while you were alive. I only saw you clipping coupons or picking out the comics. Somebody had done an exceptional job preserving you.

Your taxidermic self would return to me after we took you off life support and Daddy ordered an autopsy. Yi Ma and Kau Fu, shell-shocked by your death and horrified by the gross disruption to your physical self, hissed that because of this, your spirit might never rest.

This image of you roaming and anxious stayed with me over the years, so much that sometimes I would discover you in your rigor mortis, softened slightly, appearing suddenly. There you were when I was sixteen, in one of the back seats of your minivan during my drives to school, supervising as I checked my blind spots before I switched lanes. There you were, trapped in the longest version of hide-and-seek, tucked behind one of the curtains in our living room with your feet protruding from the bottom of the drapes, ready to leap out, laughing hysterically and shouting, *You found me!* as I passed. (I found you, yes. I am always finding you.) There you were, standing next to one of the garbage cans with your face puckered in exasperation as I sat on the stoop of my apartment in Brooklyn, having locked myself out yet again.

Hello, I'd imagine myself saying each time, stifling a *Jesus Christ, Mommy* so you wouldn't think I was ungrateful and didn't want you around. My family and I still referred to you as Mommy, all these years later. I was unsure what type of reaction you expected. Your taxidermic self rarely talked, your presence itself seemingly a threat, like the monsters you invoked when my sisters and I were young.

If you don't finish all the rice in your bowl, you used to tell me, *the Ginger Ghost will come get you.* In your seat at the kitchen table, you jerked your arms and shoulders and widened your eyes to mimic the zombie-like hopping movements of a geung si, which you frequently told us tales about. Caroline had Boogaloodoo. Steph had Mooloogachu. I had Ginger Ghost, and Dracula, and the Monkey King. They all had the same purpose, which was to instill shame and fear, and punish us if we didn't listen. You were always assigning us new monsters to shape us into the daughters you wanted.

Whenever you appeared in my life in your taxidermic state, I frantically reached for conversation. *What doing? Lei sik jor fan mei ah?* I spat out, borrowing from the way you greeted Caroline or Steph as they sat in their college dorm rooms and you stood in our kitchen, leaning against the counter and wondering over the phone if they were eating enough. But I knew each time I saw you that I hadn't brought you here just to catch up. I summoned you to remind me of the unfulfilled promises our family had made over the years to appease your spirit and send you to the afterlife. Between you and me, I kind of liked having you around, even if memories of you appeared so vividly that I felt haunted. But then I'd shake my head and blink, and you'd have vanished.

2.

Today marks thirteen years since your death. All these years later, I still struggle to acknowledge this day. After leaving my office near Bryant Park, I find myself on Chrystie Street and locked into an autopilot that I cannot pinpoint, someone or something puppeteering my limbs through Chinatown. My legs have moved my body from my desk to the subway, and to here.

I'd spent the day sifting through audio to cobble together a radio script, and now, Steph's voice is calming on the phone—*when you walk into the temple's big room, there'll be these displays on each side of the entrance. Sort of like altars*—and I break into a run, worried that I only have fifteen minutes until the temple closes. *You'll see Mommy's picture up there near Gung Gung and her mother.* My legs weave around shoppers who have paused at the outdoor vegetable stands to inspect the daikon and bok choy. The Mahayana Temple is near the base of the Manhattan Bridge, and when I get there, the hum of traffic washes Steph's voice away.

I gotta go, I say to my oldest sister.

OK, she says. *I love you. I wish I was there. Maybe we can have a call later with Caroline?*

Yeah, I say. And then: *Love you too.*

In the intersection, drivers lay on their horns. The long honks bounce off the temple's brick façade, which is crowned with red Chinese lettering; off the Orientalist marquee made to look like a roofline in China; off the tourists who wander inside to gawk at the giant Buddha. I'd read earlier that until the mid-1990s, the building housed a movie theater that showed old kung fu flicks and pornos. I wonder if these tourists have any clue that the temple isn't so old.

In the lobby, across from what used to be the theater's ticket counter, a young couple gestures at a vessel stuffed with fistfuls of burning incense. They lift their children one by one to show them the ash. They take a photo.

I follow an elderly woman past a sign that says NO PHOTOS and into the cavernous hall. A towering Shakyamuni Buddha takes up nearly the entire back wall, seated where a movie screen once hung, surrounded by vases of mums and lilies and platters of pomelos. Behind the Buddha's head is a pale blue ring of neon light backed by illuminated flames.

Like a Vegas Buddha, I want to say out loud, immediately feeling guilty.

Across the room are the two memorials that Steph mentioned: walls lined with canary yellow prayer strips slotted into neat rows. On each paper is a thumbnail-sized photo of the deceased—now an ancestor—along with their name. In front of these images are carefully arranged offerings of oranges, paper cups of coffee with their lids bent back, and takeout containers filled with cheung fun and yau char kwai.

Studying the hundreds of faces, I realize that I might not remember what my gung gung and po po looked like. And what if I couldn't recognize my own mother? I might mistake their faces, reduced to tiny, pixelated images, for someone else. It is tight-lipped smile after tight-lipped smile, pallid expression after pallid expression.

I move to the other memorial, wondering which photo of my

mother's I might find here. I recall one that I have of her in my apartment. It was taken on my parents' wedding day, and they stand in a rose garden in Elizabeth Park in Hartford. My mother wears a long-sleeved satin cream dress with lace sewn along its bodice. She holds a bouquet of Damask roses. She and my father have matching boutonnieres pinned to their chests, their foreheads shiny, smiles plastered onto their faces like wax figures.

X

The last time anybody from my immediate family visited this temple was in 2004, shortly after my mother's death. My father, Stephanie, Caroline, and I drove from our home in Connecticut, and I sat in the back seat, dazed. We left our house at dawn and arrived two hours later in Chinatown as storekeepers rolled up their metal doors. My memory inside the temple is hazy, but I recall that we were joined by our mother's siblings and our cousins.

The lights were off in the main room. My sisters and I huddled together and clutched one another's hands. My father must have been sitting on his own. I could not see; there was too much smoke from the incense. The monks sang incantations, and their voices echoed in ways that made the space feel impossibly large. Lids heavy and overwhelmed, I let myself be lulled to sleep.

After the ceremony, my kau fu and yi ma handed the temple employees a photo of my mother to be included in one of the altars. *That way,* their thinking went, *someone would always pray for her.*

X

As I inspect a row, my worry spikes. I can see a scenario where the monks had removed my family's photos because we hadn't visited, and another where I couldn't recognize my own family's faces.

And then, there my mother is: toward the upper-left corner, not far from the top. Her photo is grainy. She looks directly at the camera, surprised, like she had been caught stirring up trouble. Her hair is short, her glasses reflecting with a sliver of light. Her photo is below her parents'. I recognize my po po and gung gung from the identical pictures that sat on top of the television in our kitchen, their expressions stern all throughout my childhood when I watched hours of *The Simpsons* instead of finishing homework. My mother had been here all along. From her spot on the wall, she had observed the temple's guests for nearly a decade and a half.

Unsure what to do, I bow three times. I sink to my knees on the stool in front of the memorial, and I face my mother.

For the first time all day, I feel I am in my own body.

This is the thing about grief: Despite how much we want to forget—how much we try to ignore—the dead are still here. Waiting, watching. I try to commit the exact location of my mother's photo to memory—one, two, three down, one, two, three, four over—when a temple employee flicks the lights on and off.

We're closed, he tells the tourists standing near the seated Buddha.

We're closed, he says to me.

I glance at my mother. I want to say *Bye*, or to wave, but all of that feels trite with the temple employee watching. My limbs tighten themselves again and my marionette legs return.

I shuffle outside, drawn to the sidewalk as I watch cars roll onto the Manhattan Bridge. From my vantage point, they might as well be floating into the sky. A pack of tourists and commuters carries me down the street, pulling me away from my mother as unceremoniously as I'd arrived.

3.

It is not incorrect to say that for years, the way my family grieved my mother was to avoid acknowledging her altogether. It is not incorrect to say that we hardly invoked her name or told stories about her.

Shortly after college, my father, Caroline, and Steph descended upon my cleared-out group house in Washington, D.C., for Thanksgiving. In my childhood home, my father's stacks of clutter multiplied until they overtook the space that my mother had so carefully cultivated; it crowded my sisters and me out. I reacted efficiently, diligently, which is to say that I pretended that these trips to Steph's apartment in Rhode Island or Caroline's in California were a chance to visit another part of the country.

We'd decided to exchange Christmas gifts a month early, since we wouldn't be together in December.

Caroline, dressed in a key-lime-green onesie, handed Steph and me sets that matched hers.

They're actually really comfortable, she said. She smiled toothily and pulled up the hood to show us the outfit's ears, her faded highlights a spray of lavender around her face.

The onesies were from the kids' section, which was fine for us since everyone in our family, including our father, was small and roughly the same size. Steph and I donned ours, and I was grateful for anything to distract from how cobbled together holidays had become since my mother's passing. My sisters and I stood on my front stoop to take a photo of us modeling our new outfits. In the photo, Caroline and I jam our hands into our pockets while Steph is wedged between us, her arms thrust into the air. We look so much like sisters, not just because in this image, we are dressed identically, but because the ways we hold our mouths enthusiastically, wryly, are the same.

Afterward, Steph passed out slender boxes.

I thought this might be good for everybody to open last, Steph said. There was a question in her voice, a preemptive apology that made me tense.

She had gifted us each a framed photo of our family. It showed all five of us, including my mother, in Seattle the summer before she died, and it was one of the last photos we'd taken together. We stand on a pier. The sky is muted and filled with the gray wash of color that comes from dragging paintbrush water across a canvas. It looks windy, and though it's the end of summer, we must be cold, because we're wearing long pants and sweatshirts. We huddle around my mother, who has her hands clasped in front of her stomach.

Oh, Caroline said as she pulled the wrapping paper off hers, her eyebrows shooting up her forehead as she examined the photo.

I shivered and said nothing. Our time with our mother was a past life—some version of ourselves from which we'd become estranged. When I replayed memories of her, it was as if hearing someone else recount stories of their own mother.

What's this? Our father asked, still working his fingers underneath the paper. He looked at my sisters and me, confused by our sudden shift in mood, not understanding this context. *Oh. A photo of our family?*

We held the wooden frames like they were made of blown glass. I studied my mother's face and sat in a glum silence, unsure what to say, fighting the urge to turn the photo away.

X

When I consider the ways images can wrench our grief to the surface, I think of Diana Khoi Nguyen's poems, which are wrapped around photos of her family in her collection *Ghost Of*. The book is dedicated to her siblings, including her brother who committed suicide. He is cut from every photo. Nguyen plays with these silhouettes. She cocoons him with her grief and her memories of him. She inhabits the negative space with her despair.

> *Why should we mourn?*
> Isn't this the history we want
> one in which we survive?

The first time I read her poems, I assumed that she sliced her brother out of the photos herself. I thought she didn't want outsiders to be privy to his body. No. Years ago, Nguyen told an interviewer that her brother, in a fit of anger, carved himself from all of the family photos hanging in a hallway of their childhood home. Afterward, he carefully slid the photos back into their frames.

"They foreshadowed his death, and after his death, the missing shards in the frames wounded me deeply," she said in an interview. "I avoided walking down that hall, I avoided returning to the house."

When I learned this, her grief crept into me. *I avoided walking down the hall, I avoided returning to the house.* Why head down a hall of memories if it leads to a perpetual reminder of death? I felt as though Nguyen, with her poetry, had inhabited the void that her brother had left behind, the way I now inhabit the one created by my mother.

For many years, I could not look at photos of my mother. I wrapped the one from Steph in a scarf and tucked it into my bedroom closet, underneath a box of clothes I no longer wore. The way I endured grief was to think only of the after, and not the before.

As a kid, I was certain that the images we had of our dead relatives were taken in caskets: a photographer pried open the deceased's eyes and held them there with double-sided tape. The cameras clicked, the dead person cartoonishly wide-eyed, mouth gaping. I couldn't conceive of the idea that these photos were taken in some version of the past, when the subject was alive. Looking at these ancestral photos gave me a whole-body chill, like I had come across a dead animal—one of our parakeets sprawled at the bottom of the cage, a fish floating at the top of its tank at the pet store—uncanny, a small fright pulsing, my body retracting.

Two years after her brother's passing, Nguyen decided to tackle with words the empty spaces that her brother left behind in those photos. She said that in her work, she was trying to mourn, not exorcise. When I first read this, I was startled by how much this resonated. I have never wanted to exorcise you. I am too attached; my inclination is to preserve you—to taxidermy you—like you wanted.

But, Mommy, grief is a container of contradictions. I want to expel *something*, though I do not know what. I want to rid myself of this heaviness, just as much as I want to keep your ghosts. Writing about you is a strange act itself. I am perhaps afraid of it, or at least, I dread it. Yet I feel compelled to write you into being. I am hopeful, though: I spin you out of myself and into something else.

4.

Before my mother was my mother, or before she went by Florence, she was Bo Mui. But before she was Bo Mui, she was a growing speck in her mother's uterus, and her survival was up for debate.

When my po po was months into her pregnancy with my mother, who would be her fourth child, a doctor told her that her uterus was riddled with cancer. She should abort the baby so that they could treat the cancer, the doctor told her. There was too much risk for the baby, and for her. My po po knew she was being given a choice of chance.

This was in 1955 in a village near Guangzhou.

Po Po and her husband's extended family were recently questioned by Communists. I use that word, *questioned*, because the family history is vague. As the lore goes, my gung gung's sister had zealously fallen in line with Mao Zedong's beliefs. She'd alerted the Red Guard about her family members, who were considered landowners and therefore hoarding their wealth. And so, the family was interrogated, and eventually one of Gung Gung's brothers was sent to a labor camp for a decade up north. The family was never the same afterward—especially not Po Po. This is how most of what happened to my family was explained to me over the years: in passive voice, these events falling from the sky, actions never committed by anybody, never involving motivations, revealing so many holes that I would need to fill, might not ever be able to fill.

I imagine that when the doctor told Po Po her diagnosis, her body became still, only her lips moving to repeat some resistance: *No, no, no, no, no.* The doctor told her the same facts again, emphasizing that her health was important and that she should live in order to take care of her other children.

How could I do that, she must have wondered, *and survive the guilt?*

After a couple of days, she finally agreed: The argument made sense to her. As painful as it was, it would all be for the better, she must have thought. She rubbed her belly, which grew larger with child and disease. She relayed this in tears to her other children, my yi ma, who was eleven, and my kau fu, who was three. They had an older brother, but he would later be disowned for reasons only vaguely mentioned and hurried along in conversation. It involved booze, gambling, abuse.

This baby, Po Po said, *has to leave us.*

The idea that a baby could be in their mother and then suddenly not perplexed her children, especially Yi Ma. And her mother was usually so tender and gentle, it was nearly impossible for Yi Ma to imagine getting rid of her child.

Don't do that to my sister, Yi Ma begged. *I'll help take care of her.*

Yi Ma pleaded her case for days. They had talked about this girl so much that she was already real. Still, Po Po tried drinking tonics she thought would terminate her pregnancy.

But when the tonics did not work, Po Po understood that she would have the baby. She took on a new resolve: They could try to attack the cancer after the delivery. And besides, chance was capricious. There was no certainty that treating the cancer now— or in a half year or so, after she gave birth—would make a difference.

X

Bo Mui was born after the Communists had taken over, as Gung Gung and Po Po quietly plotted their escape to Hong Kong. Spring in Guangzhou had begun, and verdant grass leapt from the ground and hyacinths fanned across fields. That Bo Mui translated to "precious plum flower" was no coincidence, I think, something optimistic woven into her name.

Before Bo Mui's birth, her life was a feat of survival, a gritty tooth-and-nail fight. It's nearly impossible for me to think about her birth without conjuring more of the poetry from Diana Khoi Nguyen:

> Still, every living body finds a routine
> no matter its damage.
> Two minutes after I was born
> > I had already made my first evacuation

An evacuation sounds right. My mother escaped both a womb and a disaster. I once discussed this poem with a good friend who recently had a baby. She told me she thought the line about evacuation referred to shit—since birth is often accompanied by a mess—that with it comes a vulnerability and a physical expulsion. I laughed upon hearing my friend's interpretation. There was something so grounding about an evacuation being paired with something as powerful as a birth.

My extended family often invokes reincarnation, both when a child is born and when someone has died. I like to imagine that over lifetimes, whenever my mother reenters the world, her body is all new and fresh, like a bloom of spring—just as her name implies. This renders my mother's comment about taxidermy so contradictory; taxidermy, after all, is about preservation.

X

As the Communist Party established its hold over China, Gung Gung took Kau Fu from Guangzhou to Hong Kong. They boarded a boat to Macau, and they continued on to Hong Kong from there. A little while later, Yi Ma and some cousins, followed by Bo Mui and Po Po, traveled the same route to the Sham Shui Po neighborhood in Hong Kong. They reunited there, making a home with extended family in a small apartment. They had split their family this way because they had heard from friends that it might make their escape easier. It was as if they believed the Communist Party wouldn't come for them if their family wasn't complete.

X

Three years later, the entire family had arrived in Hong Kong. My mother was four when Yi Ma pulled her aside one day.

Our mother is dead, Yi Ma told her little sister. Po Po's uterine cancer had returned. Yi Ma wondered if her mui mui understood. After all, for children, the idea of forever can feel like tomorrow, and tomorrow can feel like forever.

When somebody dies, Yi Ma explained, *they go on to the afterlife*. She told her sister that their mother loved them very much, and that *maybe, maybe* their mother would find her way back to them in another life.

There was always this: another chance, another realm.

As they said goodbye to Po Po, my mother clung to her father and siblings. They lit incense and prayed. The adults and Yi Ma stayed overnight at the funeral home to keep Po Po company until the morning, when they would send her to the afterlife. My mother and Kau Fu played together like it was a normal day. When dawn came, they traveled to the top of the Wo Hop Shek Public Cemetery to bury Po Po. Yi Ma, who was now a teenager, gathered my mother to her side and whispered into her ear.

I promised our mother that I would take care of you, Yi Ma said. *You're my daughter now.*

I wonder if, at four, you were old enough to experience the tinge of panic-guilt that so many people feel when someone they love dies. Did you hear growing up that, had you not been born, your mother's cancer might not have been as deadly? My gut says you must have; you were always sensitive, able to read people's emotions, folding them into your own. I have a feeling that Yi Ma tried to shield you from the knowledge of how your birth was intertwined with your mother's death. Perhaps this was not so difficult, since talking about the dead is bad luck.

X

Outside the apartment their extended family shared, Yi Ma spent her evenings after school putting off her homework so that she could corral her siblings. Their father ran a motel in Hong Kong that kept him away from the house from the early morning hours until late at night, and a relative stayed to watch over the children. Yi Ma sewed dolls for her sister and the neighborhood girls and shopped with her grandmother at the market for whatever they could afford, carrying back small bundles of vegetables. And when they returned,

Yi Ma set to work preparing dinner. She often made, as ordered by her father, a special dish for the boys in the family, something with a little bit of meat to nurture their growing bodies. I imagine that it was a thin soup with pork bone, the remaining meat boiled until tender with pieces of daikon and carrots floating toward the top. She spent hours simmering the soup she and Bo Mui and the other girls in the family were never allowed to eat.

At dinner one night, Bo Mui noticed the difference in the dishes laid out before her and her brothers. She had no meat in front of her. Only a small bowl that was mostly rice with some vegetables.

Why? she asked. Her voice had a hard edge. *Why can't I have this too?* Her father studied her as she began to wail, her cheeks red. He allowed her a few pieces of pork. She chewed with contentment, not understanding the weight of her victory.

X

For the remaining time they lived in Hong Kong, Yi Ma led her siblings up the hill at the cemetery to Po Po's grave. She tells me that she did this a couple times a year, for holidays. That she only mentions her siblings and herself in these stories conjures an image without adults, of these young children parenting themselves. They toddle between the tombstones, ducklings in search of their mother.

For Ching Ming, Yi Ma showed her sister and brothers how to observe the day and sweep the dirt from their mother's headstone until it gleamed. They ran their hands along their mother's name and dug their fingers into the crevices to scrape away dust.

On Chung Yeung, Yi Ma explained to her siblings, their mother's ghost, along with all the other spirits of the dead, were said to roam the earth in order to visit the living. They carried a whole boiled chicken, strips of uncut pork belly, apples, and oranges up the hill, and laid them on top of their mother's grave as an offering.

Yi Ma and her younger siblings bowed three times, clutching their burning joss sticks.

Take care of yourself, they said to their mother, aunts, uncles, and others who had passed. *Good luck. Take care of everyone else.* If they were hungry, they sat by their mother's grave and ate some of the offerings before hauling the rest home. Yi Ma and our family observed these holidays each year in Hong Kong, but once our family immigrates to the United States, we're too isolated, the cemeteries are too far, and it is easier to forget than to engage with this grief. We let these traditions fade.

My yi ma mentions that whenever they climbed the cemetery hills to their mother, Bo Mui's body contorted as though a spirit had entered her. She would retch, and then with an apologetic cry, vomit.

Yi Ma tries to explain my mother's reaction: This part of Wo Hop Shek was so tall—almost a mountain, in her recollection. Maybe there was a slight altitude change. Or maybe it was all of that physical exertion. Bo Mui was just a child. When I hear this story now, it's hard not to think that there was something about the cemetery that made her queasy. Like she sensed her mother's spirit around her, and she couldn't contain herself.

5.

When my mother finished high school in Hong Kong, she insisted to her father that she attend college in America. Yi Ma was already in the U.S., in a place called Bridgeport, Connecticut. Gung Gung had found her a husband, a man whose family had made the move from China to America some years before. The plan was that Yi Ma would sponsor the rest of the family to come to the U.S.: her father, her siblings, her cousins. To support this endeavor, Yi Ma's husband worked at his parents' restaurant, and eventually, she took a job in the stockroom of the JCPenney in the Trumbull mall.

Gung Gung relented to my mother's wish to apply to college. But where she went, however, was another argument.

You want to go to the University of Wisconsin? her father asked.

He wasn't familiar with the Midwest. He just knew that it was between a place called Connecticut, where Yi Ma lived, and another place called Vancouver, B.C., where Kau Fu had studied.

You can't be so far from either of them, Gung Gung told my mother. *Just go to a cheaper college near your sister.*

Gung Gung also insisted that my mother pursue a degree in the medical field. *It's more stable*, he said. *You'll have a better chance of getting a good job.* My mother knew that this was probably because her father once wanted to be a doctor. He was smart, disciplined, and worthy of becoming one, his family thought. But he finished high school in the 1930s, when the Kuomintang and the Communists were at war, and the Japanese military's invasion of China had made it more vulnerable. With the country and his family's resources depleted, a formal education—especially one to become a doctor—was no longer an option.

And so, because Gung Gung was paying the bill—and because he was her *father*—my mother listened. She enrolled at the University of Bridgeport, studied hematology, and lived with Yi Ma and her family.

Between classes and hanging out at the restaurant that Yi Ma's in-laws ran, my mother headed to study dates with classmates and let them take her to the movies. There were two boys from Hong Kong whom she liked. She was constantly flirting with them, teasing, always dressing carefully in an outfit—something patterned or floral that Yi Ma had made or brought home from JCPenney. The students were film producers and artistic types and, as Yi Ma put it to me, very handsome.

Gung Gung, who had by now moved to the States and lived with his children, didn't approve.

Don't even think about it, he told my mother. *They're going to go back to Hong Kong, and then where does that leave you?*

I imagine my mother spending time with them anyway. I wonder if, like her father, remaining in America was a given, if she understood it was now her future. Or, did she think, defiantly, about an alternate life where she grew old in Hong Kong?

X

My parents met at a tag sale in Manchester that a mutual friend organized. The friend was moving to California and needed to get rid of his belongings. The tag sale was not far from where my father had bought a house a couple of years earlier. He had a stable job that sponsored his green card, a healthy bank account, and, with home ownership, a commitment to stay in America. My mother rented a small apartment on Asylum Street in Hartford, close enough so that she could walk to the hospital where she worked as a medical technologist and drew blood. She was twenty-five. My father was thirty-one. Both spoke Cantonese, my father's Taishanese accent slipping through. Meeting another immigrant who spoke the same Chinese dialect was rare for a suburb like Manchester, where the demographics in the 1980s skewed mostly white. I imagine the tag sale: a small driveway filled with tables of lamps and records and linens and scratched, mismatched furniture. Bo Mui and Wing Shek both wore large eyeglasses that swallowed their faces. My mother's hair was loose and to her shoulders. My father was tan and wiry, all matter-of-fact smiles, a man who believed his future was great.

These days, when I press my father for details about how he met my mother, rephrasing the same question in a half-dozen different ways, he just repeats: *We were at a tag sale.* I wonder if he really has no other memories to share, or if it's too painful. He only shrugs, his way of saying *I don't know.*

But *what* happened?

I don't know.

Was it summer or spring or fall?

I don't know.

Morning, when the tag sale was just beginning, or late afternoon, when it was wrapping up?

I don't know.

How did you know it was love? Was it love, do you think?

I don't know.

Do you know what love is?

I don't know.

Did you imagine it would end like this?

I don't know.

✗

My mother knew how to make an impression, and this talent makes my father's inability to recall their introduction more stark.

Many years later, I still laugh and am amazed when I recall when my mother met Steven, the man whom Steph would later marry. My mother only referred to him as "Stephen King," a nickname that Caroline and I still occasionally invoke, long after her passing.

How long is a Chinaman? she said to Stephen King. I was in middle school, and Steph was nearing the end of college. My mother stood in the kitchen slicing vegetables. Out of nowhere, she broke into the gag, and then she fell silent, her lips curled and her teeth exposed.

How long is a Chinaman? she asked again, slowly, emphasizing each word. Stephen King scanned the room, unsure if this was a riddle; if she was making a joke about sex; if she was being a little racist. No doubt, he wondered if he should be offended since his parents were from China, and he was also a man. The punch line: The question is actually a statement. *Howe Long* is a Chinaman.

I stood next to my mother in the kitchen, and I smirked and chanted her question at Stephen King. *How long is a Chinaman! How long is a Chinaman! How! Long! Is! A! Chinaman!*

When I am new to D.C. and in my early twenties, one of my house-mates throws a party. I linger by the dining table and stack slices of cheddar and pepper jack onto crackers. A roommate's girlfriend pulls me aside to chat with one of her friends from college.

This is C.J., she says, gesturing to a guy in a button-up with his sleeves rolled up his arms. He has a generous smile and a calmness about him. He laughs easily, and in minutes I can tell he will not be one of those people who says, troubled, that they can't tell if I'm being serious when I crack deadpan jokes. We spend the rest of the night at the party, then a bar nearby, gently teasing each other, poking fun at ourselves, our bodies constantly touching.

✗　✗　✗

33

Months later, when C.J. and my father meet, there are no jokes, but I contain a laugh for much of the visit:

So where is your family from? my father will ask. I appreciate that this is not a question directed at me.

Minnesota, C.J. says.

Minnesota, my father repeats.

And then: *Lots of Scandinavians there.*

And then: *Is your family Scandinavian?*

When C.J. says his family has distant Swedish, Norwegian, and Irish roots, my father presses on: *Do you eat a lot of Scandinavian food?*

I have eaten Scandinavian food, yes. C.J. takes this in stride, trying to answer as truthfully as he can.

What food?

Oh, C.J. says, pausing, blushing. *Lutefisk. Dried fish.*

I let out a cackle, amused by this discomfort, perhaps not unlike how my mother would have regarded this.

I wonder what my mother would think of C.J., if she would have preferred for her youngest to be with someone whose family was Chinese. My guess is that she would have found him endearing; she would have appreciated his patience, his wryness, his ability to draw out my softer sides. She would have enjoyed seeing him squirm.

X

When my parents began dating, my father had recently finished graduate school at MIT and worked as an engineer at a large company in the area. He was ambitious and handsome and smart. And, by all accounts, he knew it.

I graduated from MIT, he said frequently and stood taller as he spoke. *It's one of the best universities in the world.*

My mother's cousins rolled their eyes each time he bragged. But my mother never seemed to notice.

The first time my mother's family met my father, they remarked that Taishanese people talked like peasants. I could imagine her relatives listening to him say a few words—not much, since he was shy and did not speak often in large groups—and then, they would throw a slew of jokes between them, a good-natured ribbing that would only make my father feel lonelier.

They frequently made comments like this—*We can barely under-stand your country accent!*—which I overheard rehashed in the car or at the dinner table. My father's laughter, which I would describe in my diary in high school as *sardonic*, rings out clearly in these passing memories. These jokes: Did my mother nod in agreement? Did my father flush deeper with humiliation?

X

I saw few moments of affection between my parents. Instead, I recall the two of them in our kitchen standing over me. They were bickering. Maybe laughing; some delirious hilarity caught between them. I usually couldn't tell the difference. My mother might have complained about how my father hadn't done anything around the house in weeks, how his mess was *everywhere*, how he couldn't keep a good job or earn money despite being so well educated, and how she was always coming home from work to have to cook and clean and take care of three children. He did what? He shouted back?

One of them lunged at the other.

Saat sei lei, my mother said, threatening my father's life. *Ngo sei lei.* They swerved around one another in the kitchen.

This didn't faze me. I wanted to believe that they were flirting and that this was what people who cared about each other said to one another. I told myself that their shouting meant they were emphatically in love.

Later, after Steph reads this, she corrects my Cantonese. *I don't know if she said, 'I'll starve you to death,'* she says. My Cantonese has always been poor; before I was born, my mother worried that speaking Chinese at home would interfere with my sisters' English, and so English became our default language. The three of us sisters would eventually try to improve our Cantonese, with varying degrees of success. *I think Mommy might have been saying 'Ngau sei lei,'* Steph says. *That she was going to bite Daddy to death. Like a joke. She would've thought that was funny.* Steph and I chuckle at this. Our mother and her edges. Razor teeth, humor.

X

When I ask some of my mother's relatives about the early days of my parents' relationship, they launch into something like this: *Your gung gung didn't like him. Every time he came to visit, he never talked. Just said 'hi' and then was quiet the whole time.*

When my relatives say the word *hi*, they draw their voices into a small bark, and they pin their arms to their sides so their bodies mimic my father's affectations. I wince. It's not lost on me that their movements are not so different from the Ginger Ghost that my mother conjured, wooden, inhuman.

She always say, 'When Katelin goes to college, I will live in the condo next to you,' Yi Ma tells me. She describes a fantasy my mother harbored, where she and her sister saw each other every day and she had no husband. I nod along, and a new memory surfaces for the first time in years. When I was a child, my mother mentioned often to me how she was going to divorce my father as soon as I finished high school. Each time, I froze, anxious and guilty that I now knew this secret and was conspiring against my father. Still, I wondered then what my mother's life could be like. The word *unburdened* comes to mind, now.

I bring this up to my father.

Did you ever hear of this? I describe my mother's fantasy of leaving him.

Mm, he says. *Yes.*

We sit in his living room in Wethersfield. This is the cleanest spot, now storage for my father's mail from years before, a broken chair, garden shears, a stereo set, and other discarded belongings he gathered from buildings in Hartford that he's owned for the past few decades.

When my mother was alive, this was the most elegant room in our home. My sisters and I jumped on top of the cream couches with black and maroon flowers embroidered into their cushions, and I tucked myself into a side table's cabinet when we played hide-and-seek. My mother had lined a shelf with rosewood carvings of the family's zodiac symbols—a rat for my father, a goat for my mother, a dog for Steph, a pig for Caroline, a horse for me. A baby grand piano stood in a corner. My mother had always wanted one, so she bought this on credit, the balance ballooning with interest. I recently found the receipts from the piano company; it took my mother three years and forty-eight payments to pay the piano's nearly $11,000 balance. At the time of this purchase, Lotus Garden, the restaurant that my parents had opened in the 1980s, was hurting, and my parents' bank accounts were tight. My mother asked her father for help. If he lent them money, my parents wouldn't have to file for bankruptcy. Gung Gung refused.

It's your husband's job to take care of you, he said to his daughter. *His family should provide for you.* And so, my mother turned to her credit cards. She used splurges like the piano to prove she could make it, *had* made it, by herself. She was so certain she had time to pay off her debts later.

Yes, you have heard this before, that she wanted to live in a condo near Yi Ma? I say to my father. His face is ruddy against the blush wall of the living room, his expression unmoving.

Of course, she always told me stuff like that. She says, when I die, she's going to go live with her sister.

Huh, I say.

Mm-hmm, he says. He is not wearing his hearing aid, which we had helped him buy a few years earlier. Caroline found an inexpensive one, since cochlear implants cost thousands. But he rarely wears it, seems embarrassed by it, says that it amplifies *all* sounds, and that when he speaks on the phone it produces a high-pitched noise that makes others complain. I can see my father, a practical man, assessing a situation and concluding there is no point in speaking, since he cannot hear.

His expression puckers.

He holds his mouth funny, jaw tight, invisible marbles stuffed in his cheeks. He also needs tooth implants, but his dental insurance, part of the Medicare Advantage program, won't cover the full cost of the procedure. As a result, he has spent the past two years seeking quotes from dentists in Flushing and Sunset Park who might be able to perform the surgery at a price he can afford on his own. Steph and I have spent weekends driving him around those Chinatowns, sitting in the car or in various waiting rooms while he goes to appointment after appointment. All of these dentists, as well as their patients, are Chinese, so my father hopes that maybe they can cut him a deal. But there's no such luck. When Steph brings him to a meeting one afternoon, our father is so flustered by everything—the potentially steep bills, the restless energy of the city, his aching mouth—that he opens his driver's door into oncoming traffic, the new dent on his car another costly fee.

These days, it is hard to imagine my father growing old with my mother. He is a man entrenched in his ways. As I sit before him, I see two alternate realities. In one, my mother is alive, and my parents have divorced. In the other, my mother is alive, and my parents are still together. In the latter, which is easier to summon, my mother would have taken care of my father at her own expense. He might have had better dental insurance, at least.

6.

Years after my mother's death, I find an old cache of birthday and holiday cards. They sit on top of a basket of my old Beanie Babies, which for some reason, have remained in a corner of my parents' bedroom. I'd forgotten that my parents had nicknames for one another—my mother was the general of the household and my father was the president. Much of their relationship was antagonistic flirtation. There was something between the two of them that *of course* must have worked.

In one card, the occasion unclear, my father wrote to my mother:

To the General:

Let me sleep in a little while longer.

Love,
The President

It hadn't occurred to me before seeing this card that English might be the language of their love, that their relationship functioned this way, that it never required any translation.

7.

When I was two, my mother started a new job at Travelers Insurance working out of its twenty-four-story tower. Over the past seven years, she'd shifted her career into programming, which began with night classes at the Hartford Graduate Center and learning to code. During the day, she worked at Saint Francis Hospital and analyzed patients' blood samples.

When the tower was first built in 1919, it was the seventh-tallest building in the world. My mother worked at different Travelers outposts around Connecticut, and I can imagine this: Her first time at headquarters, she cranes her neck to take in all 527 feet of stone and glass that reflects the city. She heads inside every weekday for the two years she's employed there as a database administrator, aware of how her path has been so different from her colleagues', many of them men, nearly all of them white.

Caroline will eventually have a similar job. *I wish I could have asked Mommy more about her work, but I only came to understand what it really was after she was gone,* she tells me. She wonders if maybe she's been trying to emulate our mother all along. *Mommy always talked about how she was one of the highest-ranked DBAs at work,* she says. I don't quite understand what that means, but I know that Caroline, who of us sisters speaks the least about our mother, is impressed.

✗   ✗   ✗

After my mother left Travelers to work at Aetna, another behemoth insurance company, a pair of peregrine falcons nested on the Travelers Tower and hatched three chicks. Biologists caught the chicklings and snapped bands on their legs and returned them to their parents. A reporter for *The Hartford Courant* wrote in June 1997 that these were the "first documented births of wild peregrines in Connecticut in about 50 years." Everybody was so impressed that after half a century, these endangered birds were fighting back.

There are baby birds up in the tower where I used to work, she told me one morning. *Falcons.* After breakfast, she and Steph and Caroline led me to an encyclopedia that we had on a shelf in the other room. I was in second grade. I slowly read the paragraphs out loud while Steph and Caroline filled in what I couldn't understand.

Peregrine falcons hunt other birds and animals, they summarized.

They can go as fast as two hundred miles per hour when they dive.

I pictured the falcons circling the Travelers Tower far above Hartford and hurtling themselves toward the ground as if in a self-sacrifice. Wings tucked so tight into their body like splinters while they picked up velocity, the embodiment of headfirst. The speed was heavy and shattering and powerful, and the image of a bird shooting through the sky this way left me breathless.

Not long after, my family explored a nearby town's fair, and we came across a couple giving a demonstration with their birds of prey. My mother prodded me and my sisters toward the birds. *Go look at them. Go learn something.* My family huddled around the falconers and listened to them explain what the birds ate (bats, pigeons, ducks, songbirds) and their wingspans (a large adult peregrine can have a wingspan of around forty-three inches). After, the falconers pulled heavy gloves over our fists that stretched up our arms. They coaxed the peregrine onto Caroline's, and a smaller bird—perhaps a prairie falcon—onto mine. Caroline is ecstatic, her eyes enormous and meeting the gaze of whoever's taken the picture. In my photo, I look so small, much younger than six. I am delighted, though I look shyly into the camera, as though I've been instructed—maybe by my mother—to stay still to keep the bird calm.

For months afterward, I talked about falcons as if they were made of magic. In my kid eyes, they could reach speeds of infinity; so strong and seemingly unbreakable, those feathered bullets in the sky.

I recently read that female peregrine falcons are larger than the males. This is not unusual for birds of prey. One theory posits that female peregrines evolved to be larger to fight off aggressive male falcons; they also often chose mates that were smaller and, therefore, safer. My first reaction was that they were settling; my second was that this was a matter of self-preservation.

As a child, I couldn't understand what an enormous feat the reappearance of peregrines at the Travelers Tower signified for environmentalists. As an adult, it's birds like that swooping between glass and steel that stays with me. It was humans and the use of pesticides that poisoned and nearly eradicated peregrines from the East Coast. It was humans who helped bring them back, building roosts on the skyscrapers. The falcons nesting among the tall buildings strikes me at first as unnatural, though perhaps this is a matter of adaptation and survival. The word I'm looking for is assimilation.

I wonder now if my mother's career change was in response to my father's—a realization that she would need to provide for our family. Was this the path that my mother had originally wanted to pursue years earlier when she had first arrived in the U.S., but felt she couldn't because of her father's wishes? Was it that she hadn't realized she'd wanted to study programming until then? Was she satisfied with this change? I suppose I am wondering what it means to be satisfied.

My father often talks of survival—*do whatever is necessary to succeed*—but where in this idea does satisfaction factor?

Mommy, I am asking about your happiness—and yet, I am only able to reach as far as "satisfied."

X

The first time my father tried to reinvent his career, it was to work at his restaurant.

I can picture my father before this, seated at a cubicle that would never have his name on it. He wore a pair of khakis from the juniors section and a button-up shirt that my mother ironed.

He cycled through different industries every handful of years, often taking short-term contracts that didn't come with health insurance. He was an engineer, restauranteur, programmer, financial consultant, and property manager.

Until my sisters reached elementary school, my father worked at companies that manufactured energy. At one of the firms, which produced steam power, he and some co-workers who were also from China were assigned a project that they found a more efficient way to complete. The manager learned that they had developed their own method.

Don't do this the Chinese way, the manager told them, though nobody had brought up China or that they were Chinese. *We're in America.*

My father ignored him. He continued on with the project how he saw fit.

What did you think of that, though? I ask him one evening on the phone. I had wondered, broadly, about the types of discrimination he had faced over the years. *At the time, did you find this to be racist?*

He speaks quickly, but evades the question.

Oh, there was just always little things like that, he says. *People always say things like that. You know.*

He launches into a story about you. At work—he forgets which job—your co-workers told raucous jokes. You were one of the few women on the team, and one of fewer immigrants. My father couldn't remember what those jokes were about, specifically, but it's easy to imagine. Your co-workers, most of them white, assumed you were laughing with them.

You better be careful, you know, you said. Your lips crimped. *I'm a double minority. A woman and a Chinese.*

Then, you added, your smile broadening: *Watch out, I could go to HR.*

They froze, uncertain if now they were the ones who had missed the joke.

When Daddy relays this story, he pronounces *mi-nor-i-ty* carefully, and laughs. Never mind that women aren't technically minorities in the U.S. But that you identified as such, tells me you likely dealt with many similar situations over the years. You defused your discomfort by swiveling it around.

I am surprised when he so easily supplies these anecdotes. Surprised again when he launches into another, about a neighbor who complained about my sisters swimming at a private pool club as guests instead of paying members. Surprised again that all these years later, he remembers the name of this neighbor and the name of the pool club. I cannot recall any times from my childhood where my family spoke openly about the little moments of denigration and racism that we gathered. Distance provides safety, and allows us to call these decades-old moments what they were. Now, the speed in which he recalls this makes me want to know what other stories he chooses not to share.

As my father worked his office jobs, he found himself thinking more about his own father.

I had always wondered, he tells me, *what it would be like to own a restaurant.*

×   ×   ×

My grandfather worked in seven restaurants in Havana, goes the story. He eventually became a partner at some of them. He was successful, and not only had he survived, but until his sudden death, he *thrived*.

I thought it would help me to better understand my father, my father explains to me. I had not expected him to so readily tell me about this quiet yearning he had for any knowledge about my grandfather. There was also the promise that if the restaurant did well, my father thought, he might be able to make a better living that surpassed whatever he could make as an engineer, a position which he slowly suspected had a limited trajectory for him. Money meant freedom, he always said. It meant working for himself and doing whatever he wanted.

As my father tells it, my mother had not wanted him to enter the restaurant business. He claims my gung gung seemed to think that people who worked in restaurants, or anything he considered blue collar, didn't have much of a career or, therefore, life.

In retrospect, my father moralizes, citing Yi Ma's late husband as an example. My yi jeung had worked at his family's restaurant, and as a custodian at a local school: *I always thought that was wrong, how [your yi ma's husband] helped bring the family over, and then your gung gung was looking down on him.* He keeps repeating the phrase *looking down*. His voice curdles the longer we sit in this memory. It makes me think that maybe they'd felt like outsiders together.

My father persisted and followed his curiosity; he continued ahead with plans to open his restaurant. He kept his day job—a way to capitulate to his father-in-law.

X

My mother, as my father tells it, befriended another couple also from Hong Kong. She had listened to my father's ruminations about opening a restaurant, and had struck up conversation with a woman who ran a takeout spot in town with her husband. The four of them bought a failing Chinese restaurant and renamed it Lotus Garden. The husband was a cook, but not a very good one, according to my father. The wife—my father couldn't remember what she did. He had a lot to say about the husband though: He did not seem to take much pride in his cooking and was not knowledgeable about Cantonese cuisine, which was what my father had hoped to serve. This partner was a *cook*, not a *chef*, my father kept saying, trying to emphasize his distinction between a tradesperson and an artist.

My father wanted to serve dishes like fried taro bird's nest with sliced ginger, bamboo shoots, straw mushrooms, scallops, shrimp, and squid inside, or stewed beef brisket with daikon. He wanted dim sum carts to roll through the dining room on weekends with har gau, siu mai, lo bak go, and cheung fun wrapped around yau char kwai. And for a short time, he found a chef from New York who could make dishes like that.

But, according to my father, very few chefs wanted to live so far from New York, where there was a large Cantonese population. As he put it: Talented chefs had options, which meant they wouldn't want to live in the middle of nowhere in Connecticut, where they'd be isolated in both community and familiar pleasures. It was hard to keep this chef, who was protective of his recipes and refused to share how he made various sauces with my father and the other owners.

And so, my parents did what they could, trying to hold their restaurant together.

I don't have any memories of Lotus Garden. I was a toddler when it shuttered. But for Steph and Caroline, it was their childhood playground.

In a photo from the late 1980s, perhaps a year or so before I am born, they pose for a camera at a table. My father is the only one sitting. My mother stands behind him, a hand on his shoulder. Steph leans in front of them, Caroline to the side.

My parents look tense, as though the photo itself has interrupted an argument.

She never wanted to help, our father says about my mother now. I can already feel him sliding into that place he goes when he remembers her. Face hard, agitation building.

No, I say. *She was busy. She already had a full-time job.*

She never wanted to come to the restaurant, he says again, like he doesn't hear me. *I always ask her and she says, Oh, I'm busy, I'm busy.*

Perhaps in the photo, my parents are discussing whether to file for bankruptcy. My mother looks irritated and as though she has begrudgingly called Steph and Caroline to the table, ordering them to smile. Nobody does except Steph, though her eyes are closed and her expression seems more like a grimace.

The photo is undated, but Caroline and Steph look around five and seven years old. Based on this timing, my mother might have recently given birth to her only son. Under the glare of the camera, the pale blue of her shirt blends into my father's button-up, turning them into a human Hydra.

8.

I had an especially brutal case of the flu that spread through my first grade class. On the night my fever came, I thrashed in bed and knotted the sheets, my body doused in sweat. I sobbed in that way sick kids do: snot all over my face, eyelashes soaked, dramatic hiccups. My eardrums pulsed with an infection. At five, I had no idea what was happening.

What if I die? I asked my mother.

She tried to soothe me back to sleep. I leaned into her chest. She wore her usual nightgown, an oversized T-shirt printed with Garfield's face, his mouth hanging open near a thick slice of lasagna. She broke from me to confront my father, who stood by the doorway.

Lo Gung, she hissed. The hall's fluorescent light flooded my bedroom. I cried louder. My father had insisted the day before that my parents didn't need to waste money or time bringing me to a doctor, since my body would take care of this flu on its own.

Do something. Your daughter is sick, my mother said. We were always his children whenever she demanded he have more urgency—or *any* urgency.

Do something, she said again. She hurried back to me.

I did not know this then, but my parents had recently filed for bankruptcy. Lotus Garden had shuttered. Properties that my father bought decades before were vacant, or he could not collect rent and was finding himself—and our family—deeper in debt. Credit card companies sent my mother stern letters canceling her accounts. She saved each one and stacked them on her desk as reminders. Though she had recently started a new job at Aetna, she was struggling to stretch her new salary to caulk our family's financial wounds.

My mother's eyebrows, plucked to near extinction, pinched together.

I turned to her and wrapped my arms around her neck.

I'm sorry I'm not better, I said. *I'm sorry I was born.*

I bawled.

Don't say that, she said. *Never say that. We worked so hard to have you.*

✕

About three years before my birth, my mother discovered she was pregnant with her third child. When the ultrasound revealed the baby would be a boy, she and my father were elated. My mother especially understood from her childhood that in Chinese families—hers, at least—baby boys were always beloved.

My mother settled on the name Jonathan, which Steph and Caroline picked. She thought that if her daughters chose their brother's name—if she spoke frequently about him—it would help the transition.

They'd have someone new to look after, she constantly reminded them. Caroline wouldn't be the baby anymore. She was a big girl and had a lot to teach her little brother. And Caroline, who was born in December, would share her birth month with him. He'd be the year of the dragon, which was particularly auspicious. My mother was always invoking our zodiac signs to confirm or disprove our behaviors, and she assured Steph and Caroline that dragons got along well with dogs and pigs.

I can imagine our mother driving Steph and Caroline to Lotus Garden to meet our father. He'd been there since five p.m., after his shift at a nearby power plant. He bused tables and checked the kitchen inventory.

In the car, our mother turned to her girls and told them the news: *You two have to be good girls, OK? We're going to have a little boy in the family now. You have to teach him to be as good as you, right?*

My sisters nodded.

OK, Gah Leen? She asked Caroline, who stared out the window.

OK, Mommy, Caroline said.

Wun Lee, is that OK with you? She tried to meet Steph's eyes in the rearview mirror.

Yes, Steph said back.

My sisters will not have a chance to be the older siblings to Jonathan that my mother had hoped. But the fact that my Chinese name, Gah Lee, is a mix of theirs, and that they chose my name, Katelin, tells me my mother must have prepared them for my arrival in a similar way. (It will be Caroline who—sometime in high school—comes up with my nickname, Kat, because she thinks it is hilarious when combined with our last name.)

X

In the middle of the night as the rest of the family slept, my mother's uterus began to cramp. It was only month seven of her pregnancy. She shook my father awake.

Lo Gung, she said. *It's happening.*
From here, my family's memories diverge.

When I speak to my father about that night, he can't recall much of what happened next, just that he brought her to Saint Francis Hospital, where they had originally planned for Jonathan's delivery. My father doesn't remember making arrangements for my sisters.

Caroline is sure that someone—a babysitter?—came in the middle of the night to watch over them.

Steph recalls that one of my father's relatives, a woman in her seventies, had lived with them for a few months. My parents' full-time jobs, plus their attempt to salvage Lotus Garden, left my sisters at home often with this aunt. My sisters mostly remember that this aunt usually lived with my father's family in Chicago and that she once insisted they eat their cereal with orange juice.

When my parents arrived at Saint Francis, they learned that my mother's doctor was vacationing in Florida. The resident physician was flustered. What should he do? Should he try to deliver the baby this early? It would have to be by Caesarean section. Should he wait? The resident insisted he reach the attending before making any decisions.

Nobody at the hospital had expected this.

After hours of prolonging my mother's delivery, the doctor and nurses pulled her into an operating room. Jonathan was born within minutes.

My father says that the pediatrician tasked with keeping Jonathan alive was excellent at his job. My mother had told my father this;

when she worked at Saint Francis as a medical technician, she'd heard of this doctor. But the doctor must have known that Jonathan, frail and in crisis from the start, would not survive.

Jonathan died at one thirty p.m. He was alive for only an hour and fifty-six minutes.

He's dead, my mother sobbed. She balled a pillow and heaved it across the room at a nurse. I know this detail because it is the only one I recall my mother telling me about Jonathan, and I never asked any questions. I was afraid to confront the possibility that had my brother not died, I wouldn't have been born—and that just talking to my mother about her son would trigger her regret and render me a mistake. How strange it is to think about my existence as a debt to my dead baby brother.

X

You said Jonathan was alive for a couple hours, I ask my father over the phone one afternoon. *Do you remember what Mommy did during those hours he was alive?*

He pauses.

She was in the bed in the hospital, he says finally. My mother held Jonathan for a little while, cooing and crying at the sight of his tiny form. And then: *The doctor just brought him to me to hold on to him because he knew he wasn't going to survive.*

How did the doctor know he wasn't going to survive?

Probably from experience.

Did the doctor tell you?

At first, I didn't want to hold it. My father ignores my question. *And the doctor said, 'Oh, that's OK. You can hold him.'*

His use of *it* is likely a vestige of Cantonese being his first language; it does not distinguish pronouns in the same way as English. Still, the way *it* turns my brother into something inanimate makes me flinch.

Why didn't you want to hold him?

Maybe my father thought that holding the son he knew would die would be too burdensome.

He was premature, my father says. *I wanted the doctor to take care of him. Probably, he handled a lot of premature babies and he knew the chance of survival was not that great. It was a long time ago, so I think right now the technology improved by a lot.*

He sounds wistful, like he's wondering what might have happened today. But it is hard, nearly impossible, for me to know definitively what my father thinks.

I ask him how he told Steph and Caroline about Jonathan's death. His response comes fast:

We just tell them, he says. *When it's dead, it's dead.*

I say nothing for a few beats.

Do you think about Jonathan a lot? I ask.

Well. Sometimes.

Really? What do you think?

If it's not going to be, it's not going to be, he says. *What can you do?*

But what do you think about him, when you do think about him?

My father is quiet for so long that I worry our call has disconnected, or that he's grown tired of this conversation and hung up.

Daddy? When you think about Jonathan, what do you think about? I shift in my seat. I am sitting at my desk in my apartment in D.C., watching out the window as elementary-aged children chase one another on a school playground across the street. My father is probably in the family room on the couch with his feet propped up on an ottoman, surrounded by the books and grocery store flyers he's meant to look through for months.

Just normal things, you know? But then since he didn't survive, there's nothing I can do.

But what's 'normal things'? Like what you'd do if he was alive?

You know, normal things. What baby boys will do.

Like what?

Probably, well, I didn't think so far ahead, he says. *Just the small things, when they're young.*

I ask him more questions—*What do you imagine your son to be like? What would you want to do with him now?*—but his answers shrink, the pauses in our conversation lengthening. I want to know if the way he would father a son would be different from how he has fathered me.

X

On the morning after Jonathan's birth and death, Steph and Caroline climbed out of bed and scurried downstairs to look for our parents. They were still gone, my sisters discovered. Our aunt tried to run them through their morning routine—sit down, eat breakfast, get washed, get dressed. But Steph and Caroline weren't interested. They were distracted and wanted to play.

That's when our aunt told them the news.

BB sai lo, she told my sisters.

Steph was stunned. She thought it was a cruel joke and punishment for her and Caroline misbehaving that morning. How could baby Jonathan be *dead*?

Hours later, our father brought my sisters to Saint Francis. They took one look at our mother, her body bandaged, and they knew our aunt had told the truth.

X

Steph and Caroline remember Jonathan's wake the most clearly. My father, at first, forgets that it happened at all. He insists he and my mother immediately had Jonathan's remains cremated, though that wouldn't happen for another fifteen years. In Steph's memory, *We hear the baby died, and then we bury him.*

At Jonathan's wake, my mother tried to drape herself over Jonathan's casket. She reached for his head. She tried to bring her nose to his. In Caroline's recollection, he was impossibly blue and gray. My mother wanted to trace the shape of his mouth and cheeks and his infinitely small self. But Yi Ma and a cousin pinned her hands to her sides and herded her from the casket. They did so gently; my mother's body was still tender and healing from the incisions. She yanked from their grip and grasped for her son, howling. Steph says that our family stood watch, unsure how to console my mother, whose grief had split her open.

Later that day, my family buried Jonathan at the Cedar Hill Cemetery in Hartford, about a ten-minute drive from our house. They chose a plot at the top of a hill. They inscribed his tombstone, a modest one that lay flat, including his middle name: Love.

X

I've asked my family many times why Jonathan died.

He just came too early seems to be the consensus.

But when I sift through some family records from my father, I discover a copy of Jonathan's death certificate. My brother's cause of death is listed as tracheal agenesis. It is a rare condition where the windpipe fails to develop. It often results in premature birth and, usually, death.

I am perplexed; this answer had been so easy to find, and yet it upends the story my family had always maintained about Jonathan's death. I'd assumed that a lack of proper medical attention killed my brother—the doctor on vacation in Florida, the inexperienced resident. I had never considered the possibility that from the start, Jonathan only had a slim chance of survival.

At the bottom of his death certificate, there is a stamped date from when my parents had requested this particular copy. January 10, 1991. Just a moment earlier, I had come across this same stamp and date on my own birth certificate. Only a few months after I was born—and a little more than two years after Jonathan's passing—my parents must have visited the health department and requested these records, celebrating one child's birth and honoring another's death.

My father recently told me that after Jonathan died, my gung gung warned my mother against trying to have another baby.

Two children is enough, he told his daughter. *Your body is not strong. Don't risk it.*

That my mother chose to have me—despite her aches and her father's wishes—seeds in me a worry that perhaps my birth weakened something within her; my body taking from hers. I want to tell myself that this is irrational. But my mother's own entry into this world, regarded with fearful apprehension, seems to be a family prognosis.

For years after Jonathan's death, my sisters and I accompanied our mother to Cedar Hill, stopping first at the large pond near the cemetery's entrance. I'm not sure where our father was; he's often absent from memories like these, and I can't tell if that's because he wasn't present, or if my mind has excised him.

My mother brought stale Wonder Bread, and she showed us how to tear the end slices into pieces and toss them into the water for the mallards and Canadian geese. She pointed out the drakes, with their bright, bold feathers, and the hens, with their trail of ducklings waddling after them.

Over the hill, not far from the pond, we stood by the stone with Jonathan's name. We bowed a few times, my sisters and I mirroring our mother. She mumbled at the grave and invoked her own mother.

Take care, OK? Your po po is also there. She'll look after you.

And then: *I love you. I love you so much.*

X

I've kept one childhood memory of my father at Cedar Hill. All five of us were there. It was Mother's Day, and after my sisters and I cooked breakfast—pancakes shaped like hearts—my family visited Jonathan's grave.

We were headed toward the cemetery's exit when my father pulled Mashed Potato—named because my mother thought the van, which was white with wood paneling, resembled potatoes and gravy—to the side of the road.

Lotus, my father exclaimed. He gestured at the pond, which was carpeted with magenta blossoms. He hopped from the van and fell to his knees at the lip of the water while he reached for the flowers.

His hands plunged and yanked out fistfuls of mud. We crowded around him.

Gah Lee, he said to me. *Run to the car. See if we have a hammer or a shovel. Something to dig.*

He thought he could harvest the roots. He'd use them for a soup with red dates, peanuts, pork bones, and thin slices of lotus tubers. He was already listing off all the possibilities, leaning farther into the water.

Lo Gung. My mother's voice was a warning.

I did as I was told and skipped back to the van. This was an adventure similar to when my family went camping and we tied fishing line around chicken bones to catch crabs, which we boiled on the camp stove and ate for dinner. I pulled a flathead screwdriver from the trunk and sprinted back to my family, pumping my arms and legs as hard as I could.

My father skewered the earth with the screwdriver, over and over. We stood near him so that if he slipped into the water, we could drag him back to us.

9.

When power cut during thunderstorms, you untangled yourself from my arms to play hide-and-seek in the darkened rooms of our house.

Come and find me, you said to my sisters and me during every storm. You raced from the room to hide.

Noooo. We wailed and reached for your legs.

Come and find me! you repeated. Your voice faded into the walls. We fumbled as we waded through the humidity that dampened the house.

We crept into the living room, where we suspected you waited, and rubbed our dirty toes into the short fringe of the carpet. We took in the profiles of the potted fern and jade plants illuminated by the gray light from the window. *Behind those would be a good hiding spot*, we whispered to one another. Thunder rattled the house, then lightning split the sky with a shock of yellow. We whimpered.

Where are you? we said to the plants.

We parted the fern fronds. There were only inky outlines of more leaves.

Where are you? we said again, our voices unsteady.

Then, a giggle rose from behind the couch. It flickered, your laughter striking an entire matchbook. You sprang from where you had crouched this entire time.

I'm here, you bellowed. We screamed and giggled while we scattered in search of our own hiding spots.

Come and find us, we yelled while we tucked ourselves behind doors and underneath beds.

I will, you shouted. *I'm coming to find you.*

In high school, after you are dead, I think of those hide-and-seek games as I walk past the living room and up the stairs. I imagine taxidermic you, stuffed and stitched and posed in a kneeling position behind the couch. I worry that if the light shifts, if I look too closely, I will see your face in the shadows.

Jesus Christ, Mommy.

10.

You were in bed, at Saint Francis Hospital in Hartford, where you once used to work and where each of your four children were born. Your body was inflated, like someone had pierced a hole in your arm and pumped helium into you. A slow swell. As though if it didn't stop, you'd burst.

Thinking of you this way might be disrespectful, I know. This makes you more balloon-like than a mother. But it was unnatural to see you attached to tubes and needles with fluids seeping into you.

I wanted to crawl into your bed and have you hold me like you always did, to return to when you slept in my room and I pretended to snore while you read your kissing books.

X

I was thirteen when my mother's hospital visits began this time around. I had just started my freshman year at a new high school in Glastonbury, about a twenty-minute drive from where we lived in Wethersfield. The school had an agriculture science program, and it was not far from where I had taken horseback riding lessons for the past five years, after begging my mother. I was fixated on horses, like many young girls; but unlike many young girls, I had worn my mother down enough to agree.

I liked that horses provided a place to direct my energy, and that they never demanded anything of me. They didn't mind that in groups or in new places, my throat often closed while I grasped for something to say. I preferred the interiority that horses allowed: I read novels from the library about girls who rode; I pored over textbooks about different breeds and memorized their characteristics. I was proud of each piece of trivia I collected: Icelandic horses had heavy, double-layer coats and were small, but technically not *ponies*. A pony is 14.2 hands or smaller. A hand is a measurement used on horses, and is about four inches. There is no such thing as a brown horse; horses that appear brown are bay.

For years, I rode an old horse with a bowed back. He was a cross between a Morgan and an Arabian, which was probably why his owner had named him Sheik. His coat was a deep bay, and he had a diamond on his head and massive ears that gave him the appearance of a donkey. He was not handsome, and this, along with his slow and stubborn nature, made him unappealing to other kids. But I loved him and trusted him. I was not a great rider, anyway, and though he was not flashy and was too frail to jump over large fences, I was too anxious to want to do that in the first place.

I spent hours cleaning his hooves and brushing his coat. With my fingers, I worked through the tangles in his mane and tail, conditioning them every few weeks. He was gentle, and because my mother worked out a deal with his owner, I rode him as many times a week as I wanted. He was, basically, mine. My mother brought him bags of apples that she picked from our backyard, stroking the velvet of his nose before she lifted the pieces of fruit to his mouth. He plucked the slices from her palms with his whiskered lips, tickling her into laughter. Perhaps my mother saw the way that this hobby drew me out of myself, but she could not always fight her resentment. I understood this was expensive, but at the time, I had no idea she had dipped into her retirement account to fund it.

When she drove us home from the barn, she fired her critiques. *You should be more outgoing,* she said, mentioning a friend who was my age and also rode at the barn. *She's so talkative, and she meets everybody so she can ride their horses for free. You should talk more. Be more like her.*

In the back seat, I couldn't form any words to respond, which irritated her more.

During other drives, she tried to channel her worries into plans for my future.

You can become an equine vet, she frequently said, already supplying what veterinary schools I could apply to after college. I can't figure out now if this was suggestion or edict, though the message that I was to make this obsession with horses *useful* was clear.

Sure, I told her. *That seems great.* I was in seventh grade and barely knew what this meant. I liked this idea because it pleased her; I liked that it was different than being a doctor, which was what Steph wanted, or business school, which was what Caroline wanted. The word *want* here is tricky, because all of our career paths were influenced by our mother.

When she heard from other parents at the barn that I could switch schools and attend Glastonbury's public high school for an agriculture magnet program, my mother was ecstatic. *It's free, too,* she told my father, her decision already made. Glastonbury was a wealthy town, she knew, and in her view, that must have meant better schools. We did not realize that the program and its counterparts were the town's way of bringing a racially diverse group of students to the school—who would also leave the zip code by the end of the day. We were positioned as outsiders, referred to as the "ag kids."

Still, this high school was much bigger than my own town's. Though there still weren't many Asian kids, it would be one of the first times where my friends and I could laugh, and I could freely say to my teachers—blithely and boldly—*That's not my name. You mean, the other Asian?*

One day in the fall of my freshman year, my father called me at the barn. Though I wasn't riding that day, I often took the bus there after school. I headed to the cul-de-sac as though I lived there, while my classmates scattered to their McMansions. Those bus rides meant that I could avoid the van that Wethersfield administrators chartered to take me across the river to and from school. It was a transportation service that also ferried elderly patients to their medical appointments. It had the company name—Ambassador Wheelchair Service—emblazoned on the sides, and its engine roared as it rolled down the street.

My father's call came an hour after school had ended. Someone in the barn hollered for me to pick up the phone.

Hello? Daddy? He never called me here.

Hi, he said. *It's Daddy.*

I know who it is.

His voice was stilted. I imagined him dialing the barn's number from his flip phone in the hospital parking lot, his clip-on sunglass lenses flicked up and casting shadows on his face. He wanted to keep the conversation short since we paid for calls by the minute, and because it was near the end of September, the allotted time in our phone plan was running out.

Your mommy doesn't have that much longer to live, he said.

What do you mean? I asked. I was suddenly aware of all of the barn's noises: the clop of hooves, saddle buckles jangling, and one of the riding instructors calling out orders in the arena. I hunched my shoulders. *How much longer does she have?*

The doctors say she only has a few more months to live. It's stage four cancer, he said. *It's terminal.*

Cancer. Terminal. I turned those words around in my mouth a few times after I hung up. I didn't know how many stages of cancer there were. Later, I instant messaged this to a friend. I still recall watching our chats appear on the screen, my hope bubbling along with them. Maybe there were five, six? Seven, eight? A thousand stages of cancer?

X

That past summer, my mother had been in and out of doctors' offices to determine the source of her stomach pain. A doctor suggested she had irritable bowel syndrome and walked her through avoiding flare-ups: eat stone fruits, consume more fiber, avoid stress. At that last suggestion, I imagine my mother rolling her eyes. The aches and bloat persisted.

A few months before her cancer diagnosis, our family took a trip to the Pacific Northwest to visit Caroline, who was finishing a summer internship in Seattle.

It was my first time on the West Coast, and I spent much of the visit chattering about the mountains that stretched in the distance. I liked how people there talked about them like celebrities. *The mountain came out today. Did you see her? Wasn't she gorgeous with that sunset?*

My family piled into our rental car and road-tripped to Mount Rainier—or Mount Tahoma or Tacoma, as it should be called. We stopped along its base, and my sisters and I posed for photos in front of patches of tall grass. Steph plucked lupine and thistle, which she tucked behind her ears. Caroline and I copied her.

Afterward, we traveled north to Vancouver, B.C.

There, on a sunny afternoon, we explored the city's Chinatown.

In the Classical Chinese Garden, my sisters and I sat on a bench and studied the glossy high-rises that sprung up around the park.

Though none of us noticed at the time, our mother was nowhere to be found. She appeared half an hour later on a sidewalk outside the garden, her face pale and her jacket tied around her waist. Her stomach had begun to gurgle while my family explored the neighborhood; it was unsettled the whole trip, but this time, the discomfort was *urgent*. As my mother rushed down the street looking for a toilet, she couldn't fight her own body.

I can't remember how I learned this. I recall only that afterward, my sisters and I pretended we didn't notice. We thought that was polite. *It's OK*, I tried to make my face convey. My mother must have sensed my concern. And for her part, she also said nothing.

X

In my apartment, I have on my desk that framed photo of our family that Steph gave as a present years ago. I keep picking it up and squinting at it, as if this will help me determine the state of my mother's cancer. Each of us is tan. Our foreheads are glossy, overexposed with flash or the sheen of grease, and the picture is not centered. *How much did her body hurt here?*

Right before my family had this picture taken, we had finished dinner at a tourist spot where we dug into a bucket's worth of steamed Dungeness crab, shrimp, and clams that we dumped onto butcher paper. My mother treated the family, exclaiming how seafood like this was special. I copied her and split the shells and sucked on the legs until I was sated, the Old Bay seasoning tingling my fingers and staining the corners of my mouth.

My parents had learned from a TV program that much of

the country's seafood—especially crab—came through Seattle. The whole trip, beneath his baseball cap and usual sunglasses, my father read out loud every sign he saw advertising crab legs.

King crab legs, forty-nine-ninety-nine per l-b, he said. *Dunj-iniss crab, twenty-five-dollars per l-b.* Except he pronounced *crabs* as *craps*, which made me, Steph, and Caroline giggle.

King craps! King craps! We repeated this in the back seat of the car. *Forty-nine-ninety-nine per l-b? Such expensive craps come from kings!* If he knew we were teasing him, he didn't react.

But if my mother is feeling unwell, she does not show it in the photo.

Our bodies are touching or are angled toward her.

Gweilo gum maan mo, she might have said, poking fun at the person we've asked to take the photo.

We all grin at this. My mother's is Cheshire Cat big.

X

One morning shortly after we returned from Seattle, my father and I sat in Yi Ma's condo as we watched my mother relay the symptoms she'd experienced in the past year to Yi Ma and Kau Fu: stomachaches, loose stool, constipation, lack of appetite, exhaustion. Her siblings had decided they'd bring her to Flushing to visit doctors who practiced traditional Chinese medicine.

I wish I'd spoken better Cantonese, because then I'd have been part of this conversation, understanding my mother's pain as she described it. Now I can only guess the words she used. Maybe it was 好劫, ho gui, which means very weary, exhausted. Or maybe it was 痛苦, tung fu, which I'd always thought meant painful but, depending on the way it's pronounced, can also mean sorrowful, sad, bitter, or poignant. I can only look these words up now, and it's simultaneously comforting, gutting.

I'm scared, my mother began to sob into her sister's shoulder. I looked away. I sensed a shift during this visit, and that my father and I couldn't give my mother the help that she required. Nothing we said—*You'll be OK, I love you*—could relieve her panic. This was a new, chaotic hurt that I tried to push away.

We're bringing you to see doctors, Yi Ma said.

We'll get through this. Kau Fu paced the apartment. *We'll see what's going on. But we need to do this fast. Time is of the essence.*

Kau Fu, with his frenetic forcefulness, was the patriarch and oversaw Gung Gung's money after he'd passed. Still, neither force nor money could solve my mother's illness, and it unsettled me to notice fear overtake a room of adults. I understood then that life would often slip beyond our control.

X   X   X

While I was at school the next morning, my mother and her siblings visited doctors in Flushing who practiced Chinese medicine. They felt her liver and told her it was swollen and hot.

You say you have irritable bowel syndrome? they asked. *This isn't it.*

One doctor suggested she head to an emergency room.

At this, I imagine my mother recoiling in denial, then fear. That would mean that whatever she had was serious.

You should listen to that doctor, her siblings insisted. *You should let us take you to an emergency room.*

My mother reached for any excuse to avoid a hospital visit, but she could not find one that her brother and sister could not knock down.

Later, at Yi Ma's condo, my aunt began to trim my mother's nails, which were usually long and carefully rounded. Though my mother left her fingernails unpainted, she inexplicably always kept her toe-nails coated in a deep burgundy or plum, one of the small vanities she allowed herself. But that evening, my mother's fingernails bent like squishy plastic and tore. As Yi Ma leaned closer to examine them, my mother began to cry.

This was when we knew something was wrong, Kau Fu later tells me. *It was unnatural how soft her fingernails were. They shouldn't have been that soft.*

The next morning, Yi Ma and Kau Fu brought my mother to the emergency room.

No more discussion about this, they said. *Just come.*

After waiting hours to be admitted to the hospital, my mother learned that despite working for years for one of the largest health insurance companies in the nation, her insurance was no good in this situation. No good because the hospital, according to my father, was in a different county and was out of network. My mother worried that a visit to the emergency room would easily swallow an entire month's paycheck or more. She couldn't afford that. She had to return home to Wethersfield to consult with my father about bills. Tuition was almost due for Steph and Caroline's schools. There was my horseback riding. The mortgage. The car payments. The credit card balances.

My mother and her siblings sat on the couch until late in the evening, their backs stiff as they solidified yet another plan. First, they had to determine what was wrong. Then, in the absence of effective insurance coverage, they would pool their resources to defeat this sickness. My yi ma would sell the building that she and her husband had bought decades earlier. My kau fu would dig into his savings account. They'd ask my father to put his properties in Hartford on the market. This wouldn't be lucrative, but anything would help; they were lucky to have assets in the first place. But whatever they did, they needed to act quickly.

Time is of the essence, Kau Fu kept saying. *Time is of the essence.*

He wrote his youngest sister a check for two thousand dollars. He knew it would not be enough to cover all of her medical bills, but it might help her take the necessary next steps. *You need to go to the hospital.*

X

Two years earlier, doctors sliced a nine-pound cyst from my mother's swollen stomach. The tumor was benign, and it made her look pregnant.

After her surgery, she was determined to resume her routines. One weeknight after dinner, she brought me to the barn. It was the middle of winter, and the temperature was somewhere in the teens. We were the only ones there.

She helped me saddle Sheik.

Do you want to ride him? I asked her. *We can just walk around the ring.*

Oh, no, that's OK. She was uncharacteristically hesitant.

Are you sure? I knew that she was curious about riding. She spent so many hours watching my lessons. Through osmosis, she gathered the basics: heels down, toes up, tuck your seat, shoulders straight, arms bent slightly, hands gentle, thumbs up.

Here, take my helmet. I strapped it under her chin so that it was snug. I led her to stand on the mounting block. From those stairs, she surveyed the dim arena around us as though she was taking in its dusty, cobwebbed expanse for the first time. I brought Sheik to her.

Put your left foot in the stirrup, I said. *And swing your right leg over the saddle.*

As my mother edged her toes into a stirrup, Sheik shifted his weight and sidestepped from the block.

I don't know, she said. She clutched the saddle's pommel.

You'll be OK, I said. *Just get on.*

I don't know, she said again. She backed away. She rubbed her belly, which was still healing from the recent surgery. *Maybe some other time.*

I was only eleven, but I understood then my mother's unspoken fear, and how she felt the need to hold her body together.

You sure? I said, hopeful. *He's so slow anyway, he won't go anywhere.* She looked at Sheik, and then me, and shook her head.

×　　×　　×

Later that night, as we did most evenings, we sat in front of the computer in a drafty room off my parents' bedroom and played a game called Horse Land. It was slow with our dial-up internet, but together, we cared for our own fictitious horses. We named them after ones from real life: Sheik, Peaches, Snipper, and Razz.

After I went to bed, my mother continued with Horse Land, casting aside her usual rounds of mahjong or solitaire. She sat in the dark, the screen illuminating her face as she dragged her cursor over different horses until she, too, knew everything about the dozens we owned, including how much to feed them and when they needed their stalls cleaned. And because they were pixelated creatures, she was unafraid of riding them. Here, the pains in her stomach had no effect. Money was no matter. Under my username, my mother entered competitions where she and our horses leapt over fences and won ribbons. She owned a bustling stable that had a surplus of funds, and she made me into an expert rider. I wonder now what plans she had for us in this game. If she looked at the roster of other players and saw this as a competition, or if there was a pleasure that she derived from cultivating this online life.

I grew bored and stopped playing before my mother died. I became more interested in instant messaging friends.

Whenever she asked if I wanted to check on our Horse Land stable, I shrugged, barely looking up from my chats.

Nah, I said, *you can go ahead and play later.*

All these years later, I visit Horse Land's site and find it defunct. There is no more game, no more pretend riders or stables or horses. Still, I like to think that the Sheik, Peaches, Snipper, and Razz of

Horse Land are alive and have long outlived their real-life counter-parts. Maybe, somehow, my mother has been there in front of a computer, clicking "feed" all along.

X

A few hours after my father called me at the barn to tell me of my mother's diagnosis, the two of us visited her at Saint Francis. My sisters had sprung into action that afternoon. Steph was driving back to Connecticut and had announced she was taking a leave of absence from medical school to help care for our mother. Caroline, at our mother's insistence, reluctantly agreed to stay in Pittsburgh to finish her last year of college.

I was also angling to take time off.

You just started high school, my mother said from her bed. *You can't just stop going.*

But I'd rather be here with you, I said. She ignored me.

What did you learn today?

I don't know, not much, I said. *I went to the barn, though.*

Oh, yeah?

Yeah. I didn't ride.

Her eyes were glassy, and it was difficult for me to look at her face. Instead, I stared at her hands, which were jaundiced. I thought that, maybe, she wished she could have come, that she hated being excluded from my routines; after all, ever since Steph and Caroline had left for college a few years before, she had directed all of her energy toward me.

I wanted to ask how she felt, to talk about her diagnosis, or to plead for her to live longer.

So, do you think I can get a horse? I said instead.

I didn't know what else to say. I'd always wanted a horse, and often asked for one. I thought that if I showed my mother that I was dedicated enough, eventually she would get me one of my own. I'd gone so far as to calculate her salary and subtract the amount I thought caring for a horse would require.

You have so much left over, I had said in past conversations. *We can definitely afford to get me a horse.* I didn't understand that when she told me how much she made, it wasn't because she wanted to brag. It was because when she first came to the U.S., sleeping on her sister's couch, the prospect of a steady salary that could push our family into the middle class seemed so distant.

Maybe we'll get you a horse later, she said in the hospital. She always said this whenever I asked. It was an easy script that we fell into, me with the request, her with the deflection. But now, I understood that it would never happen. I leaned closer to her. I gripped her hand, a hiccup of panic forming.

She doesn't have much longer to live, my father told me over the phone. I saw how unlike herself my mother seemed now.

"This isn't my mother," I later wrote in my journal. "This is someone else."

What's going to happen when you're gone? I blurted out.

I don't want to talk about that, she said slowly. *Not right now.*

She shrunk into her pillows.

X

I thought I'd have plenty of time to ease that question into a later conversation. I pictured you and me in the family room on the couch that we'd turned into your bed. It is the same place where you once jokingly requested that I have your body stuffed after you died. You slept here for a few weeks before your diagnosis when climbing the stairs became too exhausting.

In this scene, you talk softly, and I try to remember every word. I'm a sophomore in high school by now. You have held on for an additional year.

I'll get through it, you say.

Yes, you will, I say. We believe what we tell one another.

Even in my imagination, I can sense our worry hovering.

What happens if you're gone? I replace my previous *when* with *if* and I modulate my voice to sift out any concern.

Just in case, you say, *I want you to know that you will get through this.*

Here, you break into a speech. You say something affirming that I carry with me for decades.

All my Chow girls are so smart, you used to tell your daughters. So maybe, in this hypothetical address, you might begin: *You're going to grow up to be so strong and smart. You're going to be so successful. You're going to be so happy.*

I know that these are generic platitudes. But my brain can't assemble better words. I am scared that I do not know you enough to guess what you'd actually say.

X

When I ask Steph what she talked with our mother about in her last days, Steph says that in Saint Francis, our mother had started to hallucinate and had become paranoid. Steph shares this with me and Caroline over a series of texts: Our mother was frequently soiling herself. Steph stayed a night at the hospital with our mother and helped her to the bathroom. They stood by the sink, my mother clutching a railing as Steph sponged her legs, then ass. Humiliated that she could not control her bowels, our mother was certain that the nurses were whispering about her. She told Steph that she could hear the mother of Steph's boyfriend judging her, too. She was worried that she'd be replaced by Steph's future in-law. Our mother knew these thoughts were not rational, but she could not stop them.

I think that this was our last night alone together, when she could really share her thoughts with me, Steph tells Caroline and me about that night. *We both thought she would have more time...I think we spent much of the night not really talking.*

But Steph and our mother did have a conversation that, in my eyes, seemed *final*. One afternoon at Saint Francis, our mother asked to speak with Steph alone. She seemed more lucid in this moment. She told Steph that she wanted to be buried in the same cemetery in Fairfield as her father and brother-in-law.

Steph recalls feeling confused. That cemetery was an hour away from where we lived; the cemetery in Hartford where Jonathan was buried was only ten minutes from our house. It had rolling hills and resembled a park. The Fairfield cemetery was small and sandwiched between a busy road and a neighborhood. Whenever we visited the graves of Gung Gung or our uncle, we heard the shouts of children playing and the creak of swing sets or trampolines. None of this mattered to our mother. The Fairfield cemetery was just two blocks from Yi Ma's condo. Maybe our mother thought that Yi Ma was the most filial of us all, that she'd always pay respects to the dead—and with greater frequency than our father. Maybe she knew that Yi Ma would tend to her grave and continue to care for her in death.

There's something else, too, my mother said. She held Steph's hand and began to weep.

Our mother had always expected that she would be laid to rest with Jonathan. So if she was to be buried in Fairfield, she reasoned, we would need to have Jonathan's remains exhumed and cremated.

Can you bury his ashes with me? Our mother asked Steph. *I'll finally be able to look after my baby. A mother shouldn't have to be separated from her babies.*

Steph leaned close, uncertain why she was the one given this responsibility.

Yes, Steph said, *of course.*

11.

The dining tray was stacked over my mother's body with a plate of pot roast and steamed carrots, along with a slice of cake. *Seinfeld* was on TV and George was complaining to Jerry about something that my mother would have normally found hilarious.

She ate in silence and eyed the dishes, calculating what would stay in her stomach and what was too tiresome to chew. She cut a square of the roast. The *Seinfeld* laugh track rose. Outside her room, it was already dark and the Manhattan high-rises across the street glowed with office and apartment lights.

Kau Fu had pulled her from Saint Francis sometime the week before. During the short time she'd been at home, she remained beached on the couch and listless while her siblings and my father called Sloan Kettering, the Mayo Clinic, and other hospitals known for their cancer research centers. When they didn't return our calls, my uncle persuaded a cousin's wife—who had co-workers who knew people at NewYork-Presbyterian—to help us get my mother admitted there. When I was at school, Kau Fu and a cousin's wife hired an ambulance to drive my mother the two hours to New York. I came home that afternoon to find our place empty, though her soiled sheets were still tucked around the couch cushions.

Steph, my father, and I were in the hospital's lobby on our way home when I realized I'd left my coat behind.

Back in my mother's room, her movements were sluggish as she pushed carrots around her plate. Her skin, in the minutes we'd been separated, somehow had become duller. I'd caught her without her mask on; it was as if she had watched us leave her for the night, and she'd let her expression tumble into the grimace that had been there all along.

It was then that I understood what a terminal diagnosis meant. In journal entries, I wrote about this frightening new clarity: "All these doctors weren't just a figment of my imagination, all the visitors— people who came to see my sick mother—weren't made up, either." I had tried to pretend that none of this was real, but I knew I could no longer maintain that fantasy.

Hi, my mother said.

I forgot my jacket. I gestured to the coat. It was thick fake suede and it swallowed my shoulders, making me look younger than thirteen. It was a hand-me-down from my mother's cousin, Lai Yi Ma, who sometimes showed up to family gatherings with bags of her old Coach purses and leather boots that she distributed among the relatives.

On TV, Jerry opened the door to a harried Kramer. He was all slapstick force, all wiry arms that stretched everywhere and palms that hit the doorframe. With my eyes on the TV, I bent to kiss my mother's cheek. She smelled stale.

Can I have a bite of that cake? I pointed to the slice on her tray.

Sure, she said. *It's German chocolate cake.*

I slid a piece into my mouth. It was treacly sweet. I was mid-chew when I remembered.

They're waiting for me downstairs, I said. *Bye, Mommy.*

I took another bite and headed for the door.

I love you as high as the sky, she called after me, invoking the expression of affection she often told my sisters and me. I heard this from the hall and turned back into her room.

I love you as high as the sky and as deep as the ocean, I said, still chewing her cake, not at all aware that this would be our last conversation.

12.

I haven't wanted to kill you, so I haven't written about your passing. I can write around your death. I can write about the events that inch up to it, and the ones that illuminate its aftermath. But ask me to write about the day itself, and I can't. I can't. I can't. It's like killing you. I want to keep you, in memory, alive.

But since this is about losing you, I need to try.

X

If I want to summon the feel of my mother's death all these years later, I listen for the sigh of the ventilator. Specifically, the mechanical *whir-whir-whirr*ing it makes when her body gives way and allows the machine to breathe for her. At Saint Francis, she was more rubber and latex than human. At the New York hospital, we were past that. Now she was a robot having a panic attack. Her automated lung. A big sigh of breath into a paper bag, slowly deflating and then inflating.

I felt the warmth of my mother's knuckles.

She is here. I took this body heat to be a sign of life, and I later wrote about this moment in my journal. "We're going to be alright." But my mother's hands were warm only because I'd been holding them.

X

It's OK, it's OK, we told my mother in 2002 after the surgery to remove the cyst.

It was like I delivered a baby, she said when she came home from the hospital, unsure how to break the worried silence. She sat on the couch in the family room beside me and closed her eyes. A couple of years before, tired of looking at the stained pink couch, its blue and green flowers faded, she bought a sofa cover from Marshalls that was the color of pine needles. She spent hours at the kitchen table with her sewing machine, trying to make it fit. She couldn't get it right. The itchy fabric popped off the cushions too easily, and she constantly had to tuck the cloth back around the pillows. Now, as my mother let the couch hold her, she didn't care that the cover was askew, or that the room was cluttered with towers of newspapers.

Later I followed her into Caroline's bedroom, where she now slept. She called each of my sisters.

What doing? she asked them in a cheerful voice. It was jarring how sticking to her usual scripts—the shortened sentences, the same chirpy lilts in her voice—made this call seem normal.

I'm just taking it easy, she said after a few beats. She sat on the edge of the mattress and looked out the window at the neighbor's fence. She tried to pull a smile onto her face, but her lips caught on her teeth and formed a snarl.

Good, I heard Steph exclaim. The conversation moved on to what Steph had eaten that day. I watched my mother slump into her familiar rhythms.

It's OK, it's OK, my mother told Lai Yi Ma at a relative's wedding just a couple of months after her cyst was removed.

I didn't hear about this story until my mother was long dead, but as Lai Yi Ma told me, the two of them sat next to half-eaten plates of dessert. I imagined my mother staring at the bowls of sweet red bean soup with tapioca while the bride and groom swished their hips to Cantopop on the dance floor. She wasn't joining them because her stitches were still sensitive and she didn't want them to tear.

How are you? Lai Yi Ma said. She and my mother were similar ages, and of the cousins, they were the closest. My mother took a slice of orange and tore into it with her front teeth.

Insurance is so expensive, she told Lai Yi Ma, remarking how the doctors told her she should return for follow-up tests. My mother gnawed on another piece of orange.

Lai Yi Ma set her spoon on a plate.

Ah Mui. She covered my mother's hand with her own. *You need to go to the doctor.*

It's so much money, my mother said. *They want all these tests.*

Money doesn't matter, Lai Yi Ma said. *The only thing that matters is your health.*

X

Mommy, I know that I'm still drifting from your death—that writing about the illnesses that led up to your last moments is not the same. Let me try again.

At the hospital in New York, I pulled a chair up to your bed.

It's OK, it's OK, I said to you and our family.

Hi, Mommy, we're here, Steph said. *It's Stephanie and Katelin and Daddy.*

Caroline is catching a flight from Pittsburgh tonight, Steph offered. The machines beeped in response.

My father sat on the other side of the bed. His face was frozen as he searched his bank of memories for a solution or any indication of what had gone wrong.

He'd spent the past evening dozing in a chair, waking every now and then to tend to his wife. Steph's story about her night with our mother makes me realize that my father's last one with her had not been restful. We have never talked about this, but I realize now that it must have been nightmarish and soaked in a surreal worry.

That morning, my father had helped his wife with breakfast. She sat propped up by her pillows while he carved her waffles into squares. He dipped them in syrup and brought them to her mouth. His lips parted automatically, not unlike how he used to feed us daughters when we were little. That role reversal must not have been lost on her.

Suddenly, mid-chew, a piece of waffle caught in my mother's throat. She began to choke. Her eyes watered and the monitors screeched. She looked around the room and gasped.

My father, unsure what to do, repeated his nickname for his wife. *Ah Mo*, he shouted, *Ah Mo*. My mother's body spiraled into cardiac and respiratory arrest. By now, the nurses had rushed to her side. They ushered my father from the room and placed defibrillator paddles to her chest. They sent a violent charge through her that shook the bed. Then another. And another.

Her body rippled with energy. Though she was unconscious, her heart resumed beating.

It was midmorning when I understood the end had begun. I was a hundred miles away in a European history class. I pressed my face onto the desk, not bothering to pretend I was paying attention to the lecture. Something about World War II.

That morning, Caroline was in Pittsburgh, a couple of months into her senior year of college and learning about different programming languages. Steph was home in Wethersfield, washing the dishes and readying herself for her day. That's when Daddy called Steph to relay the news. Key words: *waffles, cardiac arrest, respiratory arrest.*

By the time Steph's message reached me at school, our mother's body had settled into its new rhythms. By the time Steph and I were in the van racing down I-95 toward Kau Fu's house, where we would then drive with him to the hospital in New York City, the entire family had been alerted. By the time we reached my mother, the chaos of the day had flat-lined, and we soon understood there was nothing to do but wait. We had so much time now.

X

Through the gaps in my mother's hospital gown, I saw where the defibrillator irons singed her. I wanted to touch where her flesh had burned, to will her to wake and to gather her in my arms the way she used to hold me.

For hours, we sat by her side. I worked my way through a copy of *Howl's Moving Castle* I'd found in the lobby. I was captivated by this world of wizards and scarecrows, tearing through the pages with the same speed my mother used when she read her kissing books. I wanted to know if the young girl would be able to save the wizard, curmudgeonly and cranky, from his curse, and if their love would free him. (I fear this novel does not, like many, age well. Howl strikes me as a bit of an ass, and a misogynist.) It was a world of hope and joy and magic. I wished I could cast a spell and use this power to cure my mother. I wished I could travel back in time to warn her about her sickness.

When I finished the book, I left its world and was thrust back into my grief.

It's OK, it's OK, I told myself as I realized where I had been all along.

Meanwhile, Steph journaled in the margins of a medical school textbook. Caroline had just arrived and settled into a chair while she held our mother's hands.

Occasionally, our father stood over his wife's face. He slid one of her eyelids back and peered at her pupils. When he returned to his seat, stroking her arm in apology, disappointment heaved itself onto his shoulders.

The TV hummed in the background and countered the dings of the machines. The sitcoms I watched at home were on: *Seinfeld*, *The Simpsons*, *Malcolm in the Middle*. My family angled ourselves so we could see the screen. In that moment, we were briefly returned to our kitchen table, our whole unit bent over our bowls, an occasional patter of laughter dotting our silence.

When I call Kau Fu a decade and a half later to ask questions about my mother, he mentions our attempt at distraction.

We were so mad, Kau Fu says. *It was so disrespectful how you guys were watching TV and smiling. It made me so mad I didn't want to come in the room and be with my sister.*

In his eyes, my family's laughter meant we didn't care if my mother died, that the fact that we turned on the TV above her unconscious body for our entertainment was sacrilege.

You let this keep you from being with your sister? Seinfeld kept you away? I want to ask my uncle, but I shut my mouth. All these years later, he still froths with resentment.

X

In the New York hospital, my family congregated in the reception area. We folded our limbs into chairs to sleep while another family prayed in a language I couldn't place. They clasped hands and rocked back and forth. Was this a family that regularly turned to their god or gods, or was it now that they were driven to do so? My family did not pray out loud. We begged in silence.

We had been in the hospital for a day and a half when the last of my mother's relatives had reached the hospital. The adults in the family had decided, per the doctor's recommendation, that we would take her off life support.

Time is no longer of the essence, I wanted to shout.

Time could fuck right off. Time could *wait*. There was no such thing as time anymore. There was just our panic, which were thick, humid days slapped against our chests. I wanted to hurl my copy of *Howl's Moving Castle* at the waiting room wall.

This is what's best, Caroline said at one point. *She would have wanted this done.*

Steph nodded.

I felt far away.

It wouldn't be fair if we didn't. Caroline's voice trailed off, as if she were trying to convince herself. *Not fair to her, not to anybody.*

Katelin, Kau Fu said, as our family filed out of the waiting room to the ICU. *You should stay here. You're too young.*

He pressed his hands to my shoulders to keep me in my seat.

No, I said. *No.* I shrugged off his grip and searched the room for my sisters, but they had already left with our father.

You shouldn't see this, my kau fu said. *You're too young.*

Please, I begged. I began to sob. *No, no, no.*

I tried to stand again. Hands, from a cousin's wife, locked me in place.

I want to be there, I said. I yowled and twisted in my chair. *I am old enough.*

Please. Please! I repeated as my uncle retreated to the ICU. I did not care that the other families stared.

Defeated, I fell silent.

When my family emerged, their faces ashen, my body bolted from the waiting room. It was the quietest I'd heard the ICU. My legs propelled me past the nurses and into my mother's room. It was empty. I turned and looked down the hall behind me.

There my mother was, already strapped to a gurney. Her body was draped with plastic. The nurses had stuffed her mouth with gauze, which had turned the color of rust from the blood that rose from her throat when the intubation tubes were removed. She was alone.

✕

Your body was limp and blue, and the sight has been locked into my memory. Here you were. Here I was. Here we were. I reached for you through the plastic. I don't want this to be how I said goodbye. Years later, when I think back on this specific memory, it is the silence that emerges fastest. My anger and alarm have been strained and sifted, carefully remade into something more containable. But the absence of sound wrenches me back. As if I'm watching a home video and suddenly, when I come across you, limp, the audio cuts. This rattles me each time, but it allows me to see you in clear focus.

X

After we took my mother off the ventilator, my father ordered an autopsy. I still don't understand why, exactly, despite asking him. Autopsies aren't standard. They're usually reserved for deaths considered unnatural or suspicious. I can picture, though, this scenario: When the doctor declared my mother dead, she asked my father routine questions. The two of them were alone and my mother's family gathered elsewhere, inconsolable and already shouldering my father out.

He was the one who had to steer our family now. There was no alternative; he was the father, we were the daughters, and what he said must go. The doctor asked whether or not our family wanted the hospital to perform an autopsy. She expected my father to say no.

Yes, he said. More is better, he always believed. The death of his wife was no different. If there was an opportunity to learn more, and it was free? *Sure. Why not?* Though just seconds before he had no opinion, he was adamant now. He wanted from his wife's death all the answers he could not receive in life.

This, I would write in my diary in the coming weeks, made my mother's siblings more furious.

How could you do that? they asked my father. *Her spirit will never be able to rest.*

X

Hours later, Kau Fu stood at the end of his driveway with my sisters and me while our father waited in the car. It was after midnight.

Nothing will change, your brother said. He drew me into an embrace and shoved my head into his armpit.

Nothing has changed, OK? he said to your daughters.

OK, Steph said.

OK, Caroline said.

OK, I said.

13.

For my mother's funeral, we followed the template that she and her siblings created when her father and Yi Ma's husband died. We bought a casket similar to the one that she said that she liked. It was glossy and made of cherry wood. It reminded me of the car she'd pined for but never could afford: a Cadillac the color of hot cinnamon candies that had a boxy butt and a square face. She constantly referred to car grilles as their mouths and taillights as their butts, categorizing their expressions as she saw them: *That Honda has such a happy face*, or: *That van has such narrow eyes, like it's suspicious.* But she liked the Cadillac's perky expression. She thought it suited her, the way she always wore a hint of a smile.

One day you'll get a Cadillac, Caroline, Steph, and I assured her.

A red Cadillac, our mother said.

Yes, a red one, we promised. *Your favorite color.*

For good luck, and prosperity, too, she said. *Maybe one day my daughters will be so successful they can buy it for me.*

Yes, sure, of course. We were also hopeful.

Six days after she died, we stood in the funeral home's parking lot around a metal bucket. We burned joss paper and fake money. This was one of the few grief rituals that my sisters and I knew how to do on our own. Each Lunar New Year, our mother led us in cutting objects out of tissue paper that we would burn to send to Jonathan in the afterlife: tiny shirts, a car, shoes. One year, I cut him a tissue horse, with a saddle and boots. We watched this incinerate and lingered near the bucket until the paper was ash and we were certain our gifts had made it through this postal service for the dead.

Inside, Steph, Caroline, and I approached her casket and laid three pieces of cloth that we'd bought at Jo-Ann Fabrics over her body, so that she'd be warm as her spirit moved to the afterlife.

Our mother's face was caked with a foundation that was a couple of shades too light, which made her mannequin-like and somehow sicklier. She wore a gray L.L.Bean dress that had a collared neck and was made from cotton. My sisters and I chose this outfit because we thought it was our mother's favorite, and she had frequently remarked that it was so comfortable. We wanted her to rest easy in death.

But the dress was short-sleeved and didn't cover her arms, which looked unnaturally orange and plastic.

Yi Ma approached Steph.

You dressed her in that? Yi Ma asked. *It looks so cheap.*

She quivered and her normal softness was gone. She was already a frail woman, but after her sister's death, she was unable to sleep or eat.

When Steph relayed this to me and Caroline, we weren't sure if we should hug our yi ma or recoil in shame, so we did both.

I wore the flower that my father's sister-in-law had crocheted out of indigo yarn. One evening not long after our mother's death, our baak leung appeared on our doorstep. She and her son had driven hours from Toronto, and our father had forgotten to mention this to us. He needed someone from *his* family to help plan the funeral and my sisters and I needed a maternal figure, our baak leung insisted. She had spent the past few days propelling our family through funeral preparations, admonishing us when we weren't sure how to proceed.

As my sisters and I greeted other mourners at the funeral, Baak Leung peered into the open casket.

It looks like she still might have some life in her, Baak Leung told Steph. She pointed to the blush on our mother's cheeks. *She might still be alive.*

Watching this, I wanted to scream.

No, Steph said. She drew herself back.

Dead, Steph said. Her voice sharpened. *Sei.*

Alarmed by Steph's tone, Baak Leung turned again to search our mother's face for signs of life.

Did you just hear that? Steph said after she excused herself. *She tried to tell me that Mommy was still alive.*

Huh? Caroline said. *She actually thinks that?*

That's really fucked up, I said. This aunt, with her gray, frizzed hair matted around her head like a helmet, looked more corpse-like than our mother.

My sisters looked at me sharply. I shrugged and suppressed a laugh.

What if Baak Leung was right? What if you weren't dead, and you suddenly sprang from your casket? These days, when I think about your funeral, I conjure this, you standing before us:

You guys were trying to bury me alive? you say. Having thrown everyone into sudden chaos, you break into a seismic, full-body laugh. Then, you look down at the polo dress.

What the hell is this? You demand. *When I really do die, put me in something that's not so cheap, OK?*

You blink your eyes a few times, your movements hard and theatrical.

X

During the funeral service, Steph, Caroline, and I stood beside our mother's open casket and shared a few stories. I mentioned how, after nights at the barn, my mother and I stopped at the Burger King drive-thru on the Silas Deane Highway for an order of extra-large fries. She let me sit in the front seat. We passed the bag of hot fries between us and licked the salt from our fingers. We rubbed the grease on our jeans and finished long before we pulled into our driveway. I liked this small luxury; it was a secret we kept from Daddy and everyone else. It was our ritual, and I was often more eager about the fries than the barn visit itself.

After, we trickled out of the funeral home and Steph turned to me.

Why do you have to always talk about food? Steph asked. *Why couldn't you have talked about something nicer, told a nicer story?*

I dunno, I said, confused by her irritation. We each took a tiny packet containing a Werther's hard caramel and a nickel. *I thought that was nice.*

I slipped the candy into my coat pocket for later. The day before the funeral, my sisters and I spent hours wrapping the gold candy and coins in strips of white printer paper. My mother had taught me how to neatly fold the packets when we were preparing for Gung Gung's funeral. She ran a fingernail over a fold to sharpen a crease. Guests were to take one of these envelopes after the wake, she had explained, and on their way home, they'd spend the nickel and eat the candy to pass along good fortune and to sweeten the bitterness of death. When she told me this, she popped a Werther's into her mouth, smiling to show me that it was OK. I did the same, savoring the taste of buttery sugar, confused how anything could soften death.

x   x   x

It rained as we buried our mother a row and a few plots away from Gung Gung and Yi Ma's husband. We opened our umbrellas, but the storm drenched us anyway. I wanted to wave my arms and yell at the sky, to scold it for its absurdity. *You couldn't have waited an hour?* Instead, my family and I turned our backs and listened to the groundskeeper crank my mother's casket into the earth. Chains clanking, gears groaning, rain thrumming—sounds that will forever evoke the memory of you leaving.

X

A few days after we buried our mother, we returned to the funeral home to retrieve the items we had left. The miniature white packets. Photographs of her from years before. Extra memorial cards.

At home, we set the box of Werther's and nickels on the dining table. Over the next few months, I unwrapped them. I dropped the coins into a jar of change you started years ago to save for the trip we never took. Each time I ate one of these caramels, I mumbled an apology, trying not to think too hard about how, exactly, this might disrupt your spirit.

PART TWO

1.

In the weeks after our mother's funeral, well-meaning neighbors and friends brimmed with platitudes. They lingered on our front steps with their cars still running in the cul-de-sac. They carried casseroles in platters that I'd forget to return and that would remind me of my family's grief each time I used them.

One woman arrived around dusk. Evenings grew gloomier each day and the light receded earlier the further we were marched into fall. She was the mother of one of Steph's high school classmates. She had expensively highlighted hair and pale skin, and she clutched a cerulean prayer blanket that her church group had knit for us.

You are all so young, she kept saying, as if we needed reminding. *Your mother was so young.*

Steph and Caroline leaned on either side of the doorframe and listened to the woman. All through the weekend, we scrubbed the house and tossed moldy food from the fridge. We exterminated anything grimy or dying or dead with a vigor that first stunned and then soothed us. It seemed our father was constantly out of the house or tucked in the office off his bedroom. I had no idea what he was doing, and I didn't ask.

She's watching over you, now, the woman with the blanket said. *She wouldn't want you to be sad. She'd want you to be happy.*

My sisters offered the woman bland compliments while they fanned out the blanket's folds.

So soft, Steph said, always dutifully polite.

This will be...useful, Caroline said, never one for insincere or saccharine niceties.

I hung back in the hall. This visitor was the type of woman our mother would have poked fun at as soon as she left. When Steph was in middle school, she invited this woman's daughter to our house for her birthday. My parents bought Roy Rogers, Steph's favorite. We watched in dismay as Steph's friend slid the fried skin from the chicken and discarded it before eating.

Aiiiiiiy. She's the mother of that girl who didn't eat the skin? our mother would have said, personally offended. *Who teaches their kids that? What's the point of fried chicken if you don't eat the skin?* Then she'd launch into a poor imitation of how the woman drew out her words. *She thinks we're cold or something? That we need that tiny blanket? Chi seen.* My mother would smack her tongue against the roof of her mouth, and we'd titter conspiratorially.

But in that moment, I thought that Steph's friend was lucky to have a mother who crocheted blankets and prayed for other people's children. Imagine what she did for her own kids. It didn't matter if she was a good mother, whatever that meant. Being *alive* was what mattered.

These house calls thrilled and confused me. Before our mother died, we rarely had visitors. My parents did not have friends whom we invited over for dinner or saw casually. We weren't like the other Chinese families in these suburbs, since we didn't attend church or speak Mandarin. We were our own island. But these visits made me hopeful that we might gain a community, though I knew these drop-ins would eventually come to an end. I felt greedy and guilty for wanting something positive from our mother's death.

×   ×   ×

Hours later, swaddled in the prayer blanket, I turned this woman's words over in my head.

Watching over you.

Wouldn't want you to be sad.

Other adults—the guidance counselors at school, neighbors—said similar things. I often didn't respond. When I did talk, I blurted out details of her death regardless of how they fit into conversation: that she technically died of cardiac and respiratory arrest and not cancer. Her passing was relevant to everything. I spoke in chronic caps lock—*MY MOTHER JUST DIED TWO WEEKS AGO!*—and I noticed that adults often struggled to find the right words, unsettled by my abrupt declarations, then concerned when I smiled earnestly to prove I was OK. My guidance counselor wrote me a hall pass that I could use whenever I wanted, which I flashed liberally until I graduated. I used it to lie in the nurse's office and stare at the ceiling when I found class boring. I napped. I cried. I wrote in a notebook and sketched poems about my mother's death that I would later share with my English teachers for feedback; this act allowed me to express what I could not, or did not want to, say at home.

In conversations likes the one at our front door, adults tested their consolation.

She'd want you to be happy, not suffering.

I couldn't blame them for saying such things, but each time someone said my mother was watching over us and would have wanted us to be happy, I privately disagreed. To have been happy would have been to disrespect her life. After all, we were only just surveying the rubble after the catastrophe. We understood now how everything had shifted: There would be no more visits with our family; no more of her cooking; no more talks about our futures and how we needed to do *more*; no more burrowing into her shoulders for hugs. And from the practical mind of a thirteen-year-old, there would be no more horseback riding after the checks my mother had written before her death ran out.

Still, those assurances:

She's watching over you.
She's with you every day.
She's everywhere.
She's alive in your memories.

Despite myself, I took their words literally, my newborn grief latching onto every word. My imagination gorged itself on this hope.

X

I conjure you from the underworld, part taxidermy, part ghost. Your expression toggles between something comical and something frightening.

I want to think that you don't mean me harm, but I wouldn't blame you if you lashed out because you were mad about your premature death. When you're not dropping into my life, you are somewhere vaguely above—heaven, perhaps, though I'm not sure if either of us believes in it. You stomp around in the attic of our family's grief. The thrums and rattles from your footsteps constantly punctuate our thoughts.

As Steph and Caroline and I clear out your desk at your office, or call the cell phone company to change the name on the bill to Caroline's, or visit the cemetery to burn more incense and joss paper, or research how to order a tombstone, I have a flash of something that feels like memory, though it never happened. In it, you are irate about the L.L.Bean dress. You will always be a little annoyed about this outfit.

Why? you ask repeatedly. You barge into my mind, a frenetic four-foot-eleven Kramer, slapping my mental doorframe with your hands, limbs flying this way and that. *Why this?*

You keep tugging at the hem, then the sleeves. Your agita is my indigestion.

You couldn't have buried me with a sweater? you ask. *What if I get cold?*

You run your fingers along your arms to show that it's chilly. I find myself missing, of all things, seeing the soft flaps of your triceps, and how they looked like deflated balloons. There is a gentleness in the taxidermic, ghost-you, though you are mad. I prefer this irritation to the agony and indignity of your death; to your being sad or needy or worried about all that you're missing in life and all that you'll never do.

Eventually, your ghost will find this outfit situation amusing, and we'll joke about how you are perpetually underdressed in your L.L.Bean ensemble. (Whatever *eventually* means.)

I know that you are cold. But it never occurs to me until now to burn tissue cutouts of clothing to send to you. As a teenager, I was a rude host. I could've made you a jacket or a new dress that way. I could have made you rich.

2.

The Saturday before my fourteenth birthday—*MY MOTHER JUST DIED TEN DAYS AGO!*—Steph and Caroline headed to the grocery store to buy ingredients for a birthday cake made from boxed mix and two cartons of ice cream, our mother's recipe. On their way out, Steph shouted, *Baby! Baby!* from the foot of the stairs to wake me. I recorded in my journal how she shouted like our mother, making her words long. *Baaaaaay-beeeeeee. Baaaaaaaaaay-beeeeeeee.*

Our mother had a special way of calling for things—animals or us. If she was outside looking for our cat, Moo Cow, she shook a container of treats and bellowed *Moooooooooooooooo, Mooooooooo Cow*, the first *moooo* undulating like she was a backup singer whose chipper *ooooooooh* was the true star of the show. Sometimes she added our last name, *Chow*, to convey her urgency. Caroline had named Moo Cow. She chose it defensively, when she learned that eight-year-old me wanted to call him something she found corny, like Duke or Prince. Moo Cow soon associated our mother's call with treats, and it became impossible to summon him without imitating her.

After my mother's death, I stood every night on the back porch before bed. I hollered the cat's name and pulled her voice from the bottom of my stomach and threw it at the yard.

Moooooooooooooooo. Mooooooo Cow Chow. I scanned the trees. I felt ridiculous, like I was summoning my mother. I imagined her scurrying to the door on all fours with her back hunched. Her eyes were wide and unnaturally golden.

Jesus Christ, Mommy.

In a half decade or so, I will realize that I have all but forgotten how you sound. The only way I recall the pitch of your voice and where your vowels sharpen then soften is when I remember you howling the cat's name.

I woke slowly, still in the haze of a haunting dream. I listened to my sisters back the van down the driveway en route to the grocery store.

"I had a really odd/scary dream which unnerved me," I noted in my journal, which had a fake lock and, on the cover, a repeating pattern of stilettos and purses. The recent entries were a mix of recording what my family had done in the aftermath of burying my mother—the cemetery visits, the burning of joss paper—and the tiny dramas of freshman year, including which boys I crushed on, and what they'd written in the condolence card my English teacher had passed around.

"Mommy came back alive, or something," I wrote, "like she was never dead."

In the dream, my mother and I were on a road walking toward the barn. It was dusk. We were on foot. She wore loose clothes that hid the weight she had gained in recent years, and her hand cradled her stomach.

"We were walking behind people with horses. They were slow, and me and Mommy were fast, so we passed them," I wrote. "I wanted to ask, or mention...how strong she seemed. IDK what she said in turn."

When we reached the stable doors, I glanced over my shoulder, but she was nowhere to be found. I wrote that when I woke, I had a "droopy feeling"—the crash after a high, a heaviness, another wave of loss—as if my mother had died again.

✗

When I was in elementary school, my mother borrowed a library book for me that gave me nightmares for days. I cannot find the title now, but I remember that in the early pages, the protagonist—a girl about my age—watches her mother disappear. Her mother seems preoccupied and unwell. They walk outside somewhere near their home. Suddenly, the air feels different and her mother is gone. She has a mother, and then she does not. In order to explain away her absence, the girl believes her mother has vanished into a parallel world. I was disturbed by this uncertainty and that there was no goodbye. It felt violent and sinister, and reading this book instilled in me a preemptive longing for my mother. I turned to her then as she lay in bed next to me, engrossed in her kissing book. I threw a leg and arm around her.

Mothers provide, she often said. *I'm the provider.*

She made a fist and thumped her chest to show her strength. She filled such basic needs for us just by being alive. She was the general. She was the one who strategized our futures and led us to win wars. With her, we were safe.

For years, my mother asked Steph about two of her friends—sisters, whose own mother had recently died from cancer.

How are they doing? she'd say, her tone not too different from the lady with the prayer blanket. We knew that she only asked because they were motherless girls. But just the thought of them stirred within me some secondhand panic, like their tragedy could filter into our own lives. These days, whenever I hear those names, I think of them as the girls with the dead mother.

Not you, I wanted to say to my mother at the time, because this worried me. *This would never happen to you.* But I stopped myself, because saying that sort of thing out loud only invites trouble.

It took me years to realize that my mother had also grown up motherless. By the time I understood this—and gathered that this was a worry of hers, that she would die before all of her children were adults—she was long dead and her fear was my inheritance.

✕

On my birthday, my sisters asked me to stay seated at the kitchen table after we finished dinner. They pushed fourteen candles into the cake, which was frosted with rocky road ice cream and had wedges of pistachio ice cream inside.

OK, don't look, Sticky, they said as they put something in my arms.

When I opened my eyes, I saw a wooden jewelry box. They'd discovered it when we cleaned out my mother's cubicle at the insurance company and had hidden it from me for the past week.

It's from Mommy, they said and helped me slide it from its packaging. *We think she was saving this for you.*

It was rectangular and made of faux rosewood. It had a single lid that opened like a loose jaw to expose a mouth of velveteen slots for rings and earrings.

All I could see was a casket.

Oh, I said. I tried not to recoil. I was fourteen now, and though I still slept cuddling my childhood stuffed animal—a toucan my mother had mistakenly named Ducky—I considered myself an adult. I wondered if this was a test.

Thank you, I heard myself say. I pushed the corners of my mouth up and I made my voice light. My sisters relaxed.

This is perfect, my mouth said. And then, I began to cry.

Each time I opened the box and stared into its maw, littered with my costume jewelry and a tiny fake-onyx necklace you'd bought for me at a gift shop on that trip to Seattle, I thought of you in your casket. Your hands were clasped on your stomach and your engagement ring was still on your swollen finger. Your coffin, the largest jewelry box. Your body, the gem.

You suddenly are across the kitchen table peering at me over a pile of wrapping paper.

Happy birthday, Chin-na Chow, you as my ghost mother say. You invoke one of my nicknames, a derivative of *Chinchilla*, which you and my sisters had called me because when I was young, I was so small and, in your eyes, cute. You hadn't wanted to miss my birthday; you wanted to keep your claim as my mother. I shrink back. You lean closer and make the face. You flip your head back and caw with brutal, bracing laughter. Your teeth are Colgate white.

3.

In the Cedar Hill Cemetery in Hartford, there is:

An eighteen-foot-tall pink granite pyramid with an angel standing in a doorway. Her head tips toward the sky and her wings bend open. It's a memorial for Mark Howard, who died in 1887. Howard was appointed by President Lincoln as the first internal revenue collector of Connecticut.

A statue in memory of a toddler who died in 1905 for which Cynthia Talcott's parents commissioned a life-size carving of her face. Her head floats toward the top of a small cross-like marker. It looks as though she stands at a wooden cutout at a carnival and pushes her cherubic face into it for a photo.[1]

The Colt memorial, commissioned by Elizabeth Colt. At forty feet tall, it soars above the other monuments, hoisting its bronze angel into the sky. Colt's husband was the inventor and industrialist Samuel Colt, who mass-produced revolvers and died in 1862 during the Civil War. Upon his death, Elizabeth Colt became one of the richest women in the U.S. The monument to her husband, where she would later rest, cost her $25,000 and set trends in the cemetery.

Memorials dedicated to a man named Yung Wing, who died in 1912. Yung's markers sit in the family plot of his wife, Mary Kellogg, and there is an unassuming obelisk for the couple, which is inscribed with Yung's name in Chinese. There is also a plaque from the Chinese government applauding his work in starting the educational mission.

And, from 1988 until 2004, a flat headstone dedicated to a newborn named Jonathan Love Chow.

4.

My father held the square tin as though it were a gift he'd just received, his elbows bent, box in both hands just below his chest. As he approached the van where Steph and I waited, it looked for a moment like he wanted to shake the container to determine if it held a watch, a candle, a glass figurine. In reality, it was a canister of ash and bone fragments. A debt he owed to his dead wife.

A month after her funeral, the three of us were at Cedar Hill so that my father could pay for Jonathan's remains to be disinterred, then cremated. It struck me then how many transactions were necessary in mourning. So many invoices to be paid over the past few weeks: the obituary notice, the funeral services, the casket, the flowers, the burial, the death certificate, Jonathan's disinterment and cremation, and, eventually, my mother's monument.

Steph and I waited for our father in the car, not speaking as we watched the smoke drift from the building's chimney and fade into the trees. I wondered who we were witnessing take on another form.

As we left, bursts of gold and crimson scattered throughout the cemetery. The monuments obscured the groundskeepers and their leaf blowers, which made it appear as though ghosts had kicked the foliage.

At home, Steph and I took turns standing at the microwave

to reheat bowls of a thin broth with pork bones, boiled mustard greens, and winter melon. I warmed crispy noodles in a pan and we slathered them with a gravy of fish cakes and bok choy we'd made the previous weekend. We ate these without speaking, spooning rice into our soup and slurping loudly, chomping on the noodles with visible, audible relief. Afterward, the TV still blasting the *Nightly Business Report* with Paul Kangas, our father carried the tin with Jonathan's ashes to the family room. For the next decade, my parents' only son would sit at the base of the fireplace behind a jungle of wilted and rotted plants.

X

Watching my father clutch his son's ashes, I understood the weight of what he held. One can grieve a person, place, or ideal. All of those things have heft. The word itself, *grieve*, comes partially from the Latin *gravare*—to "make heavy; cause grief." *Heavy*. Like the realization that his wife and son were not ready to leave their lives behind; that each of us was scared of death and all that it would bring; that with it, our sense of home—the people who made it, the paperwork that codified it—could easily be upended.

Freud wrote famously about mourning and melancholia. These two types of grief were distinct from one another, he posited in an essay from 1917. Mourning had an end in sight; a person in mourning had a grief that adhered to a specific person or object. But melancholia was an ongoing state—pathological, almost. The melancholic may know they have lost something, but not exactly *what* they have lost.

The scholar Anne Anlin Cheng puts it this way in *The Melancholy of Race*: "The melancholic eats the lost object—feeds on it, as it were." *Eats*, *feeds*. As though those who have internalized loss become ravenous in their hunger for sustaining their grief. It bloats them, but they continue to feast. Perhaps, instead of asking if I am exorcising or taxidermizing you, I should ask if really, I am taxidermizing myself. What within my grief am I afraid to lose? It is the idea of her, of course. Here, so many years later, I can't shake her death and don't seem to want to in the first place. Eats, feeds, eats, feeds—insatiable.

But Cheng's broader argument is that identity formation—and racial identity formation in particular—is melancholic itself and is shaped by the push-pulls of loss and recovery.[2] I get this. The immigrant family tries to preserve a history and a life that the surroundings resist. They try to invent a new way of being while always seeking a home within the negative space.

I find this melancholy in the story of Yung Wing, who was buried in Cedar Hill not far from where Jonathan first rested. So many historians tout Yung's firsts: that he was the first Chinese immigrant to graduate from Yale; that he wrote what was arguably the first Chinese American memoir, before a "Chinese American" identity was called such. But it is Yung's existence in Connecticut and the question of his belonging that I find most compelling.

As a child, it was hard for me to imagine that anyone alive centuries ago in Connecticut looked like my family. Wethersfield's borders had placards that delighted in how it was established in 1634 and therefore the "most ancient" town in the state. On elementary school field trips, we toured the homes of white men named Joseph Webb and Isaac Stevens that were built in the 1700s and preserved with assiduous detail. It was impossible for me to feel as though my family, or anyone who looked like us, had roots here. We felt so new and had no community outside of our relatives. I did not know that there were immigrants from China of my great-grandparents' generation who lived and died not far from where I was born.

While at Yale, Yung was granted American citizenship, which was unusual in that era, considering that many Chinese immigrants in the American west were denied such, and the passage of the Chinese Exclusion Act of 1882 would make that xenophobia and racism law. It was perhaps, as some scholars argue, the privileges and proximity to whiteness that a prestigious institution like Yale afforded Yung.

Still, Yung struggled to find work after his graduation. His sponsors had hoped that, following his time at Yale, he would return to China to continue their mission work. The scholar Robert G. Lee once made a distinction about immigrants: A foreigner was "innocuous" and temporary; an alien had no desire to leave and was therefore considered a threat. I had previously considered both labels—foreigner, alien—to be similarly derogatory, practically synonyms because they both served to otherize immigrants. But an immigrant's permanence so quickly can eradicate any veneer of welcome.

After years of traveling between China and the U.S., Yung eventually made a life in America. He married a white American woman named Mary Kellogg, and he started the Chinese Educational Mission, which had the seemingly contradictory goal of helping China stave off Western imperialism by bringing young men from China to the U.S. to study science and math. When the Chinese government disbanded the mission because officials feared the students were simultaneously becoming too Americanized and facing too much discrimination, Yung turned to diplomatic work. During a visit to

China, Yung agitated for progressive reform, which in 1898, led Empress Dowager Cixi to put a $70,000 bounty on his head. Yung fled to Hong Kong and tried to return to the U.S., but the American consulate refused to admit him. The secretary of state retroactively invoked the Naturalization Act of 1870, which denied American citizenship to nonwhite people, in effect stripping Yung of his. But with the help of friends, Yung found a way to sneak into the U.S. despite this law. Though Yung Wing would spend his last years in Hartford, he would do so without a country.

I stop by Cedar Hill one recent fall when I'm passing through Connecticut on a road trip by myself. On Yung Wing's grave are the plastic remnants of grocery store flowers that someone had left behind. That his grave continues to be honored a century later moves me, along with the significance of its location in Hartford.

I have not come across in-depth accounts of Yung's funeral—just brief mentions that a friend and pastor of the Asylum Hill Congregational Church in Hartford led the services. Considering that he was Christian and that Hartford did not have much of a community of Chinese immigrants then, I suspect his burial at Cedar Hill Cemetery lacked Chinese customs. I'm curious if this was what he had chosen—he'd be near his wife, after all—or if he had requested that his remains be sent back to China, where his parents and siblings rested, only to have the circumstances of his isolation prevent this.

Most of the men who came as laborers to America's western states tended to be buried according to Confucian rituals. In many cases, their remains were returned by ship to China so their final resting place could be among family. Bone repatriation, it was called;

the word *repatriation* saying a lot about one's so-called rightful country.

That Yung Wing's body rests in Hartford—and that the Chinese government recognized his remains there with a plaque—might give him the last word on the matter of his citizenship. This barbs me and feels both like triumph and defeat. I know, after all, that where a body rests says so much.

When my mother told Steph that she wanted to be buried in Fairfield instead of in Hartford, I understood this decision logically. But it showed that my family's epicenter had shifted, and that perhaps our anchor had never been our home like I'd thought. It had always been our mother. We still had the physical remnants of the life she'd built for us, which itself was a feat, but in spirit, we understood it had left us.

X

Each of my family's Lunar New Year celebrations from my childhood blend together. We took the photos of my mother's parents and my father's mother that sat on top of the TV and propped them on our kitchen table. The absence of my paternal grandfather's photo underscored to me how my father seemed fatherless. All I knew was that my paternal grandfather had left China for Cuba to work in restaurants and had died there. We did not have an image of Jonathan—a photo would have been too gruesome, given his condition—and this, too, vanished him from my mind.

The new year was one of the only Chinese holidays my family observed. In the days that led up to it, my mother scrubbed the floors and vacuumed between the couch cushions. She hauled a stool to the center of the kitchen and she trimmed our hair. On New Year's Eve, she rushed home from work to finish the last details. It was jarring how, since Lunar New Year was not a recognized holiday in our town, it often fell in the middle of our everyday routines, rendering it both mundane and disruptive. My parents bustled about in the kitchen, preparing groceries from the sole Asian supermarket in our area. They soaked bok choy and gai lan in the sink and rehydrated dried shiitakes to fold into glass noodles. They warmed a whole roasted duck in the oven; they boiled a chicken in a stockpot, its head and gnarled feet taking turns bobbing at the top; they scraped the scales from a red snapper to prepare it to be steamed. My sisters and I took breaks from homework to chop scallions and ginger, which we sprinkled on top of the steamed snapper or doused with scalding oil to serve with the silky chicken. I helped lay out all of the platters on our kitchen table. My father reminded us what each one symbolized.

Before we ate, we pulled on our winter coats and my father slid open the back door and set a metal can on the deck. There, we built a small fire and burned joss paper and the tissue clothes we'd cut for my parents' ancestors and Jonathan. Afterward, we stood before the spread and lit joss sticks for each relative, bowing three times together.

We have to make sure they have a chance to eat, my father would say as he gestured to what we had cooked.

I rushed through the motions, unsure what I should think as I bowed. *Was this prayer? How does one pray? Should I try to invoke a higher power, or the dead?* I never asked my parents if this was symbolic or if maybe they believed our dead relatives existed in another dimension. So I studied the plates before us. I never imagined these ghost ancestors like I did my mother, but I wondered then if they were scarfing down what we'd steamed and blanched and stir-fried.

One year, while we waited for the joss sticks to finish smoldering, our doorbell chimed. My sisters, who remember this story more clearly than I do, said a crew of firefighters or police had gathered at our front door. A well-meaning neighbor worried that our house was burning. I don't know how my parents reacted. Embarrassed, probably. Bemused, maybe, if they didn't think too hard about it. Later, they would share the story theatrically, cheerfully, at the next family party, drawing chuckles.

X

Not long after we brought Jonathan's ashes home, my father dragged his headstone from the van to the backyard while I was at school. I hadn't noticed that we brought the marker from the cemetery in the first place; my father must have returned to Cedar Hill by himself to retrieve it.

He deposited the stone near our back deck in one of the overgrown garden beds clogged with bull thistle and cheatgrass. He likely moved efficiently, not pausing to allow any sentimentality to seep through. He did not bow; he did not offer any words to his son. After all, it was a tombstone that marked nothing. After all, his son's ashes were inside our home, to be buried later at his wife's grave.

I discovered the headstone later that week when I hauled the garbage cans through the yard to the street. Jonathan's marker sat flat in the garden bed.

Whoa. I jerked back and barreled into the house. *You put Jonathan's gravestone there?*

Hey, my father said. *Where else would I put it?*

He didn't want it inside, and I couldn't blame him. That would only invite trouble.

It just looks like, I said, waving my hands, flustered, *I don't know, it just looks like you buried him here. It looks like a grave.*

Whether my father could or would acknowledge it, he cultivated his grief this way: He let the vines stretch thick and run amok over his son's stone. There was something stunning in how the vegetation persisted, the whole scene so easily confused for decay.

5.

In the months after our mother's death, Steph, Caroline, and I drew plans for her tombstone. We buzzed with giddiness, delirious and relieved that we were honoring her as best as we could. Steph and I sat at the kitchen table for hours to sketch lionhead fish, because our mother had always liked them, and because they'd symbolized abundance. We made a heart that surrounded Jonathan's name; stalks of bamboo, which represented, among other things, luck. We included cherry blossoms and a lotus flower, and our family's last name in an intricate seal. We emailed our renderings to Caroline in Pittsburgh, who sent back adjustments, drawing new fish or reconfiguring the placement of words. In this process, the three of us piled on everything we considered special. We included the phrase that our mother had often quoted to us, which we recited back to her: *I love you as high as the sky and as deep as the ocean.* This was not a forty-foot monument like some of the ones in the Cedar Hill Cemetery, but as we sent the design to the engraver, we thought that it might as well have been.

6.

When I was a kid, my family spent most weekends at my uncle's house.

As soon as we arrived, we were to immediately greet Gung Gung where he sat by the unused fireplace in the living room. My grandfather smoked cigarettes in the armchair that only he ever occupied. Cataracts had transformed his eyes into blued, cloudy marbles, which made it hard to tell where he was looking. The family lore was that his brother was a part of the Triads in Hong Kong. The other story was that Gung Gung's parents were killed by Japanese soldiers during the invasion of China. They beat his father and raped his mother, I heard vaguely as a kid, not understanding what that meant. I later learned that the Communists were likely the ones responsible for my great-grandparents' deaths, but my aunt, still fearful of China's Communist government despite living in America for so long, hesitates to confirm.

As my family arrived on these trips, Gung Gung folded his newspaper, which Kau Fu bought from Flushing. Gung Gung permitted my sisters and me to hug him.

See how big they've gotten? our mother said. *Look how big.*

Gung Gung scanned our faces. I don't know if he rarely said anything to my sisters and me because he had nothing to say, or because he knew we could not speak much Cantonese. He took my fingers in his hands and pulled on each of them to crack my knuckles. He nodded in confirmation of some unspoken idea. I stood still, unsure if I'd passed his test.

One afternoon, I sat on the floor near Gung Gung as he read his newspaper and smoked a cigarette. My parents and aunts and uncles played mahjong in the living room. My sisters were at a movie with our cousins. Occasionally, Gung Gung tapped ash onto a tray, and the paper rustled between his fingers.

He turned a page and studied it. Slowly, he lowered his cigarette to one of the photos, watching the newspaper burn in his hands for a few seconds before he snuffed the tiny flame with his bare fingers. I would later learn that it was a picture of Japanese politicians, and that he'd singed holes into their eyes, only satisfied when their faces had incinerated.

Most mornings of our weekend visits to Kau Fu's, while Steph and Caroline hung out with our older cousins, my mother let me tag along with her and Gung Gung to McDonald's. This started when I was a toddler and continued until I was in first grade. The two of them drank coffee from Styrofoam cups, and I ate a hash brown and sausage McMuffin. They talked in low voices, their Cantonese flowing too fast for me to understand. Occasionally, my mother looked at me and called me leng lui, at which Gung Gung would allow a nod. I lapped this up, enjoying how often adults called me cute or pretty like this. I rolled a packet of ketchup like a tube of toothpaste and squeezed it onto my hash brown.

It takes me more than a decade after my mother's death to hear from a relative that these outings to McDonald's were often tense, the setting for a years-long fight between my mother and my grandfather. She was trying to defend her daughters, who she insisted were just as smart and talented as her brother's sons—that she was just as good as her brother.

How are your daughters? Gung Gung asked.

They're doing so well in school, my mother would begin to say, but Gung Gung would already be rattling off the most recent accomplishment of one of Kau Fu's sons—so proud that someone smart would carry on the family name. Gung Gung saw Kau Fu's sons more often, since he lived with them, so this could have just been his point of reference. But my mother had trouble accepting that. On the drive home, she tumbled into a rant about how her father favored his grandsons over his granddaughters.

My girls are just as smart, she said. Her voice was insistent and rose to a shout though nobody else was talking. Although my mother was livid, I liked how she said "my girls." So adamant and indisputable.

My mother had craved this type of declaration from her father; for Gung Gung—and *our* father—to say this about us; to claim us like that. Her love was a memorial. Obvious and unmissable, it held up our experiences and all of their blemishes as still worthy of love. Years later, I think about how I use this word and its variations—*my, mine*—after her death. *My mother died,* a new possessiveness incubating in my grasp, a melancholia that cannot be sated. Eats, feeds.

X

When my grandfather lay intubated and dying in his hospital bed, my family huddled around him. Months earlier, he'd fallen and broken a hip, and the aftermath had been arduous. His body had never fully recovered. My sisters, both in high school, held his hands. Only in elementary school and not knowing better, I tugged on his fingers to crack his knuckles when it was my turn. My mother and her siblings smoothed his hospital gown and pulled the covers tight around him.

He lived a long life, they said while weeping.

He'll finally get to spend time with his wife, who he's been apart from for decades, they reasoned.

Later, in the waiting room, morning light reflected off my mother like she was iridescent. She could not stay still and stood to pace by the window before sitting down again. Her face was lacquered with a dazed look, her eyes shiny and lips parted. Her fingers curled and uncurled around a Styrofoam cup of hot water. I sensed my mother's nerves and knew to stay out of her way. I sat myself between my sisters on the waiting room couch and leaned on Caroline's shoulder.

Most of my extended family had gathered at the hospital when a cousin, recently married, arrived with his wife. In the short time since their wedding, my cousin had fallen into a disagreement with our relatives about something related to wedding gifts.

As the story goes, this cousin took a seat and began talking under his breath, but loudly enough so that the rest of the family could hear. He mumbled some variation of *Why can't they just let us enjoy our honeymoon?*

Suddenly, my mother sprang to her feet and launched herself at her nephew.

Ng ho gum cho! she said. She was sick of hearing his chatter. He leapt from his chair.

My mother planted her feet and drew back her shoulders. With a flick, she splashed the hot water in his face.

Chi seen, he yelped. *Gik sei ngo!* The water dripped down his chin.

Gik sei lei? My mother brandished her cup like a knife. *Hui sei la lei!* By now, the other adults had stepped between them, shouting as well. Our family was used to this, our aunts and uncles often joking about the legendary Yu family temper. My mother's siblings gave my cousin napkins. They hauled their sister back. Contained her. Caroline, Steph, and I stayed in our seats, gripping one another's hands as we absorbed this scene.

7.

For much of her adult life, my mother spoke with Yi Ma nearly every night to debrief about their days and share family gossip about which cousin's kid found a new job and was making *how much* money or paying *how much* for rent. Usually during these conversations, my mother called from her spot in the basement, a burning cigarette in her mouth as she stood in the dark next to my father's power tools.

Years later, I find some of my family's old phone bills while I am looking through my mother's desk, eager to learn any new information about her:

> 3/28/2001—Yi Ma's phone number: 28 minutes. Kau Fu's
> phone number: 41 minutes.
> 3/29/2001—Yi Ma: 53.
> 3/30/2001—Yi Ma: 23. Kau Fu: 10.
> 4/1/2001—Yi Ma: 46. Kau Fu: 25.
> 4/2/2001—Yi Ma: 44. Kau Fu: 25.

Page after page, evidence of her nearly daily calls to her sister and brother. Seeing the minutes laid out like this makes me yearn for my mother and to call her this way for twenty-five minutes or ten or six or one.

Yi Ma remembers that when my mother was hospitalized at Saint Francis, they were on the phone one evening, and my mother confessed that she was afraid of dying.

It's too soon, she said to Yi Ma. It was just a couple days after my mother received her terminal diagnosis. *Stephanie just started medical school, Caroline is about to graduate from college, and Katelin is only beginning high school.*

She couldn't die now. There was too much life left.

But you've raised such good daughters, Yi Ma said.

My mother agreed.

Maybe in our next life, my mother said to her sister, *you and I will be together again. Maybe we'll be reborn as mother and daughter this time.*

The two sisters considered this.

No, Yi Ma said finally. *How about we be brothers? That way, we won't have to take care of anyone. They'll take care of us. We can just enjoy ourselves.*

My mother and her sister roared at this prospect.

8.

Mommy, I want to know what you consider a "good daughter."

There is a story that my father relishes telling about his good daughter, less good daughter, and possibly bad daughter. He does not use this vocabulary—good, bad—to describe us, but it is easy for me to conclude.

My father decided that each of his daughters needed to memorize the multiplication tables up to twenty by the time we started elementary school. He and his classmates had done so in China and Hong Kong, and it was a useful skill.

You can solve math problems faster, my father insisted, though I didn't understand what this meant.

When my sisters and I each turned five, he took a ruler to graph paper and sketched grids that we were to fill.

As my father tells the story, Steph was the most dutiful. She learned the multiplication tables in minutes with a genuine enthusiasm that my father recounts with awe. She sang out equations throughout the day: *Four times four is sixteen! Nine times eight is seventy-two! Twelve times eleven is a hundred and thirty-two!* When her first grade teacher asked the class if they'd heard of *this thing called multiplication*, Steph raised her hand. The teacher began to quiz her in front of the class.

Two times one?
Two.
Three times two?
Six.

With each answer, her teacher grew more excited. Steph remained calm.

Fourteen times seven?

Steph blurted out *ninety-eight!* Later that evening, her teacher called home to congratulate my parents on the bright child they raised. When my mother relayed this to my father, he had said: *Good. How it should be.*

When our father set the empty multiplication grid in front of Caroline each summer morning, she leapt from her seat and dashed away. She hid under her bed or behind the couch, until he dragged her back to the table.

You have to memorize this. His voice was stern, and he straightened the paper in front of her. Eventually, she filled the grid, pressing her pencil so deep into the worksheet that it scarred the table.

Nearly a decade later, when it was my turn, I didn't run. I wailed in front of him. By now, Steph and Caroline were in middle school. They were exemplary students, and Steph was already taking high school–level algebra. I was inconsolable.

I don't want to, I told my father.

Your sisters do it, he said. *You need to also. It's good for you.*

At five, I did not have the vocabulary to say how overwhelmed I was by this way he constantly invoked my sisters when talking about my future. Just because they did something did not mean I could, too. I filled out some of the grids, then resisted until my father left me to sulk at the table.

Laan chung, he says. *Gum sui pei.*

In my father's eyes, this story is one of the best examples of his daughters' personalities. I don't disagree. He must have always known that I would be the most defiant one.

Stephanie will just sit patiently and learn the multiplication tables. Caroline will try to run away but learn eventually, he says when sharing these anecdotes. And then his voice melts into incredulity: *And Katelin, wow. Katelin will just sit there and refuse.* His laughter here is like vinegar. I don't know if my stubbornness is the joke, or if it's how impossible it seems that I could be his daughter and feel this way about math. Or maybe this joke was really on me, because I was only hurting myself.

9.

Fresh out of the shower, I crouched in front of a portable heater in the bathroom. A towel hung around my shoulders, and I fanned it out to trap the heat.

Outside, the thermometer that my father nailed to the deck hovered somewhere in the teens—not out of the ordinary by Connecticut standards, but it was enough to turn our house into an icebox. Whenever I returned from school, I clicked the thermostat dial inside to sixty-five degrees or warmer, and my father returned it to the lowest setting.

Heat is too expensive, my father said.

I think it's broken, I said. *It can't be fifty-five degrees if we still have to wear our winter jackets and hats inside.*

I knew what he was about to say before he said it.

If you're cold, just wear more clothes.

What if I give you some money? I said, thinking about the couple of hundred dollars I had saved from a summer job. I already had on multiple layers: several pairs of socks, long underwear, a T-shirt, sweatshirt, fleece zip, the occasional winter coat. *What if I help pay for the heat?*

He leaned further into the couch. At the time, I didn't understand why my offer to subsidize the electric bill seemed like such an unreasonable suggestion, or why he didn't take me up on it.

In a couple of winters, a cold front would blow through Connecticut. There would be weather advisories, but as usual, my father would not turn the heat higher. Our pipes would freeze. I would watch my father head to the basement, where he'd stand in a corner for a few minutes, holding a blowtorch to a pipe before giving up.

We just have to wait, he would say when he returned to the kitchen. *Nothing you can do.*

Nothing you can do? I would repeat.

Hey, he would say. *Nothing you can do.* He dove into a rant about how, when the house was built, the developers didn't properly insulate that side of the structure. He claimed that he caught the crew removing insulation.

In this moment, I wouldn't say anything. I'd retreat to my room. I would be a senior by then, weeks from hearing back from colleges, the act of moving out of this house both a promise and a solution that was so close. For the next few days, neither of us mentioned the temperature. My father took cold showers. I washed my hair in the sink, rubbed baby powder all over myself, and later in the week, asked my friend Kiah if I could shower at her house. It was all so mundane. My father was right; there was nothing we could do besides live with it. It felt as though I was trapped in my father's car with him behind the wheel. We were spinning out on a patch of ice in the middle of a winter storm. We knew we never should have been on the roads in the first place. And yet.

X

On cold days, I used the portable heater to turn the bathroom into a sauna. Leaning against the tub, I worked on class assignments or painted my nails, which were long and round, just like my mother's. I sometimes napped, a lethargy settling.

I had recently started seeing a therapist at the youth services center across the street from the high school. After I'd sat in my guidance counselor's office, not understanding why I so often broke into tears, she had arranged the sessions, despite my father's protests.

There is no point in things like therapy, my father had argued. *Being sad is just in the head.*

That's exactly the point, I had said. *Therapy is for stuff in the head.*

My father and I didn't have the vocabulary for what our loss had generated inside of us. We were equipped only with words like *sad* and *mad*, which we attributed to living with one another, instead of any other circumstances.

My guidance counselor told me that for a few sessions, I would not need my father's permission to see this therapist. And so, twice a week, I walked across the street to the youth services center to chat with a woman named Carol.

In the beginning, I told myself I was only meeting with Carol to skip class. She had a soft, gravelly voice and seemed close to my father in age. She asked questions about my classes, which I answered with gusto. I told her about what books my English teachers had lent me, and dove into long rants about how I was terrible at chemistry and geometry, and how my father's reactions to my grades were disproportionately irate, and how frustrating I found it every time he quoted Thomas Edison.

Genius is one percent inspiration and ninety-nine percent perspiration, he would recite when I brought home failing test grades. I would insist that I didn't want to be a genius, anyway, and we would further devolve into another layer of argument. He claimed I needed to listen to him because he was the father and I was the daughter, but what did that matter when he didn't act like one?

In retrospect, talking about school to this therapist was easier than talking about anything else.

X   X   X

In retrospect, I must have understood not to describe the house in too much detail; not to mention the frozen pipes; not to make it seem as though the house was anything but messy.

In retrospect, she mostly listened, which was good, because I wouldn't have wanted another adult trying to tell me how the world worked. Though once, when I was on a lengthy tear about my father and how he kept insisting that I complete every problem in my geometry textbook because I had a C in that class, and how I kept insisting that wouldn't help me anyway because my brain had broken since Mommy died and could he stop being so controlling when none of it mattered and couldn't he just be more understanding of that and also wouldn't it be great if he helped me clean the house for once, she interrupted.

You can't change your father, she said. *Why not*, I said, and she had replied, *You can only change yourself.* That quieted me. I knew we were no longer talking about my father and our arguments about grades and the house.

In retrospect, I learned then a new vocabulary for our grief.

X

The heater in the bathroom pitched the smell of cigarette smoke toward me. A sweet musk. Yours.

I froze, afraid that if I moved, your scent might vanish. It perplexed me; you had been dead for months, and I was certain you hadn't smoked in this bathroom or anywhere near that heater.

X   X   X

Each morning you pulled a Marlboro from a pack and smoked it on your drive to work. Each night after you mopped the kitchen floor and you thought we were all asleep, you crept down to the basement for a fix. You reviewed your day and thought about your bank accounts; about our most recent report cards; about the attitude I gave you and how, like you always said, whenever I was in a bad mood I had to put everyone around me in a bad mood, too; about what your husband did or didn't do for you or the family that week; about how untidy the house was becoming; about your job and its never-ending projects. There was so much you could not control.

Sometimes when I couldn't sleep, I tiptoed downstairs and called for you. You emerged from the basement.

What were you doing down there? I said. I sniffed around you.

Nothing, you said. *Cleaning.*

You pulled me to your chest. I knew enough to be suspicious, and I could identify the earthy yellowed odor that meant you'd smoked. The next day, and the next, I begged you to quit. I crumpled your cigarettes and I whined for you to try Nicorette gum each time a commercial came on the television. Sometimes you said you would. But most nights, you didn't say anything. You just kept smelling like smoke.

I pulled my jacket around me and stole downstairs to the closet where your handbag was still in its usual spot, your wallet and loose change and old napkins tucked inside. I shoved a hand into your purse. I still didn't know, don't know, if your cigarettes killed you, but one by one I pinched them between my fingers until they disintegrated.

How was it that after your death, I was still trying to change how you had lived?

I crept back to the bathroom, my fingers reeking of sweet tobacco.

10.

We were at the cemetery where your body was buried. Nine months had passed since your funeral.

You popped up in front of our car as soon as we parked. I forced myself not to flinch in surprise. Was I the only one who could see you? You gestured for us to follow. You muttered something that I couldn't hear. My father did not react, and so I shut my mouth and filed behind. You ran your hands over your tombstone, which we'd finally had installed.

So gaudy, you said. The corners of your mouth drooped.

All these months that you waited, you paced somewhere nearby, maybe in our garage, maybe at the cemetery gates, wondering when we'd get our act together so you could rest.

You took months to make this? You jabbed a finger at your stone as if we could have missed it. *I waited so long for* this?

My taxidermic ghost-mother wasn't *wrong*. It was an unfortunate headstone. Back when we'd buried Gung Gung, my mother had pointed out which granite she'd liked in the catalogue. *India Red.* We took note. But the color she wanted was too expensive. Something about the vibrant reds that flecked the stone lifted it out of my father's budget.

So when we came across a gravestone in the catalogue that was a soft salmon color, my sisters and I turned to one another.

This will do, we said. *Close enough.*
When it arrived, it was Pepto-Bismol pink.

You examined your name in Chinese and English, then rolled your eyes when you noticed your gravestone claimed that your birthday was April 20, 1956.

My sisters and I knew that April 20 wasn't *really* your birthday; it was something your father had selected at random when filling out paperwork to leave China for Hong Kong. We knew that you preferred to base your birthday on the lunar calendar instead of the Gregorian one, but as we designed your gravestone, we didn't have the correct one. We were sorry about that.

So lazy you couldn't have figured it out? you said. *It looks so cheap. What am I, a beggar?*

These were the things my mother used to shout at my sisters and me when we hadn't cleaned our rooms or she didn't like how we dressed or she thought we were being ungrateful. We knew her temper well. If Steph or Caroline took too long getting ready for bed, or if they left their rooms messy, it wasn't uncommon for our mother to chase them from the house. Once, while I was already asleep, she stormed into the bathroom while they were getting ready for bed.

I thought I told you to go to sleep an hour ago, she said. *You were just faat mung'ing all night?*

My sisters brushed their teeth faster.

You don't need a mother or something? So ma fan. Get out! She sent my sisters skittering out the front door, brushes still in hand, mouths still foaming with toothpaste. My sisters sat on the steps until they worked up the courage to sulk back inside through the garage door, our mother ignoring them. They knew that the next morning, their friend who lived across the street would ask why they were outside so late. *Our mom was just playing a game*, Steph would offer weakly while Caroline blushed. This was the second part of my mother's intended punishment.

When I infuriated my mother, I refused to let her herd me from the house. While she hollered that I was sui pei or laan chung, I dropped onto the floor and grabbed at her calves so she couldn't push me out the door.

So many stories about her are like this that after a while, they barely register: Her, flinging my elementary school geography textbook on the floor while shouting that I am gum laan and never going to get into a good college or find a good job afterward and that I'll grow up a *loser*, jabbing at my head with her pointer finger or swatting at me with her palms.

As my father and I stood by my mother's tombstone for the first time, I squatted to examine the stone.

What is this? I asked. I traced my fingers along the curved edges of my mother's name. The engravers had chosen a font that resembled Steph's handwriting, which was neat and had tall, rounded, sans serif letters. It was a cross between Tahoma and Comic Sans, and even as a teenager I knew it was inappropriate for a tombstone. My mother's date of birth and death were both engraved in Courier New. It looked cartoonish, and the heart, fish, and bamboo resembled clip art.

What is *this?* I started to sob. *This is awful.* I waited for my father to disagree. Wrinkles slid across his forehead.

He reached into his pocket for a tissue. It was easier for me—for us both—to pretend he was sniffling because of his allergies.

X

140

On a fall afternoon some weeks later, my father and I returned home from school. We had a new message on our answering machine.

This message is for Mr. Chow, the caller said. It was the owner of the company that had installed my mother's gravestone. We needed to pay our bill and he'd been trying to get in touch with us for weeks about the missed payment. Could we call him back?

My father looked so small in this moment, shoulders stooped in his red down vest, the same one he'd worn for decades. I recognized it from my sisters' baby photos. His hair had the beginnings of silver. He was a thin man and had shaped new angles into his body by eating healthier and exercising more after Yi Ma's husband died of a heart attack half a decade ago. But grief had wilted him, and the skin on his face sagged, the bags under his eyes casting downward. I'd never thought of my father as frail or old until my mother died, but seeing him standing there, I noticed how little space he occupied. Next to my mother, he'd always appeared tall.

I opened my mouth, but my father had retreated to the family room, where he would spend the next few hours before dinner. He kept the same routine before my mother died. He sat on a couch in the near dark, the glow of an old floor lamp barely giving off any light. His laptop rested on a TV tray. A man's nasally, tinny voice emerged from his computer droning about the NASDAQ and Dow Jones average. Occasionally, my father jotted numbers in a spiral notebook or on the backs of torn envelopes. I often came across these scraps of paper scattered around the house. Knowing he wouldn't want them discarded, I stacked them in neat piles where I found them to form little cairns in the overstuffed wilderness of our home. For hours, my father remained safely cocooned by his belongings. Behind him, a row of bookcases stacked with decades-old *National Geographic* magazines and dusty statues of Guan Yin and the Buddha watched over him.

Are you going to call him? I said eventually. *Are you going to pay the guy for the headstone?*

I wasn't sure what I wanted my father to say, but I knew my tone held an accusation. I leaned against the doorframe and waited for his response. Anything would do, really. I would've taken his anger. He closed his eyes like he was willing this situation to disappear. He must have wondered how he'd become saddled with a child like me, his youngest daughter, who thought she was an adult.

Did you hear me? I asked. *Are you going to say anything? You need to pay for the stone, or do something about all of this.*

Hello? Are you listening? I started to cry. *Hello? Can you hear me?*

11.

One summer, my family road-tripped to Maine to camp near Acadia National Park. On the six-hour drive, somewhere between Boston and Portland, we pulled over at a rest stop.

Who needs to pee? our mother asked from the front of Mashed Potato.

I need to pee, I called from the back seat.

I do, Steph and Caroline said.

OK, Wun Lee and Gah Leen, she said to my sisters, *take your baby sister to the bathroom while we get gas.* I was six and could go to the bathroom by myself, I insisted, but I marched behind Steph and Caroline.

We didn't realize it then, but our mother had followed us, a roguish grin plastered to her face. She chose the stall next to mine. As I sat on the toilet, she reached a hand under the divider. She grabbed for my ankles, her fingers clamping around them while she laughed.

I screeched and leapt to my feet. A trickle of piss ran down my legs onto my shorts and her hand.

Aiiiyaaa, she said. We burst from our stalls and she met me by the sink with paper towels that she dampened with water. She dabbed at my shorts and knees.

I tensed my shoulders and refused her gaze.

A tiny smile creased her face in apology.

All better? she asked.

All better, I repeated, reluctant.

12.

A few years before you died, you went to the grocery store and printed out four-by-six photos of me, Steph, Caroline, and you. You taped each to the side of our refrigerator. In each picture, we are making the face—baring our teeth, biting down, sparks in our eyes. Steph wears a red sweater from MIT, her face splattered with sun freckles, her chin narrow and pointed. She looks like she is about to laugh. Caroline's eyes are crinkled. Her hair is cropped short and tinted electric red, which means that she must be in college. In mine, my eyebrows are two faint dashes on my forehead, like yours, and my skin is speckled with preteen pimples, which you and I battled together, applying toothpaste or creams you bought from the drugstore. In your photo, your hair is wiry and fluffed, like you used a blow-dryer that morning, though you rarely bothered with that. Your whole face looks swollen. You look unwell and much older than the forty-four years old that you are in this image. In retrospect, I see that this is cancer.

13.

Immediately after our mother's death, Caroline took it upon herself to carry our family's finances. She pooled her work-study money and savings from the summer, methodically unearthing what our family owed.

My mother, Florence Chow, passed away recently, and I'll be taking over the bill, I heard Caroline explain on the phone over and over again. Her voice was low and professional each time. She waited patiently on hold, verifying our mother's personal information to apologetic customer service representatives. She'd be returning to Pittsburgh to finish college, and afterward, she'd be moving to Seattle to work for the same company where she'd interned the summer before. Though she'd be far away, Caroline was determined to find her own way of helping the family.

Over the next few years, Caroline settled into her first job in Seattle. Her company would award her bonuses in the form of points. She'd hoard them and keep meticulous accounting. Sometimes, during breaks—the same ones where, back when she was a summer intern, she'd call our mother, who was nearing the end of her day on the East Coast—Caroline would scroll through the prize catalogue. She studied the images of model airplanes or T-shirts with the company logo. The coveted items were the electronics. She would notice a new model of an iPod that she could afford. *Would a teenaged girl like an iPod Shuffle?* she would wonder. She'd get me one this way, gifting it to me for Christmas.

I'd tug at the wrapping paper and gasp. I had stopped expecting gifts after our mother passed.

Thank you, I'd say. Caroline would push back a strand of her hair, cropped short and a muddied green from a box dye she administered herself. Her face would brighten. Of us sisters, relatives say Caroline looks the most like our father, with her rounded face, her tan complexion. But our father says she's the one with our mother's best traits—diplomatic, always knows how to navigate any situation, a solution-finder. She would beam at me, teeth shiny.

X

Not long after my family buried my mother, my kau fu called our house to talk to Caroline. My mother had not been alive long enough to use the two grand that Kau Fu had lent her. But my father cashed the check anyway and put the money toward funeral expenses.

Two thousand dollars! Kau Fu said on the phone to Caroline. He wanted the money back.

My father refused. *A gift is a gift,* he had told Kau Fu earlier.

I can pay you, Caroline said. *I can send you the money.*

No, I don't want your money, Kau Fu told her. *It has to come from your father.*

I can send it to you, Caroline insisted again. She calculated how she would use the money that she earned that summer in Seattle, plus some of the funds that had been disbursed through her student loans.

My sisters and I knew that this was not an issue of money, though.

My mother's siblings made it clear that they thought my father should have done more in helping their sister when she was sick—that he should have kept her from dying. I wrote in my journal that at my mother's memorial, her relatives "were so curt" and "mean to Daddy" and how they told me that one shouldn't borrow money to pay for funerals.

It was your father's job to take care of her, they told me then and reiterated over the years—on the phone or at rare family gatherings. I wavered between shame and a brimming, unsatisfying anger.

She's dead, I said. *This is so pointless. Why are you holding a grudge now?*

I talked back. Shouted: *Stop blaming my father.* Began to cry, hung up the phone or stormed out of the room.

I met their indignation with my own.

You don't know the full story.

Then tell it to me.

You're too young. You're just a kid.

Neither of those things matter! I wasn't too young for her to die.

X

Years later, I ask Kau Fu if he'll tell me about my mother. I want to learn more about her childhood. Other relatives had mentioned vague stories about how she was charismatic and a flirt, often with a crew of boys around her. Once, I'd heard Kau Fu refer to how my mother seemed to always get her way, and how one holiday in Hong Kong, when their father gifted all the kids oranges, my mother managed to cry enough so that Kau Fu gave her his. These were small stories; that's all I wanted.

To my surprise, Kau Fu agrees to chat. I arrange to drive the six hours to Connecticut from Washington, D.C., so we can talk in person. But a few days before my visit, he calls.

It's too hard talking about your mother, he says on the phone. He can't do it.

OK, fair, I say. *I get it. That stuff's hard.*

One summer in my early twenties, I visited Kau Fu and Yi Ma for the first time in years. I stood in Kau Fu's living room during a small gathering with his family, uncomfortable and not knowing what to say. I curled my bottom lip under my top teeth and aimed my gaze at Kau Fu. I held my mouth this way for a few seconds. I did this suddenly. As if a reflex, he made it back and laughed, the lines around his eyes deepening. But then his expression shifted, and ambivalence flashed across his face. He looked away. I wondered if this playfulness was something he and my mother originated together—if that face was their inside joke that she'd passed on to her daughters. If maybe there was something about looking at me that twisted something inside of him.

You look so much like your mother when she was your age, her siblings told me frequently when I was a kid, and then a teenager, examining my face as if in search of an answer to an unspoken question. It made me want to peel my dead mother off of myself and to step out of the bodysuit that was becoming more and more like hers.

With fits and starts, Kau Fu tells the story he'd hinted at for more than a decade.

In the years after my mother's death when I was in high school, he said, he felt guilty that he rarely saw me and that he didn't take care of me like he'd promised. But it was just too hard. So much of me reminds him of his baby sister. *Too hard*. He keeps using that phrase—*too hard*—as if it would soften me. His apology surprises me; that was all so long ago. But considering my past fury and the way I lashed out—refusing to talk to him, since he didn't want to talk to my father—I couldn't blame his tentativeness.

I begin taking notes as we talk, afraid of misremembering my uncle's words. I say little, not wanting to derail him or risk turning him away. After my mother's death, I watched our families retreat into ourselves and our corners of Connecticut.

I offer: *It was hard for all of us. For you, for Yi Ma, for me and my dad and Steph and Caroline. Everyone.*

He tells me that after I'd asked him to share stories about my mother, his mind kept returning to how she died.

How she died? I say, knowing already that our conversation will be elliptical. *You mean from cancer?*

I can't, he says. *You need to know about your mother's cancer and your father's involvement. But I can't tell you now. Maybe later. But right now, you need to respect your father.*

Our conversation persists this way. Kau Fu explains that since my father hadn't worked for such a long time, my mother had opted for a cheaper insurance plan. This is familiar territory, my mother's family never thinking my father earned enough money.

A low-class insurance, as my uncle puts it.

You have to pay a lot of co-pays, even though you see a doctor or you go for a physical, you have to pay a lot. That's why she never had a physical for three or four years, and every time she visited the doctor it was like $100 or $200, he says. He's describing my mother's HMO plan. *She hadn't been feeling well for two years and she didn't go see the doctor. And then, two weeks or three weeks before her death, she started mentioning to me and Yi Ma that she didn't feel well.*

Kau Fu says that when my mother was in the hospital, he and Yi Ma looked in her purse and discovered a large bottle of Tylenol. They found another in her car.

How painful the last stage of her cancer must have been, he said. *She must be taking a lot of those every night.*

As he speaks, I hear in his voice a familiar anger loosen. How easy it is for my family to become derailed this way.

His hurt is contagious, though I don't fully understand it. I have caught it, it merges with mine now, and as much as we've all tried to tamp down our specific strains of loss, here we are. I worry that my instigating conversation will allow grief to haul my uncle back into its pit.

What do you mean 'what really *happened to my mother'?* I ask.

He insists I call Steph. He wants her to promise not to get mad at him if he tells me the truth. He keeps mentioning how things are finally good between me, my sisters, and him—how we actually visit him now—and he's afraid sharing this story will damage our relationship.

You're so ma fan, I say to him, though my voice is teasing. What he's saying is harmless, I'm certain. This is just how he's always been since I was a child, making outlandish demands that my family either diplomatically ignored or begrudgingly humored. *Steph is at work. She probably won't care about this.*

Katelin, Katelin, Katelin, he says. He makes his case again: *Please just call your sister and ask that she not get mad at me.*

I call Steph. When she doesn't pick up, my uncle launches into his story.

Right after my mother was diagnosed with cancer, Kau Fu visited her at Saint Francis Hospital with his wife and my yi ma. According to Kau Fu, the doctor asked my mother why she never had the spot on her liver checked.

What spot on my liver? my uncle claims his sister asked.

He speaks at a fast clip. He brings up that period two years before my mother's death, after she had a cyst removed. As I had always understood it—and as she'd relayed to Lai Yi Ma—the doctors told my mother that her cyst was benign, but that she needed to return for tests.

Kau Fu has a different version of the story, one that seems clouded by his grief. He maintains that after my mother's surgery, my father reviewed her results and kept them from her. Kau Fu believed that my father allowed the spot on my mother's liver to remain untested—an act of negligence, purposeful or not. It turned out to be cancer, which slowly killed her.

But Kau Fu's logic does not add up. In reality, my mother was lucid enough that the doctors would have released any information to her, the patient, instead of my father. As Kau Fu's story went: At Saint Francis, learning of her diagnosis, my mother was apparently furious. She told Kau Fu that she wanted to transfer the power of attorney from my father to her brother. She wanted all of her funds allocated to her daughters, instead of my father. It takes me months after my conversation with Kau Fu for this to occur to me, but I wonder if my mother's cancer-fueled paranoia—the one that Steph told me about—might have contributed to this.

And, Kau Fu tells me, *a year before, your mother told me that she'd taken out a life insurance policy—one of the highest premiums.*

Life insurance?

This is my first time hearing this. I later learn that my father, who took a short-lived gig as a financial advisor, had persuaded my mother to take out a policy for them both.

Yes. You didn't get anything?

No, I say. *I mean, we got some money from her retirement account, a couple thousand dollars each, if that.*

Kau Fu lets out a huff that mottles the phone.

She didn't have the chance to switch the beneficiaries, he says.

I am stunned. Kau Fu, it seems, has accused my father of letting my mother die because of greed and negligence. I want to say, *This is absurd*, to start shouting like I would have as a teenager. But something in Kau Fu's voice, so earnest and troubled after all these years, like he might cry, sits in my chest like heartburn. My cousins tell me that ever since my mother died, Kau Fu has not been the same; he no longer hosts holiday gatherings; his mood has soured; his energy restless.

I could not dispute the way my father led our family down precarious financial paths; I could not deny the way my parents argued, their resentments festering. I understood how my mother's siblings were still furious with my father. In the years right after my mother's death, I frequently used the word *scapegoat* in my journal to describe how my mother's family treated my father. In their fury, they could not see something so basic: how my father had cared for his wife, and that he wanted her alive. It is that simple.

On the phone with Kau Fu, I try to keep my voice neutral. I am worried that if I start to cry or raise my voice, this might somehow be construed as me turning against my father, or my uncle; that my emotions might make them stop sharing stories about my mother.

Are you OK? I ask Kau Fu finally, my voice soft. *How do you feel after telling me this?*

Better, Kau Fu says. He laughs. *You know I'm like you and your mother. Explosive. As soon as we say something, we get it off our chest. We feel much better. How are you?*

I'm fine, I say. My head is starting to hurt. I look at my phone's call timer and see that we've been talking for more than an hour.

Listen, Katelin. A layer of worry has returned to his voice. *Don't get mad at your father. He's all you've got, OK? Don't be mad at your father.*

I'm not mad at him. I'm too exhausted by this to be upset, I want to tell my uncle. I'm almost impressed that after levying this claim, he still thinks that daughters should always respect their fathers. I laugh a little at this, and he begins to also.

Go to the hospital and get the records, Kau Fu says. He sounds sheepish, though relieved, and I wonder how much of what he's told me he believes, or if this is a narrative he's created to soothe his grief. He hedges one last time. *If it turns out I'm wrong, I'll apologize.*

X

When I mention to my father that Kau Fu claims he withheld information about his wife's illness so that she would die and he could collect her life insurance, my father spits out a laugh.

Ridiculous. Boo-oy.

I am in Connecticut for the afternoon, passing through for work. The two of us are in the living room. He and my uncle have rarely spoken since my mother's death, ignoring one another during the handful of times they've been in the same room. This accusation does not surprise my father.

You just laughed, I say. *So you think that's a big lie?*

We never know, my father says. He had never seen any surgery results, like Kau Fu had said. He shrugs. *We only find out when we were in the hospital, and that resident told us, 'Oh, this is stage four on the liver cancer.'*

And then he asked me, how come you guys have insurance and don't do it? The "it" he's referring to are the tests. The gynecologist was a very young female doctor, and then we saw in the experience—even during the surgery, she needed help from a general surgeon to help her remove the cysts.

My father leans forward in his seat and speaks louder. Most people would call it yelling, but he would disagree. When my sisters and I were little and he raised his voice, suddenly tense, we would say: *Stop yelling, don't yell.*

He'd lift his chin. At this point, he usually vibrated with outrage, which made the denial of raising his voice all the more vexing.

I'm not yelling, this is my normal speaking voice. This becomes such a common refrain that years later, when my sisters and I recount arguments with him, all we have to do to invoke him is lower our voices and shout belligerently: *This is my normal speaking voice, I'm not yelling.*

The doctor, my father recounts, was optimistic after removing the cyst from my mother's stomach.

They tell us that, 'Oh, it is the cyst—it was ten pounds—and benign and you're all good.' So we were happy. So we trust them. The doctor recommended that my mother return for cancer screenings, but she failed to follow through. I know that my mother, like all of us, was skilled at hearing only what she wanted. It seems likely that her doctor's suggestion for more tests might have sounded like a breezy afterthought. I can understand this. I often tell myself, I am young, my body is strong, and I delay making appointment after appointment, physical after physical, until I think about my mother, and I schedule something for the next week.

✕

I can't find documentation of how much my mother's insurance co-pays cost or what her deductibles were. But I see from the admission sheet to New York-Presbyterian Hospital that her primary insurance was "Aetna HMO," and her secondary insurance was "Self-Pay." HMOs are generally for people who don't think they'll get very sick; it's usually for young people, which makes the fact that my mother had this all the more gut-wrenching. In order to see a specialist covered by an HMO, one first must get a referral from their primary care physician. Even then, it is not uncommon for the patient to incur hefty bills that must be paid out of pocket.

Actually, my father says, bringing up the summer before my mother died, *the family doctor we go to when your mommy's stomach was all bloated, he told us it was a stomachache.*

At my parents' urging, the doctor referred them to specialists.

It took so long to get an appointment, my father says, and when they finally did, *they say, 'Oh, it's just indigestion or bloating' and they prescribe her some medicines.*

But as my mother's aches persisted and her stomach continued to swell, she returned to our family doctor. This time, she was seen by a different physician at the practice—his wife.

When the wife looked at it, my father says, she saw symptoms of ascites, which is when fluid builds up in the abdomen usually due to problems with the liver. *She told Mommy to go to the emergency room immediately.*

This doctor, my father says, had more experience with the "female body" and "female symptoms."

Why can't a female body just be a body, I want to ask my father. But I've never heard this story before, so instead I ask: *But what do you mean, 'because of the female body'?* This might be the closest my father will come to talking about sexism. *Do you mean that Mommy's first doctor just thought Mommy was complaining for no reason and it wasn't a big deal?*

Maybe, my father says. *Could be. Probably.*

OK, I say. I sink further into the couch and wait for him to say more.

OK, I say again, after a few minutes. *OK.*

X

Lai Yi Ma once told me that before Kau Fu's wedding, his future in-laws tried to dissuade their daughter from marrying into our family. It seemed all the Yu women tended to die young, they said. Uterine cancer killed my grandmother at forty-one, and other women in the family had medical histories that were so distinctly *female*—again, this word, which seems so outdated now—resulting in hysterectomies or infertility. These future in-laws didn't want this for their future grandchildren. My gung gung assured them that all of these deaths and illnesses were flukes.

It'll be OK, he must have said. But would it? Has it been OK? This worry was itself a curse, like saying the superstition out loud made it true.

X

Mommy, everybody has their theory about your death. Your brother and husband still seem to think this was preventable, if only others had acted differently. But I want to hear from you. Why was it that you avoided going to the doctor all of those years? I know that these are not answerable questions—that there is likely not just one answer—but still I want to ask: Was this a problem of money? Or dread? Had you sensed, with trepidation, something shift within your body?

Did you fume when that doctor said the pain tearing through your stomach was only just irritable bowel syndrome? Did you ever wonder if this was linked to your earlier surgeries?

Did you say, knowing your own self, but still qualifying and deferential: *No, I don't think that's right.*

14.

If we had known that your illness was killing you in the months and years before your actual death, would that have helped you live? I'm stuck on that. I keep going back to whether knowing could have stopped the freight train that was your cancer.

I steel myself while I type into Google: How much does a human heart weigh?

The first result says a human heart weighs about eleven ounces, or 310 grams, and that it is about the size of a fist. That is small and dense. For context: 310 grams is about the equivalent of two average-sized navel oranges.

When my sisters and I were children, our father peeled an orange at the kitchen table after dinner most nights. He was careful as he sliced an *X* into its skin with a butter knife, tugging it off the fruit so it looked like a flower. He handed us each a couple of pieces, which lay like fish in our palms. I tore the pith from mine and squeezed my hand around them before sucking the juice, one by one.

Afterward, my father set the peels to dry on the kitchen counter to put them in a soup, though he could never use enough. Years after you died, we still had plastic containers filled with those skins, all of them shriveled.

I Google how much a carton of cigarettes weighs because I imagine you clutching one in your hands every night, your fingers sweaty.

On Yahoo Answers, somebody asked this exact question, and one person replied that a pack weighs seven to nine ounces, and another person said, "About 7 days of your life." Both answers feel right.

X

In the months after my mother died, my father tried to sue her doctors. The doctors should pay for the mistake of her diagnosis that led to her death, as he saw it. Perhaps he was tired of shouldering the blame from his dead wife's family. Perhaps he would have done this whether or not they'd launched their accusations.

At the time, my father did not tell me about any of this. He did not mention that he had met with lawyers, likely whomever he found in the phone book with the cheapest rate. He did not tell me that he asked Steph to request and review all of our mother's medical records, though Steph was not yet a doctor.

It surprises me now that I was oblivious to these late nights, which must have stretched for months, with Steph bent over the playbook of our mother's death, trying to decipher it in order to help our father allocate blame. I wonder if Steph, like our father, appreciated channeling her grief somewhere. I did not notice him, bloated with stress before shuttling into a law office in his old suit, the same one my mother found at T.J. Maxx or Marshalls in the kids section— *Your father, he fits into teenaged boy's clothes and it's much cheaper and there's less hemming,* she often said. It was the same one he wore to our cousins' weddings, our school concerts, and her funeral.

I can picture my father laying these stacks of my mother's medical records on the lawyer's desk or a conference table with a hope that even if this could not resurrect his dead wife, it might be his redemption.

The first law firm my father tried to hire welcomed him into their office for a meeting. The lawyer listened to him recount my mother's illness—the shadow on her liver, the scans, how the doctor had told my parents that it was *probably fine*, his words. The lawyer sat on the case for months and might have continued doing so if my father hadn't called to say he was taking his business elsewhere.

The second law firm had a former nurse on staff.

You said that your wife lived two years after the discovery of that shadow, right? she asked after listening to my father's story.

Yes, my father said. *Two years ago, they say she had a shadow on her liver.*

So two years ago though, she said, *these doctors didn't know about her cancer.*

Yes.

But even if they'd diagnosed it as cancer at the time of the shadow, she still might have died nonetheless. In other words: Two years could have been my mother's life expectancy.

As my father relays this to me in his living room, he shakes his head, still in disbelief after all of this time.

I think they had a similar case that they had just lost, he says, *so they didn't want to take this one on, that's why she say that.*

Did they say that? I ask. *About losing the previous similar case.*

I think so. My father looks uncertain. *I think they say that.*

He nods as if to affirm his own story. It's not that I don't believe he was told that. It's not that I don't think he had a case. It's that I wonder if this law firm saw he was a man desperate to redirect his grief. When I picture my father trying to scrape together a case for this lawsuit, my throat clogs. I don't think I've told him this—or if anybody has told him this—but I don't blame him. For trying to sue the doctors, or for what happened.

X

Not long after my call with Kau Fu, I stay with Steph at her place in Eastchester. She pulls our mother's medical records from a desk drawer. The last time she touched our mother's files was for the attempted lawsuit, and she had written DO NOT THROW OUT in Sharpie on the envelopes in her careful handwriting. I had asked Steph about how, specifically, our mother died. My conversations with my uncle made me realize I couldn't recall basic things, like where my mother's cancer had originated.

So here we are. I don't want to make a big deal out of any of this. Steph warns me that the records don't reveal much; the cancer had already progressed too far for doctors to confidently discern where it had started. We sit on the floor and I pull the papers from their envelopes. The dates leap out first: *October 10, 2004. October 12, 2004.* As I reach the records from when you died, October 13, my eyes begin to water. I have never seen these before.

It is incredible how *sick* you clearly were and how as a child I hadn't understood. I'd known that you were in the hospital, which would have made it serious—but I didn't think that this would kill you. You would get sick, and then you would go through treatment, and then you'd be in remission, I'd decided. At thirteen, I was confident that everything could be reversed with another chance. That's what we were taught in school, and what you and Daddy believed. If you persisted, you could make anything happen. If you worked hard enough, the world was yours. So, *yes*, you would survive, as far as I knew.

Ah, I say to Steph. I slide the papers back into their envelopes. *Maybe we can look at this some other time.* There was dinner waiting downstairs and we both had work to attend to later.

Yes, anytime, Steph says, looking relieved.

The next morning, I lay my mother's medical reports on Steph's kitchen table and I scan the pages with my phone. I lean over each sheet and study the end of my mother's life nearly a decade and a half before, page by page.

On your admittance form to Saint Francis Hospital, dated September 30, 2004, the physician writes this:

"Very pleasant 48yo information specialist employed @ Aetna admitted with ascites/pain/fatigue..."

Very pleasant, the doctor described you, the day you learned you had cancer. Were you very pleasant then, as you tried to make sense of this diagnosis?

Very pleasant, the doctor described you, when you were swollen and tired and scared and realizing that the illness you had been fighting for months had actually been killing you.

Very pleasant, the doctor described you, just two weeks before you died.

Sometimes I catch myself on my phone and swiping open the records when I'm bored and my fingers are idle. I don't notice I'm doing it anymore. I tap on the scanner app while I'm sitting on the couch or waiting for a bus or at the dentist's office or the dog park and I find myself reading and rereading your autopsy report. My stomach hurts each time. I can't stop. *Eats, feeds*, my body struggling to metabolize my loss.

It says your right lung weighs 715 grams, your left 520. "In some sections, the lymphatic tumor spreads down a small distance into the substance of the lung." The first time I read this, I immediately Google "lymphatic tumor of lung" and I click over to the image results. I find only diagrams instead of photographs of real tumored lungs.

Your liver weighs 1,650 grams and the doctor writes that there is a "grossly nodular feel," and without searching this online, I know this to mean *riddled with tumors*.

The report tells me your heart weighs 290 grams. This is the part that punches through the drywall of my chest to squeeze my own.

"The heart is opened in the direction of blood flow," the report says about yours. "The external configuration is normal." Normal, sure. But if we're in the business of defining everything, what exactly is *normal*? This report is in present tense, which trips me up each time I read it. I think of your heart around right now and resting, *present tense*, on a little metal scale. Limp, still. 290 grams. *Normal? Normal? Normal?*

The average human heart weighs about eleven ounces, or 310 grams, and is about the size of a clenched fist. If I'm going off of this very specific measurement—the weight of two navel oranges, the volume of my hand wrapped around two slices of that fruit—then your heart *is*, *was*, just a little less than normal, but not by much. *Is? Was?* If I'm referring to lungs that no longer pump, a liver that no longer works, and a heart that no longer beats, why do the records talk about these pieces of you in the present? Why do I? Maybe your siblings were right. How could your spirit rest with your heart poked and prodded like this?

On your medical record, the doctors indicate that you don't smoke. An interesting omission that would be revealed as a very obvious lie once they sliced open your chest and examined your lungs during your autopsy. But you weren't thinking about that when during each doctor's visit, you shook your head at the question. *No, no smoking.*

Who cares, you must have thought. The deception would only be figured out after you were *dead*, so to you, it wasn't a big deal. Would your medical care have changed? Or would that have made insurance more expensive and killed you faster?

The records lists your medications. Dilaudid, which is hydromorphone, an opiate, a painkiller. Reglan. Aldactone. Colace, for constipation.

In high school, when I worked late in the kitchen to memorize physics equations or facts about cellular respiration, I sometimes opened the cabinet where we stored your pills. You'd been dead for months, then years, and we still hadn't tossed them out. I gripped a bottle and appraised it as though each pill could have saved you if only there'd been the opportunity. But they were just to alleviate your symptoms to make dying easier.

I wonder if—I cut myself off. I wanted to think, *I wonder if they could make dying easier for me*, but I was too ashamed to let myself finish the sentence.

It took me more than a decade to go looking for the "real" answers. I did not want to learn the gruesome way your body gave up. For so long, I feared that unearthing the real, indisputable facts—and other people's accounts of what happened—would bring a finality to my grief and, as a result, you.

I imagine your death like this: Your spirit had evacuated your body. It would exit your chest and slip down the emergency slide and into the tarmac of the afterlife while the rest of us were still buckled into our seats and strapped into our own anxieties and about to take off to some predetermined destination. There were no flight attendants to help us and no prerecorded safety videos to let us know what to do in case of emergency.

15.

When you were in the hospital, you called me to your bed.

You're taking care of the fish, right? You meant the betta fish that we'd brought home a few months earlier. I had dumped him in a vase on our kitchen counter and I named him something generic. Fred or Frank. He was blue-black with purpled fins.

Yes, I told you, *I'm taking care of the fish.* In truth, I couldn't tell if Fred or Frank had moved in days—if he'd died and his body hadn't yet reached the point where it had become buoyant. You were talking in present tense, about the *right now,* as if the pets would be around for you to take care of when you came home from the hospital.

And the birds, too?

Yes, and the birds.

And Moo Cow?

Your face was wan, and I clutched your hand. I wondered then if you thought you would never see the cat again, would not say good-bye to him, would never again stand at our back door, thrusting your face up and back and giggling hysterically to yourself as you belted out his name. *Yes, and Moo Cow.*

You squeezed my fingers and shut your eyes.

Days later, you would be dead. Months later, the fish would be dead. A year or two later, one winter morning, I would not be dead, though I sometimes wished I were. I would instead wake late for school. I could hear the van's engine roaring outside, the driver laying on her horn every few minutes, annoyed that I was late again. Downstairs nearly all of our parakeets except one lay limp, three bursts of neon greens and blues carpeting the bottom of their cage. The surviving parakeet, Blueberry, squawked and fluttered nervously. I'd had him since I was in kindergarten. The birds had been riddled by some disease or the cold, or both, and I hadn't noticed. I rushed back and forth to the cage, distraught and peering in while I tossed notebooks into my bag for school. I was stunned at these circumstances, mortified that I caused them, and terrified that all of this, no matter what, was now beyond my control. There was no getting the parakeets back. I ran to my father's bedroom and flung open his door.

All the birds are dead except Blueberry! I shouted, rushing from the house, not waiting for my father's response.

Because it was winter and the yard was frozen, my father would not be able to bury the birds in our backyard, like I'd hoped. His shovel would meet ice. So instead, he laid them in a shoe box, their little feathered bodies resting in the garage. We'd have to wait until the ground thawed before the parakeets could have their proper burial.

16.

My father, his mother, and his grandmother left Hoiping under the cover of day. It was 1953. The trees and greenery were verdant and approached overgrown. The watchtowers, grayed fortresses five stories tall that had sat for centuries in the distance guarding the village, were especially domineering that afternoon.

To avoid suspicion, Kiu Kwan kept their chickens outside so it would appear as though the family would return by nightfall to shuffle the birds back into their coop. She did not tell her elderly mother-in-law or her four-year-old son, Wing Shek—my father—her plan. They were visiting relatives in a neighboring village, she insisted. She led them from their home past the canals. Her other son, Wing Chong, was grown and had a family of his own. He had left months earlier for Guangzhou, which was a few hours away. Kiu Kwan did not have time to pack their valuables, and even if she did, would not have dared, could not have done so discreetly enough, what with everyone in this village watching.

They walked by the farmlands her family had worked for years, and around the homes of the neighbors who shared their last name, and who had begun to turn on them in recent months.

Before my father was born, when the Kuomintang fought the Communists, Kiu Kwan hid her family in the mountains and villages. She told my father stories about how cruel the Kuomintang were—how they shit on the villagers' rice supplies, forcing them to scrub away excrement in order to survive. But the Communists, as Kiu Kwan said, were at least polite during their occupation. They returned the pots and pans to their rightful places. When my father relays this story to me, he makes it seem as though his mother believed that public opinion—over the Communists' supposed good manners—led them to victory. She did not realize that once they were in power, her family would be in jeopardy.

My father's grandmother was stubborn and proud. My father says she was boastful—*she had a sharp tongue*, he says—about what her family had and what the neighbors did not. She could not restrain her chatter about what her son, Hoy Kit—my father's father—sent the family from Havana. He had lived in Cuba for the past two decades, working in restaurants there and sending part of his paycheck home, and these remittances allowed Hoy Kit's family to purchase a simple house in Hoiping. They also bought a few other buildings in neighboring cities, including Guangzhou. But while owning these buildings lifted my father's family to the middle class, it also made them targets of the Communist government.

The neighbors resented my father's family for this, and they threatened Kiu Kwan. They wanted to redistribute their family's money and to take over her mother-in-law's house. They were going to force Kiu Kwan to kneel on broken glass in front of the entire village to shame her for hoarding resources. And if still she didn't comply, they would take what was her family's—what they saw as *theirs*—anyway.

I can imagine my grandmother from the single photo we have of her: her high, appled cheekbones; her thin lips and deep-set eyes. I bet she jutted her jaw and gnashed her teeth the same way my father does, brimming with prickly resolve, as she reasoned: *Why should I have to give up what my family has?*

Understanding the choices before her, Kiu Kwan gathered her family and fled.

X

In Guangzhou, my father's family shared a couple of apartment units with extended relatives on a narrow street across from a school. Each morning, Wing Shek woke to the sound of someone pushing a cart down the road to collect excrement from the toilets. He watched this process with fascination, soon discovering other new rhythms of their neighborhood. Store owners rolling up the metal doors to their shops; the same man who stood in the schoolyard stretching his arms and legs, completing his exercises; neighbors walking along the road to complete errands. As a small child only starting kindergarten, my father, who would grow up to be a man of routines, found comfort in this consistency.

All of this—their escape, the housing—would not be possible without the money Hoy Kit sent from Havana.

My father does not have much information about his father. *My father left for Cuba before I was born. The 1920s? 1930s? Maybe. When? My mother had wanted to go, but my father say, 'Oh, you have to stay and take care of my mother.'*

I can only infer from my own research that my grandfather was one of thousands of wa kiu who traveled from the Pearl River Delta to Cuba by steamship for work. It was an arduous journey that took months. He may have traveled around the Indian Ocean and through the Cape of Good Hope, and he likely witnessed other men on the boat fall ill and die. This route was similar to the one nearly half a century before, when thousands of men from China had been coerced into leaving their homes to work the sugarcane fields in Cuba. Plantation owners who feared the revolts of enslaved men and women from African countries—and saw the rumblings of abolition due, in part, to the British blockade of slave ships—considered Chinese coolies an alternative source of labor. Between 1847 and 1874, 125,000 men arrived in Cuba from China, and 92,000 arrived in Peru during a similar time period.

I find it a strange coincidence that the Chinese government dispatched Yung Wing—whose final resting place was so near to my brother Jonathan's—to investigate the treatment of these men who were coolies. His counterpart at the Chinese Educational Mission was sent to Cuba, and Yung to Peru. Documenting the abuses there, Yung wrote in his memoir that "the country people were inveigled and kidnapped, put into barracoons and kept there by force till they were shipped on board, where they were made to sign labor contracts either for Cuba or Peru."

These men worked on sugar plantations, in mines, or as butlers or cooks, sometimes alongside enslaved men and women, though at the end of their contracts—if they managed to emerge from them—they at least owned their bodies.

Shortly after Yung and his colleague's investigations, China ended its coolie trade to Peru and Cuba.

After my grandfather arrived in Havana, he slowly repaid the people who had arranged for his travel and sent any remaining money to his wife and mother in China.

He returned at least once to Hoiping. He traveled by steamboat and made the months-long journey for my uncle's wedding. There are no records of this journey. But my best guess is that he made plans for the visit after 1945, when the Japanese military surrendered in China after occupying the country for eight years. He would not have been able to contact his family that entire time.

Toward the end of Hoy Kit's visit to China, which lasted a couple of years, my father was conceived.

He was born a few months after his father returned to Cuba— and just five years before his father's death.

X

When Kiu Kwan received a letter from Cuba that informed her that her husband had died, she took her son to the street. Hoy Kit was supposed to purchase vegetables and meat at the market for one of the restaurants where he was a partner, the story goes. When he didn't show up to work, his co-worker went to his apartment and found him on the floor. A heart attack.

Outside, standing by his mother, my father was too young to understand what was happening. Just that he should stay silent and watch. His mother struck a match and held the flame to the incense. She set the sticks in a little holder. Together, they watched the smoke rise between buildings. When his mother bowed, my father lowered his head and stooped his shoulders as well. He was only five. He did not know what it meant for his father, whom he had never met, to be dead. He just saw his mother crying. I can imagine my father unable to tell the difference between my grandfather, away, and my grandfather, dead. He was a child, and it would take him decades to consider the grief inherent in being unable to mourn a body; how leaving for another country was to risk saying goodbye to one's family for the last time. For all his kid-self knew, absence and longing were the same.

What can you do? his mother might have told him, equipping him with a sentiment he will carry for decades. *There's nothing you can do now.*

When my father speaks of my grandmother now, he almost always brings up something she had frequently told him: Though they were married for much longer, *she was only with my father for two years, eight months.*

This was a legend I knew my way around as a kid, just as it was for my father. There is a yearning here that I don't know how to access. I can't understand its shape. My grandmother missed her husband and felt bitter over the expectation and burden of having to take care of her mother-in-law and sons without the marriage she had been promised. She understood that this was a duty of hers and that many women then were in similar situations. But nobody had warned her about this pining. My father can only relay these ideas through this sentiment: *She was only with my father for two years, eight months.* So ingrained into his head that it is now in mine, that I have layered it on top of what little I know about my grandmother.

In the time they were in Guangzhou, my father's family quickly realized that moving to a larger city still could not protect them from the growing power of the Communists. Together, Kiu Kwan and her oldest son devised another plan to figure out how they could flee to Hong Kong with the proper paperwork. If they had been unable to do so, it is unclear if they would have tried to cross the water from China to Hong Kong on their own—if they thought their family, which included a seventy-something grandmother and a young boy, could survive the swim.

My father occasionally talks about a man he knew—a colleague at Lotus Garden—who trained for months to swim to Hong Kong. This man flung himself into the water during typhoons. He wanted to become strong, risking drowning during practice long before attempting the trek. Eventually, this man swam to Hong Kong with a watermelon, which served as a buoy when he became tired. After he made it safely to shore, he cracked open the watermelon and devoured it for sustenance. At this point in the story, my father seems more impressed with the watermelon's dual purpose rather than the feat of escaping China itself.

My father, still thinking about people swimming across that water so desperate to flee to Hong Kong, says: *Like what's happening at the border.*

I pause, surprised that he's drawing the comparison to Mexico himself. I say, slowly, *Yes.* I do not understand why he is not more sympathetic to what has happened, is happening, with our country's immigration system, why he does not believe that immigration laws should be more welcoming to refugees and immigrants. I tell him this.

I'm confused, I say, though we have had this exact conversation many times before.

Confused about what? he says.

Confused about why you aren't more sympathetic toward refugees and immigrants. Your family did whatever you needed to in order to get out of China.

Aiya, he says. *Only if it's legal.* I have heard him talk before about immigrants from Mexico and refugees from Syria, and how they need to immigrate the *right* way. When I ask him to explain, he keeps repeating that phrase, *the right way,* as an answer.

But policies around immigration in general are so arbitrary! I cite the Chinese Exclusion Act of 1882. *The reason why your father had to go to Cuba instead of the United States was because people like him weren't allowed in the U.S.*

Again, I hear the shrug in his voice.

Maybe so, he says.

Maybe so what?

I don't know, he says. *Maybe that's how it is.*

It is *how it is.* My voice is sharp.

But my father and his family don't have to test the waters, so to speak, in order to leave China. Through creative gaming, they claim to officials that they must head to Cuba to retrieve my grandfather's valuables, and that the only way they can get there is via a port in Hong Kong.

I have so many questions when my father tells me this. *Your family wanted to get your father's valuables, but not his remains?* I ask. *Did they have a funeral for him in China? Did they ever intend to go to Cuba?*

My father says: *We needed his money. Maybe we did some things for him in China. Probably.*

And then: *Maybe my brother did try to go to Cuba when we got to Hong Kong. I don't know.*

I don't know. I don't know. I don't know. My father frequently deploys these words when confronted with facts or questions that he doesn't want to acknowledge; they are his defense and armor. He doesn't know, or he doesn't *want* to know—I can never tell. This is another line that my sisters and I mimic with one another. It is a little mean, a little tender, as we shape our voices like his. Sometimes we do this laughing, our voices rising and belligerent, channeling our father's normal speaking voice.

17.

I did not mention to my father that it was my fifteenth birthday. For much of the evening, I thought he'd forgotten.

He and I sat beneath the fluorescent kitchen light slurping a broth he'd made by simmering pork bones and mustard greens. We ate char siu he reheated in the toaster oven, and we spooned steamed eggs with scallions and white pepper onto our bowls of rice.

After dinner, I turned the channel from the financial news to *The Simpsons*. My father pushed aside envelopes to make room on the table.

He pulled an ice cream cake from the freezer.

At Steph and Caroline's encouragement—*we made ice cream cake last year, Mommy did it the years before*—he spent hours making this cake. While I was at school, he bought a dozen eggs and a couple of cartons of blackberry and rocky road ice cream, and he set to work steaming sheets of ma lai go. This sponge cake was one of his favorite treats to get from Chinese bakeries, and in the absence of any near our home, he sated his cravings by spending the occasional afternoon at the stove with his industrial steamers from Lotus Garden, recreating his childhood snack.

Happy birthday, he said. He set it in front of me, candles glowing, the cake still warm and the ice cream still melted. It was a pile of mauve that oozed like a blister, something about the sponge's springiness possibly making it difficult for the ice cream to adhere.

A chunk of melted purple slid onto the plate. He paused, uncertain if he should fix it or sing me happy birthday.

X

Years before, whenever my family drove the two hours to Boston to drop Steph off at college, we stopped in Chinatown for dinner.

As my father navigated us through the neighborhood's narrow streets, he knocked on the van's window with his knuckles to point out the bakery he frequented when he lived here. It sold char siu baos that were stuffed generously with meat, my father recalled, along with egg custard tarts and slices of sponge cake that weren't too sweet.

This same Chinatown had been a reprieve for him when he was homesick in graduate school, and decades later, accompanied by his wife and daughters, the same few blocks provided a similar respite.

My family hardly ate out and this was one of the rare Cantonese restaurants in driving distance of our house, so my parents ordered generously, as if in celebration. They read the menu as a perfunctory measure before they asked the waiter to bring us their favorites: steamed bass slathered with julienned ginger and scallions, pea shoots stir fried with garlic, a roast chicken to be dipped in salt, crispy pork chops, and toward the end of the meal, a platter of lightly fried rice.

After dinner, we stopped at a shop and watched a woman pull gooey dough into strands. She coated them with powdered sugar, wrapping them around chopped peanuts to make dragon's beard candy. My parents bought a few pieces, and we let the threads melt in our mouths while we crossed the street to the bakery. We left with a couple of trays of gai mei bao, the stripes of coconut piped neatly across the tops of the buns. On our walk back to the van, we paused at another vendor for a paper bag of miniature egg waffles. We tore off sheets and popped them into our mouths in the car as we watched Boston's Chinatown give way to highway. I will forget about this memory until I am an adult, living in this city to work briefly at a public radio station. I catch myself affectionately muttering the street names in my father's voice whenever I visit the neighborhood, the vendors of my childhood gone, not realizing I'd missed those past visits with my family.

After Steph finished college, there were no more excuses to trek to Boston. And after my mother died, the thought of my father and me driving hours just for Cantonese food seemed wildly extravagant. Instead, my father began to clip recipes from old cookbooks and he learned to navigate YouTube for instructions.

On the couch some mornings, my father studied videos of Martin Yan or home cooks from Hong Kong as they kneaded dumpling dough or steamed zong. He flipped through his copies of Pei Mei's cookbooks, taking off his glasses to squint at the recipes in Chinese. He took notes on the back of envelopes, which I found days later when I tidied the kitchen, his handwriting scraggly and familiar.

My father rarely followed these recipes and preferred to improvise. It was better for him to read a few and then make his own way regardless of what others had tested and proven themselves. He eliminated ingredients he found unhealthy—salt, sugar, eggs—not caring if they helped the dough rise or provided structure to whatever he was making. There was a scrappiness here that I admired, despite the results.

He made his recipe for sponge cake this way, too, though his simplifications were successful.

When I was little, I leaned over the red Formica counter and helped my father crack eggs for the sponge cake. I fished shell shards from the bowl and whisked the yolks and sugar with a fork until they were fluffy. And then came the flour, which my father helped me fold into the batter. Some instructions that I've found say to add vanilla extract or baking powder, but all that isn't necessary.

I watched as my father stood on his toes to lower the pans into the steamer. The stove light illuminated him from above as though he were on a stage. The house was never quite bright enough because he insisted that we only turn on lights if we were sitting directly next to or beneath them, which left us in the shadows of our belongings. He was usually inscrutable and infrequently drew attention to himself, but in the kitchen, I could see his expressions clearly, his mouth open while he peered into the steamer.

When the cakes were ready, he cut slivers for me and my sisters, and we accepted the pieces as though taking communion.

I blew out the candles and sliced two pieces of the birthday cake. It was custardy and nothing at all like the ones my sisters or mother had made in prior years. But the labor of it—that my father had *tried*—struck me. I began to cry, anger with myself blooming and transferring to him. When my mother was alive, he had so often been on the periphery, and though I knew my reaction was ungrateful, it felt unnatural to have him try to comfort me now.

In the past, our mother made a racket out of our birthdays, sending short, celebratory paragraphs to the town newspaper. I recently found a clipping from when I turned six. In the accompanying photo, I am wearing one of my mother's dresses over a sweater and my sisters have piled my hair into a bun at the top of my head. I'm holding a bouquet of fake flowers and beaming: "Happy Birthday, Katelin. Katelin enjoys reading, drawing, singing, playing dolls, riding her bike…she also enjoys playing with her pet parakeets Moonlight, Chiquito and Blueberry…Happy birthday, Katelin, we love you!" My mother wanted everybody to know how much she cared for her daughters. My father found this excessive.

At the kitchen table, bent over the cake, I began to cry. My father patted me tentatively on the back.

Mo haam, mo haam, he said, then drew back into himself.

It was strange after a year of loss to celebrate *life*. What was the point of going through motions like this when, for instance, we'd recently learned from a relative that our mother's tombstone was gone? Since my father had refused to pay for the stone, the monument company had removed it from the cemetery.

I knew the absence of a grave marker would infuriate ghost-you further. *That ugly stone was better than nothing!* I imagined you saying. You would throw your taxidermic arms above your head, your limbs squeaky and stiff.

The time between our trips to the cemetery to visit you grew. Weeks morphed into months, then seasons, the fraction of years becoming whole. The lack of a tombstone was itself a monument to how our family had fundamentally failed you. Our inability to help you fight your sickness and how Jonathan's ashes sat in the same box, unmoved from the base of the fireplace. Your missing marker was yet another way our inaction grew into something consequential, leading your spirit further astray.

When my father doctors his recipes so much that his food is unrecognizable—*Why is the taro mashed like that*, or *What happened to the squid?*—he shrugs. *It's like refried beans! But better for you!* or *Hey! This is how you cook it!* And then: *It all ends up the same in your stomach, anyway.*

Every time he said this when I was a child, I thought it sounded like giving up. Fatalistic, too. *It all ends up the same...anyway*, as if nothing could be done to change the outcome. Not a CT scan, or a lawsuit against his wife's doctors.

For years, I thought that he was talking about our mother and her death. But now, the same conversations feel different.

Are you taking care of yourself? I say on the phone whenever I call him. *Are you healthy?*

Depending on his mood, he says, *Mm, yes*, and launches into a list of everything he bought at the grocery store or ate in the past twenty-four hours. Or if my tone irks him, my concern too badgering, his voice blunts.

Hey, he says. *My philosophy is that if I die, I die. What can you do?* He is in his house, alone and sitting at the kitchen table after dinner, about to pack up his leftovers.

Don't say that, I tell him. Why do I feel like I am trying to preserve my father before he is gone? I don't mean to sound so upset, as though I'm about to cry or scream. *Don't say shit like that.* I double down, abrasive in my fear.

But maybe, my father is not wrong. *Fine*, I sometimes want to say when we argue. *It all ends up the same!* I want to ask if he thinks that no matter what path we find ourselves careening down, no matter what schools we attend, what jobs we hold, how long we live, how much we *have*, we will become, *well, the same: dead.*

18.

Not long after my fifteenth birthday, my father's alarm clock sounded off in his bedroom in the middle of the night. The sporadic crackle from his radio sharpened the silence in the house. For as long as I could remember, he had always played the radio to fall asleep. I don't know if this was something he did when my mother still shared a bed with him, or if it was a habit he picked up after she began sleeping in another room.

He knocked on my bedroom door.

Gah Lee, he said, *hei san, wake up.* I yawned and followed him to the garage. We were headed to the cemetery in Fairfield. I wasn't sure why, just that the night before over dinner, he turned to me.

Hey. He spat tiny bones from a steamed fish onto a napkin. *Maybe tomorrow morning we can go to the cemetery to pay respect to your mommy.*

OK, I said. I didn't ask any questions.

In the van, I watched the strip malls fly by on Route 15 as we drove the hour from Wethersfield to Fairfield. I was replaying a fight my father and I had earlier in the week. We were on the way home from an after-school activity; I had a Rolodex of excuses to stay late at school so that I wouldn't have to take the shuttle or spend as much time at home. It was some variation of *I needed help with math* or

I wanted to join this club. The structure of activities felt safe and controlled and normal, despite how I wasn't excelling in classes the way my father wanted.

That afternoon of our argument, we were in his Miata, which he'd brought home a few years before my mother died. *You couldn't have gotten a car with enough seats for the whole family?* She glared at the two-seater convertible. And then, because my parents' bank accounts were separate, and because my father rarely paid for the family's expenses: *Where'd you get all this money?* He shrugged and offered to give her a ride around the neighborhood.

My father accelerated into a turn and we tipped in our seats. The roads were slick with rain and the car felt flimsy.

Seriously now, Daddy. Stop driving like this. Are you trying to get us killed? I said. I grasped at my door handle. *One family member dead is enough, don't you think?*

He paused.

Stop talking to me while I'm driving. You're stressing me out.

Don't start on stress, I said.

You have no reasons to be stressed. You're fifteen, he said. *You should be able to handle it. Adults have real stress.* I was too caught up in my own life to understand how he had accrued new responsibility—of bills, of a daughter he had to look after, of the day-to-day logistics of having a dead wife. He was no longer in the background and had emerged to stand at the front of the stage to lead the drama of our family's play.

Don't you realize that your parenting just takes away from me and my freedom? I said, as though parenting should be anything but that. *Grounding me because of bad grades for months and months until I bring them up, when maybe we both know it's not school that's the problem? What type of parent are you? How do you expect me not to be depr—?*

It's been a year since she died. This is all in your head. His driving was jerky.

Arguments like these always became so personal, some form of *If you weren't so lazy, you could get good grades.* Or, if I was home and he didn't want to drive me to see friends: *If your friends really liked you, they would pick you up and drive you the twenty minutes to their party.* Or: *You're making this harder on yourself by being sad.* Or: *Everybody dies. You can't keep going on about this.*

All in my fucking head? I kicked at the rubber rug.

Stop using that language! You have to respect me. He shouted, far from any normal speaking voice.

Respect? I said. *How can I respect you when you're so goddamn controlling?*

You should respect me because I am your father, he said. *See, Katelin, you never respected your mother. She spoiled you too much. She let you walk all over her.*

If you didn't get your way, you would whine and be manipulative like you are, and she'd baby you.

A silence fell between us as we turned onto our street.

Maybe she was too nice to you, he said. *Maybe that's why she's dead.*

I sucked in a breath.

Yeah, well, maybe it would have been better if you had died instead.

I think at the time we both believed what we said. My father found me needy and spoiled: Our mother had stretched herself to give her daughters—especially me—unnecessary things that she could not afford: lessons for horseback riding, tennis, violin, or oboe; summer camps at the town's nature center. From his perspective, I sapped all my mother's energy. For my part, I often wondered—and still sometimes do—what our lives would have been like had my mother lived and he died. Would she have remarried? Would I have had the childhood I did, or the life I have now? I hate her death for how it knocked my family down, but I hate also how I believe I needed it to become who I am.

X

In the cemetery in Fairfield, our van and the moon were the only sources of light. My father aimed the car in the direction of my mother's grave. He cut the engine and left the headlights on bright to illuminate our path. Yi Ma later tells me that it's taboo to visit the cemetery at night or late in the afternoon. *No good to do that*, she says. That's when the spirits roam, I gather.

My mother's grave still did not have a stone. It was marked only by a flimsy plastic sign, a remnant from her burial. I cannot remember now if my father said anything as we stood over her. If he mumbled about how she was up there, wherever she was, *heaven, maybe*, with all of our other dead relatives.

I rewound to the past hour when he roused me from sleep and we made our way here. Just before that, he had swung himself from the bed he once shared with you, his pillow tucked under the covers to approximate your form, his blankets still warm. In the middle of the night, I occasionally woke to a shout from his room. I would creep to the hall to make sure there was no intruder, only to discover that he was talking in his sleep, his voice loud even when dreaming. He sounded as though he was pleading. I wondered if you were visiting him then, and what you were asking or telling him. In my journal from high school, I wrote, "My father mourned in his sleep, where you seemed to haunt him most."

Standing in the path of the headlights, my father and I bowed three times before your grave. A fog settled under the moon, and our faces were constellated with silver.

19.

You should leave, Kiu Kwan insisted to her son. *If you can't make it in Hong Kong, you should go to America.*

After he graduated from high school, Wing Shek did not score well on the college entrance exam, as he put it, so he worked as a draftsman for an electric company. Five and a half days a week, he mapped out where cables needed to be laid throughout buildings in Hong Kong, and eventually found another job as an administrative assistant at another company. It was 1968, and a year earlier, a labor dispute at a flower factory catalyzed demonstrations, which later morphed into protests against the colonial British government, as well as clashes between pro-Communist factions and Hong Kong's government.

My father did not join any of the protests. He thought they seemed dangerous.

I didn't want to cause a big stir, he said. And in his view, no amount of protest would quell the Communist fervor or ease the British colonial hold.[3] All he could do was take it day by day, he tells me. He went to his job, then returned home for dinner with his mother and grandmother. Sometimes, when the summer heat was especially thick, he went with friends to see movies like *Doctor Zhivago*, seeking a reprieve in the air-conditioned theater.

You can't stay in Hong Kong, his mother insisted every week. It was too precarious here, Kiu Kwan was certain. She had a relative whose son had recently left Hong Kong for America, which had started admitting immigrants from Asia with the passage of the Immigration and Nationality Act of 1965. This law opened the door to family members of U.S. citizens and to people like him— who had in-demand professional backgrounds that the government deemed "highly skilled." Kiu Kwan had heard about this, and began to save up for my father to leave. She embroidered clothes for a small paycheck. She rented a room in their apartment to another family and learned to manage the buildings they had purchased with her dead husband's remittances from Cuba. In the absence of a husband, these properties afforded them some stability. They would also help buy her son a plane ticket to America.

But I want to stay, Wing Shek said. He had an easy life in Hong Kong and, according to him, was not a particularly good student. *I was lazy*, he says—though I can't tell if he is being self-deprecating or just blunt, both tendencies I also see in myself.

Just going to the U.S., people's life will greatly improve, you know, my father tells me. *People working overseas, they will make a lot of money—that's usually the belief.*

But there was the question of what would happen with his mother. *Two years, eight months.* My uncle, Wing Chong, had encouraged his oldest son, Denny, to apply to universities in Canada; Wing Chong could bring his other children that way. And my father had decided that once he was settled in the U.S., he would send for their mother. They had assembled a loose plan.

In 1969, Wing Shek enrolled at the University of Wisconsin–Madison, where he studied nuclear engineering. People would always need nuclear power, he figured, but the University of Wisconsin was also the most northern school that accepted him. Martin Luther King Jr.

was killed the year my father applied to universities. He read about the assassination in the newspaper and saw the occasional headline about the civil rights movement in the U.S. As he put it, he knew that America was "not nice" to Black people, especially in the South. He thought that maybe Wisconsin might be better to Chinese people like him, as though that "not nice"-ness was contained to a single region, and racism was as simple as being "not nice." This was the depth of what he knew, or at least acknowledged, on these matters.[4]

Wing Shek arrived in Los Angeles a few months before classes began. One of his friends worked in the kitchen at a restaurant there, and my father washed dishes for cash. Eventually, he traveled to Madison and meandered his first afternoons around campus. He met with academic advisors to argue about his schedule.

I don't think I should be required to take this introductory drafting class because I worked as a draftsman, he insisted to a counselor. She pulled out his record.

You went to a technical school, she said.

If you give me a test, I can do everything those students can do, he insisted. He and the counselor debated this way for a few minutes. In his professional life, he had already put classroom theory to use, so there was no need for him to waste time or his resources. The university just wanted his money, he suspected. Wing Shek increased his volume in case this woman was having trouble hearing him. In case that was why she wasn't listening.

You can do it if you work hard enough, he always heard. He was trying to project confidence. After all, America—as he believed it then—was a meritocracy.

Three years later, Wing Shek finished his undergraduate degree. The university did not offer help with job placement for international students, he tells me, and so, unable to find work, he decided he had two choices: return to Hong Kong, or remain in America and earn a graduate degree. He chose the latter.

X

That summer, before he enrolled at MIT to study nuclear engineering, he worked for a month as a porter at a resort in Wisconsin Dells and roamed the golf course and water park carrying luggage for guests and cleaning toilets. He was flattered when his boss there told him that if he returned next summer—and all the subsequent summers of graduate school—he could train to be a manager.

Hearing his story, I grow defensive and suspicious on his behalf. *But you would've had a graduate degree*, I think but do not say out loud, not wanting to dampen his memory. *Did they think you weren't capable of getting a job?*

They like me, he says. He is proud all these decades later. He knew he wouldn't take the offer because there was no reason for him to return to Wisconsin, but there was flattery in being wanted.

Afterward, he slowly made his way to Massachusetts. He stayed with extended family in Chicago, where he worked at a print shop and occasionally helped at his cousin's restaurant. As the summer ended, he boarded a plane to Boston, where he would begin graduate school nearby at MIT.

It was well into fall when Wing Shek found a rhythm with school and work. He had spent his first few months in temporary housing and had finally moved into a more permanent spot. Only then did he reach out to his relatives in Chicago to give them his new address.

How is the restaurant going? he asked a cousin.

We didn't know how to get ahold of you, she told him instead. *Your mother is dead. Died a few months back in August.*

Wing Shek called his brother, who by now was living in Toronto with his children. Wing Chong was almost three decades older than my father, their lives so separate.

According to my father, my uncle had done the cursory work of trying to reach him. But when Wing Chong was unsuccessful, he decided that since *he* wasn't returning to Hong Kong to attend their mother's funeral—the costs of traveling too high—my father probably wouldn't have wanted to, either. Their mother's funeral carried on without them.

My father says his mother went to the hospital because something was wrong with her throat. Cancer, perhaps. He isn't sure.

One of my father's nephews, who was in Hong Kong when my grandmother passed, tells me she had a bad stroke. That's what killed her.

When I ask my father to confirm this, he frowns.

I don't know, he says slowly. *Possibly.*

I feel the need to apologize for surfacing another uncertainty. I am struck by how few details my father knows about his parents, in their lives and in their deaths. And how for so many years, I have been this way, too.

X

In later years, when I ask him if he has any records of his own father, he shakes his head. After I prod a few more times, he finally tells me this anecdote. About a year after my grandmother's death, my uncle called my father to ask if he wanted any of her belongings. My uncle was moving to Toronto and needed to do something with their mother's clothes and valuables, which included letters from my grandfather in Cuba.

You can just throw it out, my father said. *I don't need you to send me any of that.* His rationale was that it was too expensive to mail a box of nostalgia across the world. But as my father tells me this, there is regret in his voice, followed by a clamorous silence.

This is what my father is left with—six details, including three indisputable facts: His mother was sick and she may have had cancer. She may have had a stroke. Either way, on August 16, 1972, she died in Hong Kong. She was only sixty-six.

20.

When my father first toured the buildings on the edge of Hartford's South End on Franklin Avenue, the real estate agent assured him that these properties would bring steady income.

It was 1988. He had only called the agent to inquire more generally about apartments, and he balked at first when he was led to a nearby commercial space. There was a garage, a bodega, a used Jaguar dealership, and a massage parlor that billed itself as a "leisure and health spa." He would eventually find another apartment building not too far from there. These properties, the agent claimed, would bring steady and easy rent; they would quickly pay for themselves.

All of this, though, for $1.1 million! My father thought our family would never be able to swing the down payment. He and my mother had full-time jobs, but they also had two children to support and were hoping for a third. Lotus Garden was leaking money and had already forced them to file for bankruptcy just a few years earlier. But the properties, he hoped, could be a solution to all of our family's financial problems.

It was a good deal, insisted the agent, who had a friend at the bank who could set my father up with a mortgage. Coincidentally, the agent also knew the owners of the property and could make sure the current tenants stayed.

My father—who often now says that *nothing in the world is free*—could not believe his good luck.

×　×　×

He thought that owning an apartment building in a city—any city—seemed straightforward and was smart business. Real estate ownership was a perk of living in a capitalist country; he wanted to take part. As he'd seen with his mother in Hong Kong, rental income could float the family in hard times. He'd heard get-rich anecdotes about old acquaintances taking risks on businesses that had proven successful. When I was a child, my father often mentioned a former colleague who, in the 1970s or 1980s, asked him to invest in a sandwich company he was helping start in Connecticut. Would my father want to open a franchise? *No*, my father had said. He couldn't spare the money. And besides, *Sandwiches? Why would there need to be a fast-food chain for deli sandwiches?* At this point in the story, often triggered because we had driven by one of the restaurants, the yellow and green logo a taunt, my father would laugh and shake his head. *Bo-o-ooy. It was really something.*

After conversations with the real estate agent and the loan officer, my father shuffled our family's finances and his own savings to accommodate the hefty down payment. He sold his share of a small storefront in Hong Kong that my grandmother had left to him and his brother when she'd passed. My father drained his savings, which he'd promised my mother he would use for our education. It would all be OK, he reassured her. They were fortunate that they had these resources; not many people were this lucky. He'd recoup everything.

My father, however, did not understand real estate or Hartford. He'd heard the real estate agent refer to the area as an *old Italian neighborhood*, and perhaps there was something inherent in this description—the perceived charm, the whiteness—that the agent thought might add to the allure. But this coded subtext was likely lost on my father, who often becomes oblivious to everything else in conversations when terms like *money* are involved.

The agent's depiction of the neighborhood was only partially true. Though Franklin Avenue had once been an Italian enclave starting in the early 1900s, the street's demographics had already started to shift by the time my father toured those buildings. This might have contributed to the agent's eagerness to sell the parcel of buildings to my father, this immigrant from Hong Kong with questionable credit, whom the agent—a white man with his network of white mortgage lenders and white sellers—could not place in his own racial order. Or, perhaps, my father—so clearly *not from here*—and therefore clueless about the buildings, the businesses, and the history he'd be inheriting, seemed like an easy mark.

The census data of the blocks where my father's properties sit tell a familiar story of white flight. The neighborhood, up until the 1980s, was nearly all white, until it became increasingly Latino, many of its residents Puerto Rican. And a couple of decades before that, when laws that prevented Black residents from securing mortgages were lifted and Black people began to move into Hartford, their white neighbors headed for the suburbs and sold their homes in the city for less than what they were worth, undermining property values. This exodus hurt Hartford's economic health for years to come and racially segregated the city even further.

Hartford was once considered the wealthiest American city. Following the Civil War, and starting in the nineteenth century, it was known as the "insurance capital of the world" because—as my mother's work would attest—there were so many companies headquartered there. That was another era, though. The city had not seen that type of affluence in decades.

In drives along I-91 through Hartford, my family passed the old Colt Armory, which had been vacant since 1994. Its iconic blue onion-shaped dome and enormous brick complex—rebuilt by Elizabeth Colt after it burned in 1864 in a rumored arson by Confederate sympathizers—sat next to the highway. The building's emptiness was eerie and apparent from our car. Near the armory was a billboard my family always read out loud when we drove past: HARTFORD: NEW ENGLAND'S RISING STAR. In high school, I found that slogan peculiar, if not desperate. It was an unsubtle attempt to hoist Hartford into an economic center—to attract large businesses and their potential employees. It was a billboard sponsored by the Hartford Image Project, a marketing group that created the slogan. The group also funded developmental projects, which resulted in the demolition of some public housing units in the process. The slogan seemed both condescending and a side step of the issues that made Hartford's poverty and its disparities across race prevalent. In a way, it reminded me of the showiness of my parents' own markers of class—my mother's slow payment of the baby grand piano and her purchase of a Land Rover in order to compete with her brother's new Lexus—despite the reality of their finances.

X

One of my earliest memories of summer mornings as a kid followed this pattern: Steph and Caroline were at their summer jobs and my mother was at Aetna. My father had stopped taking new office jobs—or perhaps they had stopped taking him—and his button-up shirts collected dust in his closet. He would manage the properties full-time, he insisted to my mother, since his alternatives for making money were dwindling. I woke late to the sound of him downstairs on the phone. I heard half of the conversation.

When are you going to give me my money? he said.

You need to give me my money.

You owe me so many months rent.

A pause.

This IS my normal speaking voice.

I'm not shouting, he shouted.

Other mornings, I listened to my father talking into a pocket translator that he bought from Ocean State Job Lot. He was always trying to speak Spanish to his tenants, some of whom were from Puerto Rico or the Dominican Republic. He thought he was being clever, or polite, like he would have been tickled if someone tried to speak to him in Taishanese.

Hola. ¿Cómo estás? ¿Tienes dinero? he said.

He typed something into the machine.

Dinero, the little machine said in its robotic voice.

Dinero, he would say slowly, stretching each syllable. *Din-AIR-oh. Hola. ¿Tienes dinero?*

Why not sell? my mother frequently asked my father, anxious because these buildings were only earning our family more debt. *Why not? You're not making any money from these properties. They're more trouble than they're worth.*

My father often pointed out two tenants who mostly paid their rent on time—a man who ran the bodega, and a woman who operated the massage parlor. They asked him for very little, he said. This was miraculous to me, since it seemed there were constant roof leaks or ruptured pipes, which my father insisted on fixing himself because he said he could not afford to hire professionals. This just compounded the problems. My father kept these properties to similar standards he had for his own house. This left much to be desired and surely outraged his tenants, and the city would later take issue with this when they condemned one of his buildings. The remaining apartment units that my father rented out slowly emptied and, for the most part, remained that way. The bodega owner would stay for decades, only leaving when he bought his own storefront down the block.

Good for them that they were doing well enough to get their own spot, I say on the phone when my father tells me.

Mm, he says. I'm uncertain if his tone is one of approval, or if he's upset about his lost rent.

X

When somebody rents something from you, my father says, *you cannot control them*, so he does not ask questions. He insists he does not care who rents his properties—where they come from, what they do, who they are—as long as they can pay. He has the impossibly hefty mortgage and the bankruptcy on his shoulders, and so he takes what he can get.

One evening when I was in middle school, I was on the phone with a friend while the local news was playing on TV.

A reporter was talking about a spa and health club that the FBI, the IRS, and local police had busted in Hartford. It had acted as a front for a brothel for decades, the reporter said, and had made millions of dollars in profit. The reporter stood in front of a building that looked familiar, with its boxy shape and twin panels of windows surrounded by tan stucco. And then I saw the sign—with our home phone number—hanging by one of the windows. FOR RENT 860-xxx-xxxx.

That's the building my dad rents out to people, I told my friend. *It's on the news!* I dug my fingers into the carpet and tugged at the fibers.

At this moment, the confounding calls to my house suddenly made sense. The home phone would trill, and I would answer, standing in the kitchen along the red Formica counter with a ball-point pen in hand, ready to record a message for my parents.

Chow family, I answered, as instructed by my sisters. *May I ask who's calling please?*

You got girls? A man asked.

Huh? I said.

Girls? You got girls?

I think you have the wrong number.

These calls didn't come often enough to make me wonder too much, but still so frequently that I registered them.

Weird. I returned to the kitchen table where Steph and Caroline were bent over their textbooks.

When I was in high school, I asked my father about these properties. He needed my help hauling trash from one of the vacant buildings.

Did you know about it? I asked.

What, he said.

You know, I said. *The spa.*

Hey, he said. His voice picked up volume. *They tell me, it's a spa. Why should I think it's not?*

I didn't reply.

Besides, he said, narrowing his words into a point. *It's none of my business to ask.*

Eventually, when I am in my late twenties, I visit my father's house to sift through papers on my mother's desk, looking for anything that might help me understand her better. I am perplexed to find a sun-faded section of the *Hartford Courant* sitting on top of old bills. *Brothel Customers May Face Charges*, March 31, 2004. Had my father left this here for me after one of our conversations on the subject? Had this newspaper been one of the last things my mother had reviewed at her desk?

"There could be a lot of nervous johns out there," the article begins, "now that law enforcement officials say that hundreds of former customers at a closed Hartford brothel could face charges as part of an investigation into one of the most lucrative prostitution operations ever seen in the city."

You must have followed the news of this sting closely, though I cannot imagine your reaction. Shock? Anger? Anger feels right. I wonder if that's what made you demand that you and your husband fill out bankruptcy paperwork again, finally formally evicting the women who ran the spa and brothel, who owed tens of thousands in back rent. This all surfaced in the last six months before your death. That this was the background to your sickness made me hurt for you and Daddy both.

X

My father uses an argument about *depreciation* to defend his attachment to objects. In his view, he cannot put these buildings in Hartford on the market because they are valued at less than half of what he originally paid. He still refuses to sell our family's old cars that either no longer work or are beyond repair—a Chrysler New Yorker, his totaled Miata, my mother's old Land Rover, and the minivan—because he thinks each will only get a few hundred dollars.

My father let our cars rust in our driveway for decades until a new family moved in next door after I left for college. They complained that the cars were parked too close to their yard. *Was he still driving them?* they might have inquired, passive-aggressively. They planted hedges to block his house from their view. Their message was clear: my father's presence was driving down their property values. Their requests must have finally shamed my father into moving the Chrysler to the empty garage in Hartford, and their row of shrubs grew nearly two stories high. Each time I see them when I visit my father, I flush with embarrassment.

If my father felt cheated by the real estate agent, he never said so. He just tells me now: *Yeah, probably he was no good, probably he worked with the guy at the bank to get me a mortgage because he knew he'd get a commission. And probably he worked with the owners of the building too to set a high price.*

He also says: *I never would have been able to get a mortgage without that guy.*

I can't tell from this if my father is grateful or bitter; if he feels scammed or like a scammer. His buildings in Hartford—save for another auto repair shop and a small church that has moved into the massage parlor's former space—sit vacant. But then he says, as if to shake himself out of regret, *That's life though. What can you do?*

So many other people couldn't have gotten a loan, I say to him years later when we are talking about these buildings yet again, and

I am echoing my mother's sentiments and suggesting that he sell them. Our conversation moves in circles. *None of the people who have rented from you would have gotten those loans from that guy. This was by design.*

We are talking about the difference between his story, an immigrant from China by way of Hong Kong, and the stories of some of his tenants, immigrants from the Dominican Republic or refugees from Liberia. We are talking about racism, or at least I am, though I can never be sure with my father.

Well, he says in the tone he uses to cut our conversations short, *it's a fact of life.*

I'm not sure if it means that he disagrees with what I've said, or if maybe he is bothered by it.

Other facts of life:

In 1974, at the urging of local activists, federal attorneys sued some real estate firms in Hartford, West Hartford, and Wethersfield, alleging that the firms had "steered" white people away from properties in racially diverse neighborhoods in Hartford and encouraged buyers who were Black or Puerto Rican. The firms denied any wrongdoing, but formally agreed to comply with the Fair Housing Act.

According to Census data from 2000, in Connecticut, 48.1 percent of people who identified as Asian owned their homes, compared to 72.5 percent of white people, 36.5 percent of Black people and 28.1 percent of Hispanic people.

In 2017, a report on the Greater Hartford area found that of the people surveyed who received high-cost mortgages, 3 percent were white, compared to 10 percent who were Latino, or 12 percent who were Black.

X

In my father's eyes, he was trying to help our family survive. He had always considered himself pragmatic. He told me constantly when I was a teenager that it didn't matter how I solved problems in physics—I could use calculus equations or I could brute-force the answer with my confounding boxes and diagrams—because the destination was most important, not the process. It all ends up the same. But what if, I often asked, it didn't start the same? Life is not an equation. Is it any wonder that his version of survival seems so lonesome? I keep wanting to pose this last question to my father, but I don't know how.

21.

I struggle to recall tender moments between my parents. I ask my sisters what they remember, and one of the first things they mention is a game we played each time we came home from Marshalls or Bob's, where our mother took us school shopping for the year.

Guess how much it cost, our mother asked my father. She held up a shirt that she bought for him from the boy's section of Marshalls. It was a polo, with the actual Polo logo.

Guess how much, I echoed. I glanced from my father's face to the shirt. Sometimes my mother instructed my sisters and me to hide what we had bought. My parents' finances were such that everything my mother made was the family's and, also, his. But everything my father made was his.

The shirt was on sale. Purchased for something like $8.99, original price $30.

One dollar? my father said.
  No. My mother frowned. *It's a nice shirt.*
  Three dollars? he said.
  No.
  Four?
  No. Irritation slipped into her voice.

Five? He always low-balled the answers, entertained by this game. He thought my mother could have gotten a better deal if she'd looked harder. Tried harder.

No.

Six?

$8.99, she snapped.

Wah, he said. *So much.*

I can still recall his laughter here, derisive, acidic.

22.

After the last customers were served, the staff crowded in the kitchen for family meal.

I had just started working at Green Tea/Green Olive Bistro, a restaurant not far from my house. The owners, Cindy and Denny, were my parents' age. They'd immigrated to the U.S. by way of Hong Kong and Vietnam, and for the past couple of decades, they ran another restaurant that was also called Green Tea in a neighboring suburb. For their new venture, they rented space in an old Uno Pizzeria, the same one my mother had pointed out whenever we drove home from the grocery store. According to her, that location was tough for any restaurant, including a national chain like Uno, since it was tucked in a sleepy strip mall plaza and not visible from the turnpike. That was one of the problems with Lotus Garden, my mother was certain: its relatively isolated location compounded by other issues. My mother's comment lingered each time I walked into Green Tea/Green Olive for my shifts as a hostess.

But Cindy and Denny were optimistic. They wanted to make the most of the pizza ovens, so they hired a chef who had defected from a popular spot in New Haven that was known for its clam pies. They used the word *fusion* to describe the concept, and I could tell they were eager to try something new. Maybe, they hoped, the idea could catch and give them the success their first restaurant had not found.

When I saw the menu, though, I understood that it was a restaurant with two separate kitchens, little merging together. On one side, there was a kitchen where chefs turned out plates of General Tso's and orange chicken—American Chinese takeout food, as my father called it. On the other side were the pizzas, which customers hesitated to order, remarking to me how novel this was while I smiled blandly and poured them water. (These same customers, not surprisingly, were also the type to compliment me on my English.)

I spent my shifts tethered to the hostess stand, snacking on broken fortune cookies and counting how many people I'd seated, the numbers for the evenings rarely reaching more than forty or fifty guests. I knew this was not optimal and that Green Tea risked a future like Lotus Garden, which now only existed as boxed-up dishware and dusted paper menus in my family's basement.

Over the months that I'd worked at the restaurant, I'd developed a protectiveness for it. It was kitschy and so earnest in its pursuit of what Cindy and Denny thought diners might want, though ultimately, in the eyes of its customers, it was overpriced pizza and Chinese takeout. But I found comfort within its walls, in the ways Cindy and Denny were determined to ensure its survival by incorporating elements they hoped would create a sophisticated or exciting ambiance: the jazz band that played each weekend evening; the flaming scorpion bowls that the bartender, a young woman from Hong Kong studying epidemiology at a local university, whisked throughout the dining room.[5]

I often tried to coax my father to the restaurant toward the ends of my shifts.

Just come, I invited him. *Get something small, I'll pay for it. Just sit and listen to the music.*

He visited once and sat in a booth by the bar. He studied the entire menu and remarked how expensive each of the dishes was, and asked what the staff would eat for family meal later.

He had an exuberant, uncomfortable energy about him. There was a wistfulness that I would see amplified when I took him to Cindy and Denny's original Green Tea a half hour away, which served dim sum and had a modest clientele that spoke Cantonese.

At this original Green Tea, I watched my father take in the space. He sat, his mouth slightly ajar, and surveilled the waitstaff as they carried metal trays of har gau and siu mai to tables. He craned his neck to get a better look at the chicken feet, not uncommon in Cantonese restaurants. But Cantonese restaurants were not common in suburban Connecticut, which made this all the more impressive. I understood then that my father was seeing the version of Lotus Garden that never surfaced. This moment unearthed the parallels between us. I was drawn to Green Tea for the ways it reminded me of my parents' restaurant, and how it might provide answers to some of my unspoken questions. My father had done the same when he'd opened Lotus Garden, curious to understand the father he'd never met, hoping that my grandfather's successes would transfer to him. I am not sure what answers, if any, my father gained. If Lotus Garden had allowed him a closure or a closeness to his father, or if it only emphasized their distance. It is always strange when a child realizes that they are attempting to recreate their parents' path with their own; something uncanny within these movements, embedded within it a contradictory worry of recreation and a hope of carrying out a wish that had not been fulfilled.

But Green Tea/Green Olive would not last. This seemed clear to me long before it became true.

X

A memory from when I was five:

It was a summer evening that was thick with humidity and mosquitoes. My father broke stalks of sugar cane into small pieces with a cleaver. He drew the blade back and slammed it into the cutting board until cane splintered. I winced each time. He handed me a small piece while he popped another into his mouth.

Ho sik, he said.

Ho sik, I agreed.

This is like candy. This is where sugar comes from. Make sure you chew out all the juices. He demonstrated, his teeth macerating the fiber. *They grow a lot of sugar cane in Cuba.*

I was young, but not too young to know that this was where my grandfather had lived. At the time, I did not understand how grief could be consumed, how food was one way to process a memory, or the absence of one. My father could not speak of what questions the cane made him ask about his own life. All I could taste was sweet juice, which I sucked from the woody pulp until it was dry.

Mimicking my father, I whacked the trash can open. I spit out the cane.

X

During family meal, I filled my plate with leftovers from service, along with blistered green beans with soy sauce and black bean paste; chicken, sliced and sautéed with carrots and other leftover vegetables; a tender beef stewed with daikon that was soft like a pat of butter; a soup with a thin broth and briny, boiled knots of seaweed. In Cantonese, I answered the chefs' questions about my family and where they were born, laughing when they teased me about my lack of fluency and promising that I'd work on my pronunciation.

Our dishes in hand, we fanned along empty tables. The band that Cindy and Denny hired was finishing their set, the last few customers readying to leave. We ate in companionable silence. When everybody came together at the end of the night like this, it felt familiar, something joyous and relieved in how we bent over our plates. It was amazing how we could create our own space this quickly, even if temporary.

X

Whenever I take my father for dim sum or to a Cantonese restaurant, I let him pick what we'll eat. He enthusiastically reads the menu out loud. I always expect him to order in Cantonese or Taishanese. When he does not, when he instead asks for another napkin or a pot of chrysanthemum tea in English, I am perplexed. Maybe he is self-conscious about his fluency these days. Maybe he worries he doesn't know the right slang. His Chinese finally emerges when the waitress asks what dialects he speaks. A familiar conversation in Cantonese unfolds.

My father sits up straighter, enthusiastic and eager to have a rare audience when the waitress poses these questions to him:

Where were you born?

What is your last name? How do you write the character for Chow?

When did you come to the United States?

Oh, your daughter lives in [Seattle or Boston or New York or D.C.]?

Oh, there's no good dim sum where you live? Where is that, again? Connecticut?

Yes, such a shame. You should visit your daughter more. She'll treat you.

Ha ha ha. You're right. A daughter should always take care of her father, ha ha ha.

X

After the staff meal, Cindy gathered leftovers into quart containers.

For your daddy. She pushed a bag into my arms, insistent. When I first started at Green Tea, Cindy had asked about my parents, and after I mentioned that my mother had died, she made sure I left my shifts with plenty of food. This small act was so comforting in its matter-of-factness; though it made me long for my mother—to be mothered—it did not highlight her absence, which was a relief.

When I returned home, my father and I fell into a routine we had only recently established—as though working at this restaurant had provided us an armistice. He'd rise from his seat in the family room, where he'd spent my whole shift watching a documentary about space travel or a war or whatever the local PBS station aired. While I took off my shoes, he pulled the containers from the bag and appraised each one.

At the kitchen table, I watched my father spoon soup into a bowl. He chewed on a tangle of seaweed while he lifted open the container with the braised beef. Steam fogged his glasses and the gentle scent of star anise floated across the table.

They gave you a lot of meat. Approval lined his voice.

I arranged the rest of the food in front of him. The school year would start again in just a few weeks. I hoped that in less than a year, I'd be far from this house.

Under the dim kitchen light, watching my father slurp the soup, I understood I was witnessing a memory in progress—of the two of us, separately, recalling this moment, and of our future selves returning here to this scene.

23.

I drove through Wethersfield's surrounding towns in your old van, slowly, cautiously, leaning into the newfound independence that a license afforded. I did not want to be in the house. The house was diseased, dark and sickly and sad.

I was lucky that my father let me use the van, that he hadn't gotten rid of our old cars, that he added me to his car insurance policy without much begging on my part. Driving meant I could be away from the house, which was good for us both. I had no curfew, or at least I ignored my curfew and any of its potential consequences, and I often stayed out late and slept at friend's houses.

I drove from my weekend shifts at Green Tea, and from my job at a high-end clothing store near the high school.

I drove to the bagel shop where a friend worked, and the gelateria where another had a couple of shifts each week.

I drove to therapy, my counselor agreeing to see me for free after she moved to private practice and did not accept our state insurance.

I drove home from school after tennis, after band practice, after study sessions.

X X X

Slowly, and often without a map, I navigated the highways and streets around our house. Intuition and years of watching you and Daddy in the driver's seat led me. I flipped my blinkers on hundreds of feet before I turned. I looked over my shoulders multiple times, anxiously, before switching lanes. I wanted to yell out to the empty rows of seats behind me, *Girls, all of you help me merge, OK?* the way you had, as if invoking the child selves of my sisters and me—as you. You had always turned driving into a team sport, starting most trips by holding up a packet of Wrigley's and asking if anyone wanted any *gums*. Your tendency to pluralize everything was contagious, as if you were delighting in the bounty around you. *I want some gums*, my sisters and I hollered back at you, a chorus.

Before I unlocked the car, I did as you had frequently instructed me, Caroline, and Steph: I peered in the back seats and under the van to make sure no one was hiding there. You had heard stories of dangerous men lurking beneath women's cars in grocery store parking lots. *Somebody could be waiting to getchu*, you told me, your usual playfulness gone. Yet when I checked those spots as a teenager, I was not only worried that I would find a threatening man—I was anxious that I would find you.

Route 2 was one of the only freeways that didn't scare you, Mommy. That you had sat in this same driver's seat years earlier never escaped me. This muscle memory that guided me—it was not just mine— was our version of autopilot.

A year before, when I was fifteen, I wrote in my journal: "My father once told me, 'Success makes a person survive.'" He repeated this frequently when we argued about college—where he thought I should apply (all the Ivy League schools), where he thought would actually admit me (definitely not any of the Ivies, possibly not our state schools, despite my honors classes and decent grades).

I was never sure how to respond when he leaned on this phrase. When you died, we had clutched at whatever it was that might translate to survival. My father thought accolades or money would do the trick. At the time, this confounded me; it did not seem we had either. I understand now that is all relative. We had what my father had always hoped for when first moving to America: a house with a mortgage, a seemingly assured way to go to college, enough food. This ascent up the so-called societal ladder, made possible because American law had so conveniently decided he was the *right type* of immigrant, was enough for him.[6] My father wrote on my financial aid forms that he spent $500 on food a year, and to him, this was due to frugality and not a sign of poverty; our dependence on the state's Medicaid program for healthcare was a product of circumstance, not class. This was his rationale, which he passed on to me, which would take me years to question.

On my way home from hanging with friends or school, I drove the same route you took from the barn, my left foot bare and tucked under my right leg and my shoes kicked under my seat. After midnight, Route 2 to Wethersfield was dependably empty. I let its stillness comfort me. The Glastonbury woods and the Connecticut River snaked black underneath the pavement and the concrete bridges. On summers, I rolled down the windows and crooned along to whatever CD that Kiah or another friend, Meg, had burned me. In many of these moments, I felt calm and contemplative, and the loneliness that often registered instead felt right. I would miss these moments later in life; how freeing it felt to be by myself, with so much in my future feeling like a possibility.

Success makes a person survive. But considering the two of you and where we had wound up, I wasn't sure I could agree. And besides, why stop at survival? I wish I could ask you. Why not want something more, like joy? But maybe this is what you thought you couldn't have; maybe this is what you wanted your daughters to have as our legacy.

24.

The thought of leaving home did not come without guilt. I knew that once I moved away, it would just be my father and the balloons. Steph and Caroline had brought some home years earlier for his birthday, and afterward, he and I had let those balloons bob in the corner of the family room. They eventually gravitated toward the fireplace on the back wall. Simple physics probably explained why the balloons began to list: air from the chimney had created a vacuum, maybe. But I was never good at physics, and had to read my textbook many times over to understand the most basic problems. Instead, I preferred to imagine there was some spirit clenching the strings in her fists. Slowly tugging them closer. You, with your face locked in concentration.

I shouldn't have to do this, you seemed to say. *Why am I the one doing this?* Your shoulders slouched in defeat.

As the balloons shriveled, they came to their own resting spots at the base of the fireplace, folded gently over the tin box of Jonathan's ashes to make a shiny, crinkled blanket. As if you had wanted the remnants of our birthday celebrations to keep your dead son warm. As if you understood we had forgotten, or were close to forgetting, what you had asked. But a lethargy had settled into our remaining family, and the wilted balloon only obscured Jonathan from our sights. Together, they would linger as my father's companions.

25.

A few months after I graduated from high school, my father and I stood in front of Old Faithful with dozens of other tourists. We leaned against a fence and waited for the geyser to erupt. Old Faithful, true to its name, is a "highly predictable" geyser. It erupts twenty times a day, 60 to 110 minutes between its blasts of scalding water that soar 184 feet.

I thought it was a little cheesy how we waited an hour for this *thing* that would only briefly appear. Like we were at a zoo, anticipating the emergence of a great animal in an enclosure, only to see it immediately turn and scuttle back to its hiding spot.

I watched my father watch the geyser opening.

I watched other tourists watch the hole.

He looked so much like a dad then, with an SLR camera strapped around his neck and his signature faded blue baseball cap and clip-on sunglasses flipped up above his glasses.

Look, look, he exclaimed. The crowd around us cooed as water punched from the ground skyward, and I felt a brief awe watching it spit hot water and steam.

For many years, geologists weren't clear how, exactly, Old Faithful's underground functioned. But in 2017, a team of scientists from the University of Utah used tiny sensors to measure the vibrations in the ground that the geyser created when it erupted. From that data, they discovered there was an enormous hidden reservoir full of hydrothermal fluid and more than 79 million gallons of water that fed Old Faithful. When I read this, I liked it immediately, this idea of a source of energy and power sitting latent until it was needed. The quick draw of power, the inevitable and consistent return. It felt hopeful.

My father bared his teeth giddily, his gold and silver fillings glinting. And then, like all the other tourists, he brought his camera to his face.

Here, I felt a pang. A longing for you. You would have wanted to see this, too. You would have watched your husband, then noticed me observing the both of you. Your eyes alight, you would blush, then try to deflect my attention by commenting on one of the other tourist families. How parents didn't seem to notice their small children toddling to the edges of the boardwalk, how if it kept on, you would walk over there and point this out. Despite your critiques, you were a woman who understood delight, not immune to the wonders of this place.

Wah, you would have exclaimed, thrilled at the sight of the geyser and surprised still after the wait, *ho dai.*

My father had mentioned a few weeks earlier that he'd always wanted to see Old Faithful. *Might be good to see*, he'd said. *Why not, since we're there.* All casual, like it didn't matter to him, the most direct way he'd ever communicated his wants in years.

So there we were at Yellowstone. We were in the middle of a cross-country trip from Connecticut to Seattle, where I'd soon start at the University of Washington. For the past week, we'd been on the Amtrak watching cornfields and mountains fly by. At one of the stops, we splurged on a rental car and took a short trip to Yellowstone.

You can see the country this way, my father had said as he bought our rail passes. This was cheaper than flying, and we wouldn't have to worry about paying for checked luggage. The idea was that after he dropped me in Seattle, he'd loop back across the country by himself. There was so much distance between where the train was taking us and our home, further from you. My relief grew.

During lengthy stops, we climbed down to the platform to stretch our legs and take long inhales of fresh air. We barely spoke—not about what we were seeing; not about how I was moving across the country for school; not about how we were getting tired of train food and, worse, train bathrooms; not about how for the first time in twenty-seven years, he'd soon be living by himself. The latter was something he'd have to deal with on his own in a few weeks when he was home, creating a life in the negative space. For the time being, we stretched our legs across our own rows of seats and used our coats as pillows and slept restless nights, our hands clutching our valuables.

X

We stopped at a Chinese restaurant near Yellowstone for lunch. It had wood-paneled walls flecked with grease and a menu with all the usual American Chinese fare. We shared plates of moo goo gai pan and beef chow fun and ate them with bowls of rice. My father asked the waitress if they had spareribs, though they weren't listed on the menu. A few minutes later, she set a small metal plate of glistening barbecued ribs in front of us—leftovers from the staff meal. We chewed on the ribs and spat the bones on napkins. We paused only to wipe the grease from our lips, grateful after days of eating microwaved pizza. At the time, I thought my father insisted on eating here because he was curious about how others had pulled off their Chinese restaurants, but in retrospect, I wonder if there was a comfort—and a safety—in somewhere familiar.

When I see my father in places like this—national parks or other mostly white spaces—I feel a tinge of irony. Like our presence here is a tiny yet long-formed act of resistance.

In 1870, the Washburn Expedition came across what is now known as Old Faithful. They admired this geyser, and eventually created Yellowstone National Park.

In order to attract white visitors to Yellowstone, park officials falsely claimed that the indigenous people who first lived on that land—who were pushed out and forcibly removed—were afraid of the area because of its evil spirits. They would avoid the park, therefore making it *safe* for visitors. This supposed fear was untrue, as evidenced by the many archaeological sites throughout the land that link back to tribal nations that include the Crow, the Blackfeet, and the Shoshone-Bannock, among others. Instead, the myth only reflected the era. Yellowstone—and national parks in general—were founded in the late 1800s as havens for white Americans to flee the urbanization happening at home. Madison Grant, who led the national parks movement, was a white supremacist. His tome *The Passing of the Great Race* served as inspiration for both Adolf Hitler and restrictive U.S. immigration laws. Grant and his followers positioned the parks this way: White people could reconnect with the land; they could flee the new wave of immigrants, and the brown and Black people, too.

I'm troubled by how our visit to parks can sometimes feel like small triumphs and how our entrance to this space is a conquest of its own. This land was never ours and it is not ours and it will never be ours. What is it about this country that makes it so that to hold something as our own is to have *won*?

X

A couple of afternoons later, the train pulled up to our last stop. In the aisle, I stretched each of my arms and cracked my knuckles. Seattle's King Street Station. I dragged two suitcases and climbed down the stairs.

We made it, I said to my father as I helped lower his suitcase to the platform.

Mmm, he said.

Mmm. I unintentionally mimicked him.

We kept nodding at one another. I shifted on my feet, thrilled and animated with anticipation. Everything felt fresh here, a reprieve after the days on the train. We took in the brick clock tower in front of us, high-rise buildings shooting toward the sky, which was expansively, platonically cerulean. I helped him untwist the backpack straps that dug into his shoulders and I led us inside to where Caroline waited. This would be my home, now. We had finally arrived.

In just a week, my father would cross the country once again. He would travel south and then east to the Grand Canyon. It was only when he'd arrived at home that he would call Caroline, Steph, and me. I took the call reclined in my dorm room on my bottom bunk, the outline of Mount Tahoma pinkened by the setting sun, a leaky, cracked egg.

My father would recall on the phone: When he was halfway down the trail, the Arizona heat was dry and overwhelming. He felt light in the head. It had been relatively cool when he'd started his walk just an hour before. But suddenly, he was drenched with perspiration. He took a sip from his bottle, which was only half full of lukewarm water. For a few minutes, he closed his eyes.

Are you OK? A hiker passing asked.

My father nodded. He hauled himself to his feet.

Aiya, I said on the phone. *Why wouldn't you bring more water?* It was less a question and more a reprimand. I should've been relieved that he'd made it home, but instead, I was pressed with worry that he'd been reckless.

Take care of yourself, I said. I wanted to shake him through the phone, to tell him that he needed to be more careful so that he could live forever.

PART THREE

1.

Mommy, I can see you now. You're in a kayak on Portage Bay between Lake Union and Lake Washington. Boathouses bob in place near the shore, and the I-5 bridge stretches across the horizon, the morning traffic dragging with it a ribbon of sound. This image comes from a photo of you on a family trip we took when I was a kid that I superimposed onto a scene of Seattle. I've only been in this new city, at college, for a few days. At sunrise, jet lag flung me out of my bottom bunk. I jogged to the water just a few blocks from my dorm.

This is such a stereotypical Seattle situation, you in a kayak. You wear a life vest that is too large, and it puffs around your shoulders in a way that makes you look neckless. The vest isn't even fastened, and I don't think you know how to swim, so this concerns me.

But you don't care. You're already dead.

Your lips curve and the corner of your eyes crinkle with roguish pleasure. You dip your paddle and bat water at your brother. In this vision, he is somehow also here in his own kayak. You and Kau Fu laugh uproariously and yell tamer Cantonese profanities at one another, the water chilly as it speckles your clothes. You're wearing that gray polo dress, though it does not bother you here. You tug at the fabric to show that it's soft and flexible. It is difficult to watch you and your brother without absorbing your lightness.

x x x

Seeing you here isn't eerie. It's hard, yes, in the way that my body braces for a crash that will deflate me. I had mistakenly assumed I'd left you behind, that the winding train route throughout the country would have derailed you.

Everything about Seattle, and its mountains, and its trees, and its lakes, and the stretch of the Puget Sound, has gifted me a propulsiveness. As though, hungrily gulping down this air, I am brand new.

X

Is this what it means to say goodbye to your ghost?

I believed that at seventeen, just by leaving home, I could begin to exorcise my grief.

Sure, sure, sure. If I repeated that enough, it would become true. We tell ourselves lies all of the time.

2.

A pain shot through my stomach for the fifth day in a row while I texted my sisters mundane details about my week. I was only a couple of months into my freshman year of college. *I can't believe I willingly signed up for a natural science class with a quantum physicist, it is actually very hard, I didn't think this would be real physics??* or *I've been getting nightmares lately, which is weird,* or *Tried out a new Thai spot on The Ave for dinner,* or *Do you think my stomachaches are just stress cramps or something?* I was heading into my dorm when a stretch of sirens sounded off in the distance and approached campus. I would later learn that a man named In Soo Chun had stopped along the oversized concrete and brick platforms in Red Square near the university president's office. For a couple of years, Chun worked for the university as a custodian. Amid the throng of students meandering to their next class, he doused himself with gasoline. Then, he lit himself on fire.

The school newspaper published a photo of Chun engulfed in flames. Seeing this image all these years later, I feel a similar revulsion and need to click away from the screen: A crowd of students surrounds a blazing mass, which upon first glance, is easy to mistake for anything besides Chun's engulfed body. Students dump water on Chun and try to beat away the flames with their jackets. Everybody looks in motion, bodies leaning toward Chun.

X

Why did he do it? many asked afterward. The university's narrative, which most seemed to accept, was that Chun was mentally unstable. A few people online wondered, though, if Chun's self-immolation was a form of protest; they mentioned that Chun was Korean, implying there might be something "cultural" at play.

I wasn't satisfied with these theories, certainly not the latter. I did not know enough to draw any conclusion, but for weeks, I kept surfacing Chun's story in all my conversations.

Don't you just keep thinking about that man, I found myself saying to new friends, the guy I was starting to date, people I met on campus or at parties.

I don't know, they said. They entertained me for a few minutes before they slid us toward safer topics, as though talk of death was contagious.

A few years later, one of my friends will write about In Soo Chun for the school's paper. Chun was in his sixties and worked for two and a half years as a custodian for the university. Chun had left behind a manifesto that revealed that he thought the university had a covert drug and prostitution ring and that there were Korean operatives who had infiltrated the custodial department. He was certain that he was being monitored. He also wrote that he had, since 1987, "seriously suffered with a thought disorder and a brain slash and a sudden black-out and memory loss."

I couldn't articulate why his death stuck with me. His circumstances were different from my parents', but something about him brought them to mind, and the way they seemed alone in their interior lives. There was the obvious connection—that they were all immigrants. But there was also the way in which their needs in life had slipped beyond notice; how Chun returned me to a defensive stance—so bothered by how easy it was to look past stories like his.

X

In a couple of years, during my winter break, my family would convene at Steph's apartment in Rhode Island, where she was completing a medical residency. My sisters, father, and I sprawled, starfished, on Steph's sectional, watching the movie *A Thousand Years of Good Prayers*.

I need to watch it as part of my honors thesis, I had announced. I was writing about intergenerational grief, so clumsily searching for reflections of my own family. *Is it OK if we all watch it?*

Wow, that's something, my father had said. *You want us to help you with class work?*

I hit play anyway. It was an adaptation of a short story by Yiyun Li. A man named Mr. Shi visits his adult daughter, Yilan, in America. Though he does not speak much English, he makes friends everywhere: with a woman on his flight, Jehovah's Witnesses in his daughter's apartment, an elderly woman in a park. Yilan has recently gone through a divorce, and ever since her mother died, she and her father have not spoken much. In her small apartment, the two of them are tense. They circle around one another, litigating and re-litigating their pasts. Yilan grew up believing her father had been unfaithful to her mother. Mr. Shi worried that his daughter, recently divorced, was lonely in America. Though Yilan's mother does not appear in being, only mentioned in conversation, her absence blankets the film.

After it ended, my family remained in our seats. We blinked slowly. My father took off his glasses and rubbed his eyes.

What did you think? I said to the room, cautious.

Well, my father began. He shrugged and brought up a supporting character, an elderly Iranian woman, whom Mr. Shi had met in a park. The two of them, both immigrants, spoke in a mix of Farsi, Mandarin, and the occasional English. *Seems to me that the father has a good, new friendship with the old lady.*

That was your takeaway? The on-screen friendship he mentioned had ended abruptly because the woman had been sent to live in a nursing home against her wishes.

My father shrugged again and announced that he was tired and going to sleep. After he left the room, Steph turned to Caroline and me.

I was so worried that this would make Daddy sad, she said. *I thought this might make him think of Mommy.*

Yeah, Caroline and I agreed, our voices flat. If we saw ourselves in the film, we did not share. All those years later, we still did not know how to talk about our mother, her death, and what it had done, was doing, to our family.

In one scene that I highlighted in my college paper, Yilan tries to explain the dissolution of her marriage and snaps at her father.

"You don't know what it's like, Dad. If you grew up in a language in which you never learned to express your feelings," she says. "It would be easier to learn to talk in a new language. It makes you a new person." As a twenty-one-year-old, I took this exchange literally, writing that Yilan and her father's problems arose from gaps in translation. I attributed this to the fact that Yilan had moved to the United States and her father had not. This oversimplification was so hopeful, as though language skills alone could remedy a father-daughter relationship. Now, watching the film again all these years later, I am devastated instead by the familiarity of the distance between Yilan and her father—how despite their efforts, they continue to talk past one another, or not at all.

X

A week after Chun's death, I woke in the middle of the night, sweaty and fevered. In a panic, I burst into the hall, freshly nightmared.

I ran into a girl I'd chatted casually with a few times. She lived a few rooms down on what my friends and I deemed *the quiet side of the floor*, where everybody kept their doors closed so they could study. She unlocked the communal bathroom's door.

Can you tell me that I'm not dreaming? I floated into the bathroom after her. *I just had a nightmare that I was possessed.*

I paced frantically by the showers. *Can you please tell me that I'm awake?*

She led me to a bench by the sinks, still carrying her bathroom caddy.

You're awake, she said. Her voice soothed me. I fanned my T-shirt and took deep breaths. It was In Soo Chun's death that had me so bothered, I was certain. I would not realize until a week later, after visiting the medical clinic on campus, that the stomach pains I had experienced for the past weeks were symptoms of a kidney infection.

You're OK. You're OK, she repeated. *You're OK.* It only occurs to me now that I had wanted somebody to tell me that for years. Your death warped me. I had not realized that all this time, I had taxidermized myself. My grief had entombed me in my emotions. It made me hyper-attuned to the ways we exchange our bodies for ash.

3.

Our first days there, my family and I roamed Guangzhou for hours. My father's head was locked into a perpetual slant upward to study the storefronts, so vigorous and lost in his gawking that I worried he'd injure himself. He scanned each street hoping to recognize anything from years ago among the endless rows of clothing and electronic stores that were dotted with the occasional McDonald's or KFC.

It was the winter break of my freshman year. I was here because my father suggested my sisters and I join him as he resolved a dispute with the properties that remained in his name. Something about needing to be there in person to sign paperwork. Something about not trusting distant relatives.

Do you gals want to come with me to Hong Kong and China? I shall take a trip around the end of the year. Maybe we can go over the winter holiday, he had emailed us. Us gals would. It was my first time in China, and my family's first trip together since my mother passed. Caroline slipped into her usual role of running logistics, and for months, she forwarded us flight deals and we debated which prices seemed reasonable.

We ambled from sight to sight, taking in the Temple of the Six Banyan Trees and wandering the next day through the city's Central Park. We examined the fruit vendors' stands and bought paper bags of apple custard and salak. My sisters and I downed Pocari Sweat, bottled milk tea, and canned drinks with grass jelly. I hummed with a delight that teetered on anxiety, all of this feeling familiar yet, in its entirety, nothing like I had experienced before. This felt nostalgic, though it was perhaps not my own nostalgia. All children live in their parents' realities or the realities of those who raise them, but to be the children of immigrants is, in a sense, varying degrees of living in our parents' remaking of the country in which they were born. How adept were my parents at rebuilding that world, and how much had they attempted in the first place? I was only beginning to figure this out.

Do you know where we are now? Caroline asked my father. I watched his eyes dart along the street.

It looks so different. His mouth twisted in the same expression of focus and discomfort that he wore when he was scrunched beneath a car trying to diagnose a problem.

For many years, I mistakenly thought this trip was the first time he'd been back to Hong Kong and China since he'd originally left. But I learned later that in 1974, when he finished graduate school, he returned to cremate his mother's remains. Since much of their family had left Hong Kong and settled in Toronto, my father resolved to have her reburied there. She would still be physically separated from her husband, whose remains were assumed to be in Havana, though nobody knew for sure. At least in Toronto, she would be at rest in a cemetery where much of her family could pay their respects.

X

At the hotel, my father requested the least expensive room. Upon arrival, we discovered that meant two twin beds, and he promptly stretched out on one and fell into a jet-lagged sleep that was punctuated with his jagged snores.

Well, I said, *this'll be interesting.* Caroline and I pressed ourselves into the other bed. I tucked in my legs and she let me curl against her like a cat—unusual, since she was always shrugging me off whenever I tried to spoon her. Steph folded herself on top of two chairs. We slept this way, fitfully, until our father woke in the early morning hours.

For the next week, my sisters and I carried out our lives in Guangzhou. We ran errands that we didn't have time for back in the States. We shopped for boots and jackets and helped Steph, who had recently gotten engaged, purchase a wedding dress. We met up with our father for dinner with his old friends or relatives. As our father made small talk with his guests, my sisters and I focused on the plates in front of us. We sucked the juice from clams steamed with fermented black beans and we stacked the empty shells on our plates. We passed a dish of silky, steamed eggs between us, and took turns refilling everyone's cups of tea. When our father gestured at us, reaching for something to say, and finally settling on what we studied or where we worked, we let polite smiles fill our faces.

X

At a café after lunch, my father and I sat at a table across from one another. My sisters had left to look for a coat for Caroline at a shop next door, and my father wanted to polish off the remaining noodles. We had not talked much in the past few months. I idly tore bits of a napkin and shuffled the scraps into a pile between us. The more time we spent here in Guangzhou, the more unsettled I became. Maybe it was witnessing my father unmoored. Or maybe it was realizing that I would not be able to observe my mother in this space, and that I would not see how she fit into this country.

Do you miss Mommy? I said suddenly.

Well, my father said. *Life…* If he was taken aback by my abruptness, it did not show.

But don't you miss her?

There's no point in wasting time being sad. Everybody dies.

He noticed my brows pressing together and he leaned back in his seat.

Ai, Gah Lee. Everybody dies.

I know.

If you're forty or seventy or a hundred, everybody dies. It's a fact of life.

But it's Mommy, I said. *Doesn't it make you sad being alone all the time?* I thought about him and his new routine: Wake up; microwave oatmeal and sprinkle sesame seeds and peanuts on top; spend the morning on the stationary bike; eat lunch while watching the actors from *The Young and the Restless* grow old; tinker with the plumbing at one of his properties; watch more financial news on his laptop; eat leftovers for dinner; sleep.

There's no use crying over spilt milk, he said.

Spilt milk! Spilt milk, I said.

Hey. Hey. I don't run from my problems. I face them head-on.

What does that mean?

It felt like a barb.

X

This was where your father grew up, my father's distant cousin told us as we pulled into to a small village. He had driven the two hours to Hoiping and he had laid on the horn every time we passed another vehicle, someone walking on the street, an animal on the side of the road.

Hoiping appeared on this cloudy day in beige and monochrome.

We stopped in front of a boxy, sand-colored house that had sat unoccupied for decades.

This is it, his cousin said. *Does this look familiar?*

Our father shook his head and stepped into the house as if reeled in, his past a fishing line; deceptive and once hooked, an inevitable and precarious path. He ran his hands along the concrete walls, everything shrouded in a thick coat of dust. The first floor was mostly empty except for a couple of chairs and busted knickknacks. He bent to pick a teacup off the floor. Gingerly, he held it with both hands. After appraising it, he wrapped it in a tissue he had in his coat and tucked it into a pocket.

Our father's cousin scaled a ladder at the back of the room. He hoisted open a hatch on the ceiling and suddenly, we were steeped in a pearled light that was filtered gray by the clouds. My father followed. Caroline, Steph, and I filed behind. We were no longer mumbling jokes, no longer exchanging looks when our father did or said something outlandish or asked the waiter or his cousin how much things cost or how much they made, no longer whispering *leeeeeng luuuuui* to mimic our relative each time he greeted any woman.

The roof was made of large tiles separated by concrete columns. Not far from us, buildings the color of cream hovered behind newly greened tree branches. Slivers of the canal appeared below.

My father and his cousin climbed higher onto the roof so they could see more of the village. They shifted their weight to accommodate the incline and pointed at structures in the distance.

Years later, when I am reaching for memories of this visit to my father's village, I sift through old albums online. Caroline has suggested I look there. *Remember,* she says, *you kept wanting to post photos and text your friends from college and high school? You had FOMO about not being with them even though we were on vacation.* In one of the photos, my sisters and I flank our father on this roof. Our expressions are abbreviated, our lips stiff and manufactured creases on our faces. All of us have fresh hair from a salon visit from earlier that week, mine newly permed, Caroline's and our father's trimmed, Steph's straightened.

We had been so interested in seeing the view from above that we had rushed through the inside of my father's first home. I wish that I had taken photos of him inside there, submerged in his bank of memories, and that I had asked him to point out, if he remembered, where he slept. Were there still remnants of the bed he shared with his mother and grandmother? Was there anything he recognized? At the time, all of these questions felt intrusive, but I regret not finding a way to discover the answers. When I ask him these questions now, so distant from this place, he cannot recall. But what is the point of recognition, if it's absent of memory or meaning? Doesn't it just become more that we hoard?

X

On our last evening in Guangzhou, the hotel's concierge knocked on our door. She had our bill. She peered into the room at the twin beds and chairs. She smirked.

Four people in here? All of you sleeping here? she said. *Why not just get another room or a bed? So cheap.*

My sisters and I blushed.

Caroline later told us that she'd thought about paying for an upgrade, but didn't want to offend our father.

I didn't think it was my place, she said. *I wish I had.* Though we were all technically adults, we still fell into our family's original order. I wondered when our father's favorite mantra—*I'm the father, you're the daughter*—would expire.

Later, in the shower, trying to alleviate the flu symptoms I had the whole trip, I began to sob. I wasn't sure what came over me. Steph and Caroline pushed their way into the bathroom.

What's wrong? they said.

I don't know, I said. *I think something's wrong with me.*

Is it your cold? Should we look for cold medicine?

No. I dropped to a crouch, suddenly self-conscious that I was naked. *Aren't you two just sad, sometimes? I always feel so sad.*

I feel like I always miss Mommy, I said. *That type of sad.*

Oh, Steph said, her glasses fogged.

Sticky, Caroline said. She reached around me and turned off the water.

Why don't you get out of the shower, Steph suggested. Together, my sisters enveloped me in a towel.

It perplexed me then how grief could still be there like that, injected into my body as if some preserving agent, indistinguishable from my insides. Diana Khoi Nguyen, the poet, wrote: "Some plants have nectaries / that keep secreting pollen even after the petals have gone." I interpreted this originally to refer to the way our bodies become locked into grief. I finally decide that this image is one of determination.

4.

I dragged myself to the dining nook in my studio apartment and leaned against the table.

It was the summer between sophomore and junior year of college, and for the past couple of months, I had fallen into a routine with my friend Lexie. I headed to my internship in the suburbs, where I worked for the third summer in a row with a cable company's communications department as part of a scholarship program. Lexie huddled at her desk in the school paper's newsroom, where she was an editor. After work, we sat in a coffee shop and tapped out free-lance assignments. From there, we hung in my apartment watching Hallmark movies or old rom-coms until the early morning hours, passing between us a jug of Carlo Rossi that we'd bought months earlier to make sangria and had since become acrid. Most nights, before the movie ended, I crawled to the air mattress that I'd slept on for the past year and fell asleep. Lexie dozed on my couch, rousing in the early morning to walk the half block to her place.

But that night, after Lexie left, I woke and was unable to fall back asleep. Still woozy and flushed from wine, I thumbed numbers into my phone. As if a compulsion, I dialed my mother's old work line. 860-636-XXXX.

I still remembered this number from all of my childhood after-noons. If I was home from school, bored and missing her, I'd call her at work under the guise of wanting to know what time she'd leave the office or what was for dinner. Never mind that she came home at six p.m. most nights and that dinner was whatever we had in the refrigerator, stir-fried a little, with rice, or a potato she diced and steamed in the microwave and covered with shredded cheese, salt, black pepper, and paprika.

Each time I called, she answered: *DBA Florence.*

DBA was her title; she was a database administrator. I loved hearing her say her own name—the delicateness of the syllables and how elegant it seemed coming from her mouth. Floor-rinse. Floor-rinse. FLOOOOOOR-rinse.

Maybe when she lived in Hong Kong and attended one of those British schools, her instructors called her that. Or, when immigrating to the states, she thought it'd be easier to take on an English name. My theory is that she chose *Florence* because she'd admired Florence Nightingale. There might have been something about Nightingale being a famous nurse—a caretaker—who was also known for her contributions to mathematics and medicine, that appealed to my mother. Groundbreaking and could not be swayed by what women did or didn't do in that era. Nobody in my family called my mother Florence, though. She was Mui Mui to her siblings; Mommy to Steph, Caroline, and me; and Ah Mo to our father. It took me until adulthood to ask after her first name in Cantonese, or to learn the Chinese characters: 余 寶梅. I already had the vocabulary to describe her, so why did I need more? Why would I bother looking outside myself for the words that she might have identified most as her own?

I had Daddy teach me, years after your death, to pronounce your name.

× × ×

Bo Mui, your husband said.

Bow Moy, I said. We repeated this for a couple of minutes, and the whole time I was sure I was saying it wrong. After all, I couldn't get my own name right.

Ngo giu Gah Lee, I'd say at family parties when I was a kid, prompted by Kau Fu because he was tickled by my pronunciation.

You're called 'curry'? Kau Fu teased, laughing into my face and pinching my elbow while I spat out my name over and over, flustered, trying to will a sense of self into place. After my mother died, I tried to convince my father to speak to me only in Cantonese. But he often had to supply both sides of our dialogues, the expansiveness of these conversations unnatural and overwhelming. Soon, my vocabulary exhausted itself, his patience also depleted, and we slipped back into the hard sounds of English.

In my apartment in Seattle, I listened to the thrum of the phone's rings. It forwarded me to an answering machine of some employee, perhaps the one who had replaced my mother years ago. I hung up. I wondered if this person had heard of my mother, or if anyone on her team still thought about her. I was afraid of what thinking too much of her might bring. I guzzled another glass of wine before falling back into bed, the air mattress buckling under me and compressing my sides in a makeshift swaddle.

I pictured calling you again. You'd pick up this time.

DBA Chow Bo Mui, you'd say, forgoing your last name for our family's.

Hi, Mommy, I'd say, relieved and ecstatic that you had been here all this time. Had you aged in the afterlife? Would your hair still, in this imagined world, be wavy? Had it grayed, like Daddy's?

Wei, you'd say. *Lei sik jor fan mei ah?*

The rest of our conversation played out in Cantonese. In this alternate universe, I was fluent and we discussed everything I'd eaten that day: popcorn chicken at the bubble tea spot I always studied at with my friend Colin; half a sandwich; three cups of coffee. I'd ask the same to you, and over the phone, you'd demur.

Oh, just this and that, you'd say.

I wasn't sure if this meant that dead ghost-you didn't eat, had no need for calories, or if nobody had recently left out offerings.

Here, I could not conjure more of the conversation. Too much guilt. Too much worry. I pushed these thoughts aside and fell asleep.

5.

The next summer, I was visiting my father for a few weeks. I woke late to the sounds of him on the stationary bike downstairs. The pedals were connected to a fan that had a gentle, constant hum that blew air across the family room while he watched a morning talk show, our rear-projection television that he bought sometime in the early 1990s shouting the latest news and family-friendly gossip. I ate an apple and leaned on the counter, brushing a pile of grocery store flyers aside to make room for myself. In the afternoons, my father ran errands. He glided down the driveway in his Miata, which was dotted with black nail polish, his attempt to hide its many scratches. He was on his way to Hartford to clean up one of the vacant buildings, trash bags and a bucket of tools jammed into his car's trunk. As soon as he left, I dampened a paper towel and cleared away the cobwebs that had grown thick and matted across his kitchen windowsill. I dumped out containers of spoiled leftovers and scrubbed the Tupperware, leaving them to dry in the dishwasher. I collected some of the detritus he had scattered on the floor in the hallways and kitchen—an old bookshelf, a smashed TV, a mirror, a chain saw, used car batteries—and I hauled them to a corner where I decided he'd be least likely to trip.

One late morning, when my father and I had nothing else to do, we set to work making dumplings from scratch. We had never done this before.

While my father sifted through his books for a recipe, suspicious of the one that I found online, he sent me down to the basement to retrieve a baking sheet so we could lay out all of our dumplings. Upon seeing my list of ingredients, he broke into his half laugh, half scowl. He gestured to the refrigerator at the groceries we already had. *You can just substitute char siu for the pork and leeks. It can be like char siu bao.*

Sure, OK, I said, not wanting to argue. In the basement, I eyed pots and pans, barely used, resting on top of their boxes. A dozen empty plastic tofu containers sat on the floor next to expired spices.

I was about to tug a tray from a shelf when I noticed something out of place across the room. A few feet from me, past cardboard boxes that were empty but still intact, lay a fish. It was real. It was dead. It was about a foot and a half long and resembled a striped bass, though it was hard to tell in its condition. The fish was positioned on a small table on top of two wooden planks that served as a makeshift stand. Its eyes were congealed, its scales peeling and fins flaky as though it had been deep fried or dipped in Elmer's glue. Its mouth hung open, which gave it the appearance that it was mid-gasp. A couple of pliers and screwdrivers sat next to it.

I tensed and backed away, though I suppose this was not in the realm of abnormal. Nothing was, when it came to my father or his house. I was confused, though, that I could not smell the fish. Perhaps the scent of the basement's mildew and the cat's litter box, which my father infrequently cleaned, were too pungent.

Why do you have a fish down here? I yelled. I grabbed the pan and ran upstairs.

It's from when Stephanie and Steven took me deep sea fishing.

What are you doing with it? I paced the kitchen to steady myself.

My father stood at the counter and mixed flour and water with his hands. He shrugged.

Well, I taxidermied it.

For Father's Day that year, Steph and her husband gifted their fathers a day of deep-sea fishing along the Connecticut shore. To them, it seemed like an ideal present: useful, hands-on, something their parents wouldn't do by themselves. It seemed especially suitable for our father, since he was always one for adventure.

But as Steph had told me a few months back, this past Father's Day, the temperature was well into the nineties. Once the boat sped to sea, it became hotter. This, paired with the rocking of waves, lulled our father into sickness. While everyone else learned to cast lines, he spent much of the afternoon sitting inside the cabin as he clutched a water bottle and tried not to hurl.

Afterward, when they returned to the dock, the boat's two-person crew took stock of their catch.

My father watched as the crew filleted the striped bass and blue fish, slicing behind the gills and removing the heads. My father's arms were probably folded, his face sunburned. He later told me that he thought the crew was wasteful, and that they were trying to keep the good parts of the fish for themselves. When they mentioned their taxidermy services—a way to remember this day, they'd said— my father perked up and listened raptly. The captain reeled off more details about the trophy mounting, and how the person they worked with—an artist—specialized in saltwater fish. My father was less interested in memorializing the day, since he'd been sick, but he was intrigued about the process itself. He could teach himself anything, he was certain, and this was no different. It would be a nice thing to have in his home. And so, my father—who had not caught any fish himself that day—asked the boat's captain for one to bring home.

Leave it whole, he said.

When he was home, he filled his laptop's browsers with searches like *taxidermy fish* or *stuffed fish do it yourself*. He skimmed a few articles, ignoring the instructions and materials list. Then he searched the basement and garage for planks of wood, Elmer's glue, and any other material that seemed helpful.

I think you should throw that out, I said. I pleated a dumpling.

It looks like it's rotting, I continued when he did not answer.

No, he said. *It's taxidermy. Some people pay a lot of money to do that to their fish.*

I don't think like that, I said, dipping my finger into the bowl of water and running it along the edge of the dough wrapper. *It looks really scary.*

He shrugged.

Hey, he said. *It's none of your business. It's my house.*

I considered taking a broom and sliding the fish into the trash. My father would be livid, though that wasn't what concerned me. I was a coward and I thought then, *I don't ever want to touch that fish.* I would be too afraid of what was living in it, or how its insides might seep out.

If my mother was still around—and had my parents stayed together—my father and I wouldn't have had to look for a dumpling recipe in the first place, and in the basement there probably wouldn't be a dead fish, its flesh soaked in preserving chemicals but still decomposing.

X

This was not the first time I discovered dead fish in this house. A year or two earlier, I opened the oven to bake brownies, and I found a tray of my father's angelfish, both of them tiny and roasted. They looked up at me, their eyeballs dehydrated and shriveled. Like crackers. He had left them on a baking sheet, days or weeks or months ago, among all the other pans that he stored in the oven.

Daddy, I called out, though he sat at the kitchen table. *Please tell me you weren't going to eat these.*

He hoisted himself to his feet and met me by the oven. I waited for him to make a joke. *They're like those cheese Goldfish!* I could see him saying in a tone woven with amusement. I had flashbacks to one of his favorite sayings: *I'm Cantonese, and Cantonese people eat anything with four legs, except for tables!* This, I worried, did not exclude pet fish.

Some months before, my family piled into the minivan and road-tripped from Connecticut to Toronto to visit my father's extended family. That weekend, one of his relatives—a niece's husband—led us to their basement, which was filled with tanks arranged neatly on shelves, pumps whirring and water trickling. He explained to my father how he raised and bred angelfish, which he'd in turn sell to pet stores for something like fifty cents each. He changed the water almost daily, fed the fish bloodworms, and kept a close eye on the temperatures and pH. As the fish spawned, he tended to their births, netted them, transferred them to different tanks, and began the process again. My father peppered him with questions while my sisters and I ambled between the aisles and studied each tank. The fish floated like ghosts suspended in air, their long, stringy fins dangling underneath them as they glowed neon in the light. They were so still and peaceful. But on closer examination, I could see their translucent side fins fluttering quickly, all chaos, as they bobbed.

Before we left, my father's nephew netted half a dozen fish and dropped them into plastic bags with water.

For you to raise them at home, he told my father.

They tucked them into a Styrofoam cooler for safekeeping during our eight-and-a-half hour drive. My father was giddy, already envisioning his empty tanks filled once more. When these fish multiplied, he could turn this into a business like his nephew and sell them to a pet store by his house.

My sisters and I exchanged looks.

Do you really need *them?* I asked. *Can't you get them back in Connecticut?*

Hey, my father said. *I can do whatever I want.*

At the U.S.-Canada border, when customs asked if my family had anything we wanted to declare, my father spoke quickly: *No, nothing. Nothing to declare.*

In Connecticut, my father kept the angelfish in a tank beside the kitchen table. It remained half full, and the water became a brackish green with a thin film that clung to the glass. The water was not between the suggested seventy-five and eighty-two degrees Fahrenheit; the pH, I guessed, not anywhere close to what it needed to be. My father had taped coins to the outside of the tank so that he could see if his fish had grown, comparing their little bodies to the size of pennies and quarters. If I looked hard enough, I could see the remaining, lone angelfish in there, hardly moving.

X   X   X

I don't understand why you baked your fish, I said. I tried to make my voice calm.

My father opened the oven and pulled out the tray. He held a crisped fish in his palm, inspecting its desiccated fins and tail before he set both on a shelf by the table. They rested by the other knickknacks he had collected over the years.

They kept dying, he said. *I wanted to be able to see the difference as the alive ones grew.*

If you dry them, don't you know that they'd contract? I said, bewildered. *Isn't that a fact of science that they'd get smaller if you baked them?*

My father didn't say anything. He sat back down and started cracking peanuts from their shells, popping them into his mouth by the handful. I joined him, cautiously studying his face. He shrugged, though I think because he didn't try to argue, he understood that this was startling—and he might have even allowed for it to be described as disturbing. This struck me as, perhaps, a matter of an attachment to the angelfish that he could not admit, of poor logic, and of his need to hold on to objects, long after they'd expired. Later, anytime I returned to his house and wanted to bake, I opened the oven, wary. At some point, I stopped trying to bake there at all. And eventually, my visits became so infrequent they might as well have ceased entirely.

X

Years later, I watch hours of YouTube videos that demonstrate how to taxidermy a fish. I wonder if my father had watched these clips.

One way to taxidermy a fish: First, slice open its body on one of its sides—the one that will not be visible, the one that will most likely attach to a board or some other type of mount. Slide a knife between the flesh and the skin, taking care not to tear it; taxidermying a fish is not a forgiving process. Make incisions by the gill and the tail. And then, gently, peel the skin from the flesh and bones and organs in a movement that's similar to removing a sticker from wax paper, but only more violent. Scoop out the eyes and also the brain. Inject the fish with embalming fluids, such as glycol ethers or ethanol, then sprinkle borax inside. Using a needle and fishing line, sew together the skin, then stuff it with sawdust; alternatively, wrap the skin around a foam mount. After all this, there's more work to be done: new glass eyes must be inserted and secured, and all of this must be painted.

My father skipped most of these steps. I do not know what he expected, if he thought that he could alter the dead to make it seem alive, or if he thought the fish that he had created looked anything like it had when it was living. I'm curious if he thought he could stop the decay.

X

Mommy: Would you have been unfazed? Here I wish I could talk to you.

So, Daddy, he did this thing with fish, I would tell you.

I read this book about the history of taxidermy, *The Breathless Zoo.* I wanted to understand Daddy's draw to taxidermy—and yours, too. In the book, there is a photo of zebras at the Natural History Museum at Tring, in England. I can't wipe the image from my memory. You would have also found it unnerving.

The zebras are positioned with their legs tucked under them as if resting in tall grass. There are eight of them, and a foal stands in the corner as if shy. Their eternal bodies look so peaceful, though in reality, they are displayed in glass cases and arranged on shelves stacked above one another. They are an uncanny family, though the author, Rachel Poliquin, points out that they are different species. *Species.* That word holds so much weight. "There are many species of sadness," Poliquin writes, which often evoke "what might have been." She continues: "While sadness for a failed dream is bitter, sadness is most acutely linked with the real physical loss of a person or thing that has passed forever from view. With this loss comes remembrance, and with remembrance a longing for the departed and, in its absence, a sentimental yearning for a token, an object, something that can be felt and touched: a material souvenir of what is no longer but lingers everlastingly in memory."

I take these ideas to refer to a nostalgia, or a desire. That despite the many reasons people had for creating taxidermy, they wanted to preserve these specimens to understand them, and also for a sense of posterity. Even if they ceased to exist—if they died out—they could still be present. Like you.

"Longing is itself a peculiar condition," Poliquin writes. "It works as a kind of ache connecting the stories we tell ourselves and the objects we use as storytellers. In a sense, longing is a mechanism for both pacifying and cultivating various lusts and hungers by creating objects capable of generating significance. And here, objects of remembrance or souvenirs are exemplary." Taxidermy itself—or rather, *poor taxidermy*—strikes me as melancholic, the way one who is melancholic clings to something, though isn't quite sure what is gone. The way one who attempts and botches taxidermy enters into a contradiction, unable to capture the *essence* of what they recreate—that being life.

You and Daddy had taught me that almost any longing could be remedied by effort, and then more effort; desires could be fulfilled if I worked hard enough or completed enough repetitions until, suddenly, my goal was achieved and whatever I'd hoped for—a good grade in school, acceptance to college, a slimmer body—appeared in my life as if by some given, definite transaction. But that outside factors might hinder these desires, and that all of the things I was taught to long for were material because they related to *achievement* or a symbol of *money*—instead of, say, *happiness* or *well-being*—wasn't apparent to me until years later, long after you had died. I resented this. I wanted to talk to you about this. A desire to preserve can't alone resurrect the dead. Holding and hoarding can't turn ghosts into flesh.

But we create these souvenirs nevertheless. This allows us, in a way, to hold our loss close. Taxidermy, after all, gives the impression of permanence. An animal that has been preserved may not be *alive*, but it remains here. Sometimes that is enough.

X

I don't ever want to touch that taxidermic fish. But everybody in my family knows that there will come a day in the next decades when Caroline, Steph, or I will be tasked with throwing away the fleshy, peeling sea bass. The angelfish, too, wherever they rest.

Do I dread touching the dead fish, or do I instead dread what it means to dispose of my father's haphazard trophy, which has over the years become a memorial to him?

6.

In the early fall of my senior year of high school, a prospective college mailed me their creative writing program's literary magazine. I dragged the book into my bedroom and I paged through the materials while sitting at my desk. I was amazed by a poem from an undergraduate student; it was unlike anything I'd read.

A couple dines by the Adriatic Sea. The title implies they're on a honeymoon of sorts. At sixteen, there is so much context I missed—like sex—that I understand now, having just reread the poem for the first time in more than a decade. The couple is buzzed. They'd been plied with liquor all evening, and one of them takes a bite from the plate of octopus they're sharing—*octopi*, according to the poem—and says, "*taste like the motherfucking ocean.*" They pitch a glass onto the rocks while the other looks on, perplexed.

I read that as a teenager and immediately I separated the phrase from the rest of the poem. There was something about the word *mother* next to *fucker*, its sharpness, how it reminded me of my own mother, who could slice anybody open with a single look.

Your mother is like Bill Clinton, my father frequently said, *and how he can say, with a smile, that someone should go fuck themselves, and they will.* His use of present tense when referring to her always cuts. This could be a product of Chinese being his first language. There are no tenses in Chinese dialects. Everything is present tense, the marker of something that has happened in the past—了, *le* in Mandarin or

254

liu in Cantonese—appended at the end of the sentence. An after-thought, in the eyes of this English speaker. When people talk to me in Mandarin or Cantonese, I frequently confuse tenses and I find it easier to assume that everything is still happening. Somebody could talk to me about my mother, and if I had no context, my tense mix-ups might lead me to think she was still alive.

When my father said the word *fuck*, his voice dropped, not sure if he wanted to commit to the swear. Reading the poem, I marveled at how something as ordinary as an ocean could take on a harder edge with those words preceding it. There was conviction. I wanted to scream, *taste like the motherfucking ocean!* in my bedroom. Or, *Look at this motherfucking mess of a house!* The phrase encapsulated something about myself that I wasn't sure how to express—this untouchable rage and despair, how just thinking those words felt confusing and reckless and scary.

I did not mind saying *fuck* in everyday conversation, or when it was aimed at someone, so *motherfucker* did not seem like a stretch. I did not understand the original violence of the phrase.

X

I thought again about *taste like the motherfucking ocean*, and *fuck* itself, when I was a senior in college. It was a few months after the New Year, and I was in the bed of a man who I'd been dating on and off for the school year. He kept breaking up with me, and we found ourselves getting back together, over and over.

But I love him, I told my friends as they rolled their eyes when I was a couple of drinks in and already weepy. I was getting *fucked* in the sense that I couldn't tell if this was something I didn't want or just didn't enjoy. He had told me about one of his fantasies, which was to be awoken from a deep sleep with me on top of him, and in turn, he enacted this on me. I found myself yanked from sleep with him crushing into my body. I willed myself to make my limbs slack. I told myself: I was lucky in that, for the most part in my adult life, I had never had to think of sex as something uncontrollable, that happened *to* me. And yet, when he rolled off of me—this person who turned me into someone I resented, someone who was needy and prone to shouting and crying and picking fights—he laughed and slapped my ass, trying to get me to smile at him. My mouth automatically turned upward, and this involuntary, nonconsensual reaction made me seethe. I pretended to sleep.

This isn't a big deal, I told myself. *This is whatever.* Still: a brittle anger cracked through me, the same one I'd sensed for months. I didn't know what to do then about my fury, and I don't know, now.

A few hours later, while I walked to a bus stop, I wanted to call you.

I wanted to cry and say, *I feel fucked.*

I wanted to describe my shame to you, to hear you say, *Shh, shhh.*

I wanted to ask if you ever felt this way.

If I wanted you gone before, I needed you now.

What does it mean to feel so far outside yourself, I wanted you to answer.

X

I didn't understand why everything always came back to you, how grief seemed to inhabit so many of my feelings, how I couldn't think about my own shortcomings or mistakes without considering our family's history.

X   X   X

That morning, I wanted to tell you on the phone, *I don't know who I am anymore,* and because it was my senior year of college and I had no plans yet after graduation and *what was the point of working so hard and taking on so many jobs and internships and loans if I couldn't get a motherfucking job.* I'd worked at the Olympics and had, over the past four years, finished a dozen internships and part-time gigs while enrolled in the university's honors program. But maybe this was entitlement speaking. Or maybe it was the lie that we existed in a meritocracy, if I worked hard enough, I could do anything, didn't need anyone.

I wanted you to say from your end of the phone, *You are exactly who you are,* for you to return me to myself. I wanted you to tell me the point of it all, and I wanted your words to hold me as a mother's.

X

Months passed. This man dumped me, again. On my walk from my apartment to campus for an appointment with my thesis advisor, I bought a bag of miniature Snickers. I devoured them one by one, crying as I tore open wrappers. Between mouthfuls, I called my father because he was the only person who I knew would pick up, because Steph and Caroline were at work and tired of hearing about this ex. I told my father how *sad* I felt about this breakup in a way that scared me.

I never talked to my father about my relationships. I never invoked them, or that thing called *love,* or that someone might stop feeling that way toward me. But I did that day.

There are plenty more fish in the sea, my father said. I wanted to ask if he felt that about you, if he wondered if he'd be able to find someone else like you. I didn't want to inflict this hurt on him; I knew there was safety in looking away.

Later, in my apartment, I began to brainstorm a way out of Seattle, and out of who I was afraid I'd become. After graduation, I'd leave the country. I'd get a fellowship to work at a newspaper in Cambodia. And then I'd head to Boston and look for work in a newsroom there. It was as far as I could get from Seattle in the United States, but close enough to Connecticut and Steph, and I heard it was a good journalism town, anyway.

I repeated those ideas every day until they became a plan. Because that was resolve, motherfucker.

7.

In Wisconsin—where I was for a week and a half before college graduation, nearly eight years after my mother's death—lightning swung in the fields and far from the interstate. I drove a rental car, my friend Lucas and another classmate with me. We wended our way south to Madison from Green Bay, here for a journalism class to cover the gubernatorial recall election. Lucas was in the back seat with his window open. He aimed his camera lens at the car's side mirror. In the reflection, he wanted to capture the exact moment the lightning collided with the horizon.

You can take your time, our classmate said as she gripped the door handle. *We're not in a rush.*

I hadn't realized I was speeding through the storm, the speedometer ticking up the longer we were on the highway. I eased my foot from the gas, but a few minutes later, we sprung forward again.

In a few days, we'd return to Seattle, and in less than two weeks, I'd be in Phnom Penh, working as a fellow at an English-language newspaper.

For now, Wisconsin:

It was strange how my father had once lived here and my mother had also wanted to attend college here; something about the American heartland must have been compelling. My father first encountered snow here. *The first time I saw snow, I thought it was really beautiful,* he recalls to me, when it has been years since either of us have been to Wisconsin, *but my classmate told me when it melted, it was really dirty.* That was the only description he could muster about the snow, that this moment of soft, gleaming sheets of white—all of it new—would soon be mussed by grime. He was always anticipating the worst; always hearing the worst; always remembering the worst. It is an inheritance I do not want.

I want to go back into my father's memory with him. I would convince him to enjoy his first snow. *Just let it be soft snow for now. Look at snowflakes on your gloves and how they're formed.*

He learned to sail on a lake near campus. It might have been the same one my classmates and I had sat by when we visited the University of Wisconsin, days before our drive in the lightning storm. I was too distracted to take in the lake and the campus. I had wondered, instead, about the possibility of a state university selling beer on campus, my mind drifting toward potential liquor and liability laws.

But my father, he figured out how to heel and tack on this lake using intuition, the wind carrying him. I realize now, as he bent his limbs on that sailboat, that his mother was alive then. He must have thought he'd return to Hong Kong to see her; he was likely monitoring his savings to see how much more money he'd need to bring her to the U.S. But he did not think about this then, on that boat on the lake. He just ducked beneath the swinging boon, adjusting to the breeze that glanced off of the water.

X

A few months earlier, one of my university's financial aid counselors called me into their office for a meeting.

I owed the school something like $4,000, the counselor told me. She was accompanied by one of her colleagues. While I studied abroad in Spain the previous year, the office accidentally mailed me an extra loan check. It was a technical detail that related to how I was an out-of-state student, but enrolling in the study abroad program allowed me to pay in-state tuition, which was a cheaper fee. This resulted somehow in leftover, unaccounted-for money.

What check? I could not remember any checks. *It must have gotten lost in the mail,* I insisted.

They read out the address. My father's.

I don't understand.

The check was cashed, one of the counselors said, careful not to assign blame. *You'll have to pay it back.*

I don't have that money. Sweat soaked my lower back. *I don't know what happened. That's a lot of money.*

The counselors assured me that I had options. I could return the money. I could borrow another loan to pay off that one, for example.

I'd always been meticulous about my loans and my tuition payments. Caroline taught me this; she'd been the one to encourage me to study abroad.

We'll figure it out, together, she'd promised. *You might not get another chance to live abroad. You should do it, Sticky.* When I arrived in Spain, she wired me $800. She included a note: *This is a gift. You should travel while you're there.* I was thrilled, and did not think then how that sum of money was not insignificant for her, only twenty-seven at the time and with her own loans to pay off.

All throughout college, I lived off of scholarships, government grants, and student loans. I juggled various gigs to cover my rent and tuition and also had tried to freelance and complete unpaid internships that mostly only kids with rich parents could afford. I did not sleep much, and I went about my life with flashes of anxiety that I was not doing *enough*. At the time, I was proud of how I thought I was doing *whatever it took* to make it. When friends who also wanted to be journalists worried about job prospects or the economy or how so many newspapers had folded, I was confounded by their discouragement. *Just apply*, I said. *It can't hurt. What else can you do besides just keep applying?* It would only occur to me later how much I'd started sounding like my father; how I believed that work and success translated to survival and independence.

Except for me, I was certain, it was less about money or success, since each of those things seemed so distant. It was more about what the promise of a career could afford me. But it was a luxury to not worry about money. I never had $4,000 in my bank account, unless it was a loan disbursement, but then, I understood the money was not mine.

I excused myself from the meeting in the financial aid office and called my father while I walked to my apartment.

Well, he said. His voice was curt.

Well?

You wanted me to visit you in Spain, and I needed money to take the trip, he said, *so I cashed the check.*

But it wasn't yours to take. The check wasn't in your name. I knew this hadn't stopped him before. After my mother died and my father could not access her bank accounts, he used her checks. When we found a few addressed to her that she had not deposited, my father signed his own name on the back and brought it to the bank. *As long as you use your signature, it's OK,* he had explained. *It shows you're cashing it for that person.*

Over the phone, he started to yell, and my voice grew with his.

Hey, he said. *I'm the father. You're the daughter. You and Caroline say, 'Oh, let's visit Spain,' and I needed the money. You wanted me to come visit you, so I come.*

You needed it, huh? I was confused and started to cry again. Was it that he'd thought that money was his to take—that he'd spent so much parenting me and that it was my turn to look after him? Was it that he was really so broke? I was not opposed to helping him. Just not like this.

You need to respect me, he said.

Respect you, I said, over and over, still shouting, unsure if I was asking a question or repeating his words or trying to will this into myself.

X

When my father settled in Connecticut a decade after leaving Wisconsin, he was nostalgic for his days there on that lake. He bought a sailboat with aspirations for towing it often to the water, either the Connecticut River or Long Island Sound. He only used it once or twice before he claimed that neighborhood kids had stolen its parts, all of which were too expensive to replace. What remains of his boat sits in his backyard by the shed, just a few feet from where our dead pets are buried.

I always forget that separate from my father, my mother had originally wanted to enroll in this university, as well. She would have enjoyed sitting on the lakeshore. She would have been a remarkable student, majoring in whatever she wanted, finding a job near Madison that paid her well and provided her and her family with excellent health insurance. Maybe in this alternate reality, she would have wound up with the man she dated when she was in her early twenties, before meeting my father. I do not know much about this boyfriend, just that the letters I'd come across years ago and have not read since were filled with pining. They were earnest and pleading, which made me think she had left him and he was eager to get her back. But the fact that she had saved their correspondence must have meant something. I imagine her in Wisconsin, possibly still with this boyfriend, though this is an unfortunate exercise in picturing me and my family's non-existence. Year after year, she would have been in awe of the snow, both as it fell and days after; in my fantasy, she would have thrived, is what I'm trying to say.

8.

It's not good, I told Steph over the phone. *Really dusty.* I mentioned how, whenever I arrived at my father's house, my fingers and eyes tingled and my face became bloated. My body always adjusted, but the initial response was concerning. I'd returned from a fellowship in Phnom Penh, and by September, I'd run out of money and needed to find a full-time job. I applied to public radio stations and newspapers along the East Coast without much luck.

Maybe we can clean out the house for him, Steph suggested, before adding, *We should get him an air purifier.*

Steph took a conciliatory tone as we swept peanut shells that overflowed from potted plants—the hulls were a natural fertilizer, our father insisted—and into trash bags. She tossed out the moldy scallions he'd attempted to grow in empty yogurt cups, the scraggles of their roots coated with slime, while I collected the empty containers of tofu and oatmeal that were scattered on the kitchen counter and in the dining room.

You'll feel better if you don't have this mess around you all the time. Steph's tone was firm but still gentle, ever the geriatrician. I circled the perimeter of the kitchen and mumbled about the potential dangers of everything that lined the floor: grocery store flyers, a yo-yo, paint cans, a fire extinguisher, lumber, an old boombox, crates heaped with crumpled papers and power tools.

What if you tripped over these, I said out loud to my father, antagonistic and worried while I envisioned him falling and unable to get back up, alone in this house.

As Steph and I worked our way through the refrigerator, my father pulled from the trash a softball-sized glob of neon orange cheese that was rimmed with soggy, molded almonds. It looked like the log that Caroline had bought a couple of Christmases earlier.

Cheese is mold. He brandished it in my face and returned it to the refrigerator. *You shouldn't get rid of this. So wasteful.* He had declared the same of the milk, too, which had spoiled, but he insisted he'd use it to make cheese. It was a familiar debate about whether or not lactose intolerance was experienced in the body or the mind.

It's psychological, my father often insisted. He cited a celebrity doctor from one of the morning talk shows.

The gas, Caroline's husband had once protested, *isn't psychological.* I interrupted the argument to pitch my head back to laugh, full-bodied and delirious, not caring if I was being dramatic or rude. Our father ignored us all.

Psychological! It's true, he insisted. *Look it up. Fact.*

Do you eat this cheese? I asked.

Sometimes, he said.

When was the last time you ate a piece of it?

Hey, he said, irritated by the quiz. *It's none of your business.*

If I pressed, he might try to make me eat the cheese, or he'd do so himself. I shut my mouth.

We want to help you, Steph said, taking her turn. She set down a pile of newspapers and rubbed her eyes. The dust was starting to get to her, too.

You're just stressing yourself out, he said, his voice growing louder. He hovered by her as she flipped through his mail.

He took her lack of response as an invitation to keep talking.

That's why you can't get pregnant. You're putting too much strain on yourself.

Steph yanked herself back as if slapped.

I can't believe you would say that, she said. She swiveled to face him. *How could you say that?*

He repeated himself. *All this stress is why you're having trouble.*

If I ever get pregnant and have kids, Steph said, *I don't want them around you if you're going to say things like that.*

My father and I watched her retreat upstairs to her childhood bedroom, and I ripped up a few pieces of his junk mail.

You shouldn't have said that, I said. *That was a really shitty thing to say. She was just trying to help you. We both are.*

He studied my face and let out a whistle.

You're trying to help me? He laughed. *Geez.*

You think this is funny? You think she's joking? You need to say sorry to her if you ever want to see your grandchildren.

In high school when we shouted at one another, I would tell him sorry at dinner the next day, and that I didn't know where my anger came from. It was overwhelming, I wanted to say, having so much *feeling* sitting there. I always hoped he'd return the apology. Instead, he would only nod. *You always had a temper like your mommy,* he'd say, matter-of-factly, as if that were the only explanation and it had not come from him.

When you do tell Steph sorry, you need to explain what you're sorry for, so she knows you mean it, I said.

I wondered if he had ever apologized to anyone; if he and my mother had said sorry to one another.

You can't say that you're sorry she feels a certain way because that puts this on her, I said. *You have to say sorry for what you said.*

I continued to toss his grocery store flyers into the recycling.

X

My mother loved reading a children's book called *Owly* to my sisters and me. Owly is, not surprisingly, a baby owl. He has endless questions about the world, and he poses them all to his mother.

"How many stars are in the sky?" He asks his mama owl. She tells him to count.

"How deep is the ocean?" He asks her. She tells him to find out.

He tells her he loves her. This time, she asks: "How much?"

To which Owly replies: "I love you as much as the sky is high, and the ocean is deep." It was, not surprisingly, the book that we insisted our mother read most nights.

It will take me years to realize that it was no coincidence that most of the books you read to us did not have human characters, that instead you chose books with talking owls or cats or dogs with hats or monsters. This strikes me now as a protective measure, that you wanted us to imagine ourselves like these anthropomorphic animals, instead of people who looked nothing like us, as if you were worried the absence of *us* in these books might hurt something within us, like it did you.

I love you as high as the sky, our mother told me and Steph and Caroline when tucking us into bed. This was a misquote of *Owly*, but we didn't notice or care.

I love you as high as the sky, we repeated.

And as deep as the ocean, she said.

Years later, when that saying has become a refrain of the Chow women that we recite when we leave the house, or when we hang up the phone, or when our mother is dying, we add a couple more lines to the verse: *I love you as high as the sky and as deep as the ocean,* we say. *And as tall as the tallest tree. And as far as space can go.* We abbreviate it to LYHSDO, appending it to our texts and emails.

Sometimes, we say this to our father, cheerily and in a never-ending competition with one another to see who might be able to get him to say it back.

Love you as high as the sky, Daddy, Caroline begins.

Love you as deep as the ocean, Steph says.

And as tall as the tallest tree and as far as space can go! I call out.

Mmm, he says. *OK.*

✗

Earlier that day, Steph had confided in him that she was struggling to get pregnant.

Did Mommy have trouble? she asked our father.

No, he said. *It was fine.*

No? She didn't have any trouble getting pregnant, or with her pregnancies?

No, he said again. *No troubles.* This, I'm certain, perplexed Steph. There was, after all, Jonathan's premature birth.

At the end of the night, as Steph and I brushed our teeth, our father greeted us from the hall.

Stephanie, I'm sorry, he said. *I shouldn't say something like that.*

Her face tightened. She spit into the sink. I did the same and pretended I wasn't listening. I turned on the tap and pushed our leftover toothpaste foam toward the drain with my fingers.

Thank you for your apology, she said.

OK, he said. *Good night.* Unsure what to do, he nodded and turned to his bedroom.

A mystified look slid onto Steph's face.

Huh, she said. *I don't think I've ever heard him apologize like that.*

Over the years, Steph was the most attentive and patient with our father. She had found a way to debate him that acknowledged his need for the hierarchy of *I'm-the-father-you're-the-daughter* to be maintained. Caroline and I had trouble with this. When disagreeing with our father, Caroline withdrew into a bemused or frustrated silence, and I tended to match my father's irritation with my own, immediately escalating our argument. As a geriatrician, Steph had developed a bedside manner—and subsequent boundaries—that proved effective on him. I was not sure our father completely understood why what he'd said had been so offensive, but I knew he felt he needed Steph, and that he understood that to turn her away would be a mistake. This apology felt unique to her.

You never forget anything, Sticky, Steph had told me multiple times over the years, when I had relayed to her and Caroline the most recent fight with our father. *Sometimes you hold on to things for too long.*

I had rolled my eyes, though she wasn't wrong. Wanting to defuse the sting of what she'd said, I pulled on my father's voice. *Boo-ooy*, I'd said, *It's fact. Why should I let it go when I'm right?*

We had laughed at the time. I had mumbled something about our histories with our father being different and how he hadn't raised her or Caroline the way he'd been required to parent me. Of course, the difference in our childhoods was our mother's presence.

X

I wish I could ask Mommy all these questions, Steph said the following morning when she and I were in her car and on our way to Providence.

I know, I said.

I wish I could ask her for advice.

She was such a good mother, Steph said.

You will be, too. My voice contracted.

She sucked in a breath and reached for my hands.

I love you, she said, barely audible. This would later become a shared phrase that we'd pass between us. In our most earnest moments, we text one another: **small voice* I love you!!!!!* We never forget the context.

I love you, I said. She was already a good mother, had always been one.

X

A couple of winters later, when I had first moved to Washington, D.C., Steph visited for a conference. I noticed as we walked along the National Mall that under her down jacket and beneath her shirt, her stomach gently curved.

Your stomach is looking round. I blundered in my eagerness to be right.

Oh, really? She rubbed her stomach. *Or maybe I've just got a belly.*

Weeks later, Steph called me and Caroline in tears. As soon as she'd returned from D.C., she'd taken a test that revealed her first pregnancy, and for days, she'd allowed herself a small hope that she'd get to have a baby. But the fibroids in her uterus were growing too rapidly, and she'd need surgery to remove them in order to get pregnant.

That's OK though, right? I tried to reassure her.

A lot of women have fibroids and still get pregnant, right? Caroline said.

Right, Steph, said, still sounding scared. Just because something was common, didn't make it any less terrifying. *Right*.

A month later, I was in my room in D.C. folding laundry when Steph sent me a text.

Her surgery had gone well, she said, and she was recuperating at the hospital in Providence. The doctors were able to take out most of the fibroids.

STEPH: 18 of them. The biggest was the size of a baseball. 10 cm

ME: wow

STEPH: do you want to see them?

STEPH: I took a picture so I wouldn't forget

ME: they let you take a photo???

ME: sure, send it

Her fibroids were lined on a metal tray, each of the bloodied bunches of skin arranged neatly in order of size. The orderliness, seeing a part of my sister laid out this way, made me recall the Body Worlds exhibit that she once brought me, Caroline, and Daddy to see. She'd found a coupon online and we'd spent the afternoon gawking at the bodies that had been plastinated to reveal and preserve all of their imperfections. I imagined Steph's fibroids that way: *Here, in size ascending order, are a dozen and a half uterine fibroids from a thirtysomething female of Chinese descent.* They resembled little brains, and I couldn't look away.

STEPH: There were so many

ME: oh my god Steph

I crawled over my piles of clothes to lie under the covers. Jonathan's death came to mind, as did my mother's fibroids, her hysterectomy, and eventually, her cyst. Her body had always seemed fragile; her ailments appearing so inextricably linked to her ability to bear children. She had died of cancer, yes, but long before then, her body was glass. I worried that this might be the same for Steph, or Caroline. Or myself.

In six months, Steph would call Caroline and me again. *They're back*, she said. *I have to have another surgery.* She steered us through a conversation about how much time she needed to take off from work, and how this surgery would be straightforward. There were thirty-seven of them now. Afterward, she didn't text me photos. I didn't ask to see.

X

Later, in my late twenties and at the gynecologist, the doctor presses her fingers into me.

I think it might be my first time seeing a gynecologist, I blurt out.

Oh, she says, trying not to appear taken aback. *Why?*

I don't know. I'd always directed any questions and needs for prescriptions to my general practitioner. I blush, suddenly embarrassed by my own inertia. I have health insurance through work, so I have no excuse. *Scared, maybe?*

The doctor incorrectly thinks I mean that I am afraid of the examination.

Oh, don't worry, she says. *This doesn't hurt, does it?*

It's fine, I say, trying to keep my voice light.

You might have fibroids, she says breezily. *Not uncommon, but just something to keep an eye on.*

OK, I say.

Not a big deal, I tell myself. But frantically, I recall Lai Yi Ma's story about our family's curse.

That is just folklore, I insist to myself. Still, old superstitions like that are spun from some threads of truth.

9.

There is a twelve-minute video that I've had saved in the cloud for nearly a decade. Every time I set up a new phone, it's the first item to appear in my photo album.

It's 2012, two days before Christmas, 12:25 p.m. My father and I are driving to Steph's apartment in Providence, which is only ninety minutes away.

We are in the middle of a conversation. I don't remember how it began, but since it's right after college when I am parsing through *identity*, I'm not surprised it develops into this:

> **ME:** Do you identify as American or Chinese?
>
> **DADDY:** I think of myself as American Chinese.
>
> **ME:** What do you think other people see you as?
>
> **DADDY:** Well, depending on who that person is, why would I care about what he feel? I am my own person, that is OK for me...
>
> **ME:** One question I never asked you was, did you ever want to go back to China or was the goal to always stay in America?
>
> **DADDY:** No, no. China has nothing for me.
>
> **ME:** What do you mean?
>
> **DADDY:** Well. That's what it is, you know. We came to Hong Kong, run away, and then it's a Communist, and Communists

are against people they call land owners, capitalists, or whatever they call it. See, Communists is a very ideal concept when people have no money—

I know then how the conversation might unfold.

He's driving, and my phone catches his profile: He is wearing his clip-on sunglasses and zipped into his oversized L.L.Bean jacket with the rip in the sleeve that over the past decade has grown larger each winter.

I gently try to prod him back to my question.

ME: Back to how you consider yourself American Chinese, or Chinese American. What does that even mean? What does that mean to you?
DADDY: Well, in America…as long as you make enough money to survive, you can do whatever you like. If you think that you have enough money, you don't have to work if you don't want to. You can live anywhere you like, talk whatever you like, and things like that. Those are the freedom that America offer people. Other countries does not have this type of freedom.

This is not unfamiliar territory.

ME: What do you think of the American Dream? What is that to you? Is that it?
DADDY: Well, depending on how you define as the American Dream.

ME: What do *you* define as the American Dream?

DADDY: I think some people define it as, you get a house and you get the freedom, you get enough to eat, things like that.

ME: I'm asking about you personally. Do you think there is an American Dream, and if so, what is it to you?

DADDY: Well. My dream is just, have enough freedoms and be happy and enough things to eat, or I can do whatever I like. Travel wherever I want to go and stay wherever I want to stay.

ME: So right now at... age sixty-four? How old are you? You're turning sixty-four, right?

He laughs in response. When I ask his age again, insisting that he answer at least this question, he makes a clicking sound and lets out a dramatic huff so his bewilderment is unmistakable.

DADDY: Oh, you cannot calculate?

ME: You were born in 1949. You're sixty-three turning sixty-four. At almost sixty-four, do you feel that you've accomplished that, your sense of the American Dream?

DADDY: It's alright. You know, there is always something you're looking for all the time. That's how we keep going.

ME: Do you think there is ever a point where you're going to wonder whether or not you've made it? What is "making it"? Are you always pushing forward?

But doesn't it imply that we're working toward something? At what point do we stop and say "I'm satisfied"? Do you ever expect you'll reach a point where you'll think you're satisfied?

DADDY: Well, I think in order for people to keep on going they have to have a target, they are shooting toward it. If there is no hope, then there's no motivation to go forward.

There is always something you're looking forward to for you to achieve in order to get motivated to achieve that goal.

ME: So what are you looking forward to? What's moving you forward personally?

The GPS cuts in. *Drive 9.4 miles on U.S. route 6.* He is quiet. The gloves he bought on extra sale from Big Lots are a couple of sizes too large and turn his hands into paws on the steering wheel.

ME: Do you know what's moving you forward?
DADDY: Oh, yeah, sure. Sure. One step at a time.
ME: What are your steps?
DADDY: Doing whatever I feel like I can enjoy doing.
ME: Do you have a goal?
DADDY: No, not a specific goal.
ME: Are you happy?

Silence.
My father looks down. He glances out his window. His jaw twitches. For some reason, I stop filming and put down my phone.

10.

Years later, a friend and I were in her car on our way from D.C. to Baltimore when I noticed a string of missed calls from Caroline. This was unusual. When she didn't respond to my texts, I called her.

Daddy is in jail, she said, relaying that our father had called her husband, the only lawyer whose phone number he knew. *He asked us to bail him out.*

What? What happened?

That's all he said. His voice mail was so vague.

We only knew this: He was in a jail somewhere. We did not know which one, or why he was there. Just that he would like us to bail him out.

There were many logistical questions that made me suddenly aware of how unprepared we were to navigate this. Caroline was with friends somewhere in the mountains and without much access to cell service. Steph was at a conference in California. I had arrived at a friend's apartment and was standing in her back stairwell.

Was he OK? Would he be OK? My sisters and I texted one another all night, our group chat filled with links to bail bond services as we tried to minimize our fears with action.

Later, we learned our father's side of the story. As he told it, he'd had a disagreement with the tenant who leased the garage space he owned in Hartford. The tenant was a smooth talker, my father kept saying, and always promised to pay rent. But the business—a car wash—was not doing well, and the tenant fell behind in rent for months. My father, being *a nice guy*—his words—didn't want to go through the formal process of evicting the tenant. He offered a deal: Leave by the end of the month and all the missed rent would be forgiven.

My father claimed his tenant announced he had vacated the space. After my father changed the locks, the tenant said he had forgotten tire rims from a Porsche that he wanted to retrieve. They met at the property to discuss. *No. What you've left is mine*, my father insisted. *It's my property now. Pay me a little bit of your rent money, and I'll let you get it.*

The tenant called the cops on my father.

Three officers arrived and insisted that my father let the tenant into the garage to retrieve his belongings.

It's my property, though, my father kept saying. *Private property.*

They asked to see my father's identification.

No, my father said. *Show me a warrant. You need a warrant.*

He was probably shouting now—no, not shouting—just talking in his normal speaking voice. He'd watched enough TV to know that warrants were required; he'd watched enough news to know how badly this could have gone.

This guy, he's such an asshole, my father claims one of the cops said, as if he wasn't there or could not understand. They grabbed his arms and shoved him against a metal gate that covered the garage doors. They latched cuffs around his wrists.

In the process, the cops knocked my father's hearing aid and glasses from his head. The lenses shattered and the frame bent. His jade pendant of Guan Yin—which he and Steph had spent hours searching for in Flushing and Manhattan—snapped. I can only describe this in passive voice; it is less painful for these small acts of violence to have just happened. If I make myself imagine, though: A cop pushes my father's face into the grate and the jade splits; a cop steps on my father's fallen glasses and the lenses crack.

Later, my father told my sisters and me that someone stole his debit card, and while he sat in jail, they tried to drain his checking account. He discovered $800 in mysterious charges to Western Union and other local businesses from the time he'd been arrested. He was so certain the police were behind this: *They're bad guys. So corrupt.*

When my father recounted the story of his arrest to me, I hesitated.

Daddy, I said. *You need to be careful. You can't yell at the police like that. Or your tenants.*

Hey, my father said. His eyes narrowed. *It is what it is.*

That guy owed me $15,000, he continued to deflect, unable to hold on to the thread of our conversation in his fury. *If you don't pay for rent, you shouldn't get to stay.*

I wanted to dismantle his anger, to demand that he talk to me, instead of around me, but I had rarely been able to do so in the past. I shared in the same problem with him, never certain that my words had sufficiently reached him. I wondered then—maybe unfairly—if my father always had this coming. If his general belligerence, his agitation, his inability to maintain his properties had caught up with him.

Mommy, what did you think about this? I cannot tell if my questions stemmed from my own resentments about how he had parented me, or the transitive shame I'd harbored for how he had kept those buildings and treated his tenants. For the first time in my adult life, I was unable to look away. Certainly, all of this had existed before. But it was never *my problem*; it was *his*, and, by extension, my mother's.

✗

The cops set the bail at $75,000. We would discover later from a lawyer that the cops charged my father with disorderly conduct, for interfering with a police officer, and criminal attempt to assault a police officer. My sisters and I did not have $75,000 between us. It felt so ridiculous to Google *How to bail someone out of jail in Connecticut*, but I was a dozen entries deep into bail bonds services, sifting through customer comments, wondering if it mattered if a bondsperson was polite or not. Caroline hired the best-reviewed one on Google—4.6 stars, eight reviews, "Great service!"—and paid the bill on her credit card.

The following Monday morning, my father was released from jail. Without his glasses, he squinted as he walked into the early sunlight. His face was swollen and his cheeks were lined with scratches.

Disoriented, my father did not recognize C.J., and tried to rush away.

Mr. Chow, C.J. said. *I'm here to bring you home.*

My sisters and I were not in driving distance of Connecticut, so C.J. retrieved my father. I hadn't wanted to involve someone who wasn't a part of our family—hadn't wanted to take anyone else's help, hadn't mentioned to the friends I was with that this happened—but C.J. and I had been together for a couple of years, and he was living in New York City and could drive to Connecticut in just a couple of hours. It made sense.

At first, my father fronted for C.J.

They shouldn't have bailed me out, my father said, referring to me and my sisters. *They shouldn't have wasted the money.* (Later, he would call Caroline, outraged: *You let me spend an entire weekend in jail? What were you doing?*)

He'd eaten a lot, he told C.J., his tone light. There were the double-decker bologna sandwiches, with so much meat and no cheese. All of that white bread. The chocolate milk. The juice.

It was pretty good, my father said, impressed.

They drove to the garage so my father could look for his hearing aid and glasses. When they arrived, a group of men were hanging out in the parking lot near the market.

Are you going to let that skinny faggot fuck you in there, one of the men laughed.

The cops going to come and lock you up again? another said.

My father ignored them and retrieved his glasses. He dusted off his hearing aid.

He and C.J. returned to the car in silence.

Maybe, my father said to C.J., when they were a few blocks away, *we can go to A-dong? It's close by, and also, it's Lunar New Year.*

I had forgotten in this frenzy that it was Lunar New Year. The weekend's events were an especially inauspicious sign for what the next year would bring.

At home, before they began to cook, C.J. documented my father's injuries, taking photos of his broken glasses and close-ups of the bruises and scratches around his eyes and cheeks. I'm not sure if C.J. knew to do this because he had just started law school, or if because he is generally meticulous and observant. His mother once told me a story, which I think about often when I imagine him with my father: When C.J. was a small child, his grandfather, who had Alzheimer's, visited them for a short while. His grandfather tried to peel a plastic banana, which was on the counter for decoration. C.J., who must have only been in elementary school, politely and quickly retrieved a real version of that fruit for his grandfather to eat. He had learned as a child how to quietly help in a way that disarmed shame.

In the photo that sticks with me, my father stands in front of a white wall. He looks beyond the camera, his eyes cast down and puffed, his cheeks scored with thin scrapes. His hair is long and covers his ears, the side part he's had for years still in place. He has not had a haircut in many months. This is the first time I've seen a photo of him without his glasses, and the absence of his wire frames makes him look gaunt and drained.

Afterward, my father and C.J. cooked the New Year dinner. They stood in front of the kitchen table in their winter coats with the back door open. My father lit incense for his parents, my mother's family, my mother, and Jonathan. He instructed C.J. to light his own sticks, and one by one, they bowed for each person.

X

For the next few weeks, and months, and years, my sisters and I take turns helping our father manage the fallout of the arrest. Caroline helps him correspond with lawyers; I ferry him to a court appointment to make sure he arrives on time; we all walk him through tangential situations that arise from this.

A few years and thousands of dollars later, my father's charges will be dropped and he will be put on probation. He begins to pay Caroline back for the bail bonds services, and the lawyer for the legal fees. Relatively speaking, he is lucky.

X   X   X

My sisters and I take turns with varying degrees of patience (Steph and Caroline, more patience and steady tones; me, no patience with my voice almost always bridging into a yell, my arms gesturing wildly, unproductively) trying to convince my father to do the many things that we think are practical or better for everyone.

For me, this includes selling his properties, since he clearly has trouble taking care of them; buying a reliable car that has four-wheel drive and brakes that don't feel like stepping on a bike pump, soft and clumsy; donating at least one of the remaining cars that sits on his driveway; cleaning out his house; selling his house and moving somewhere closer to one of us (Steph).

He waves me off each time.

This is my life, he says, smiling at first.

After a few minutes, if I keep asking questions, his face sours. He boxes his shoulders.

This is my *life*, he says again. His voice rises.

Yes, but, I say sometimes, when I think there is a point in trying to argue that his business is my business. *This is your* life. As if my emphasis on *life* will change anything. Years pass, filled with many versions of this conversation.

11.

On March 4, 1897, twenty-six-year-old Lon Dorsa was struck and killed by lightning in Nevada, Missouri, according to old newspaper reports. He left behind his wife, Neva, who, months after his funeral, had his body disinterred so it could rest in a custom tomb she'd ordered.

The tomb was made from a Missouri granite. It is massive. Twelve feet long, five feet wide, five feet high, one article says, and weighing around eleven thousand pounds.

But what is unusual about this stone is not its size. Dorsa requested a Bible be placed on top of where her husband's head would rest. And with a key, she could unlock and slide the Bible aside to reveal a glass pane, through which she could peer into her husband's face.

Notable also is that she kept a photo of him by his body.

"If the body should be stolen and another substituted, even a stranger could quickly detect the robbery," a local newspaper reported in 1905, when Lon Dorsa's grave had become a road-side attraction, "for all visitors, of whom there are hundreds yearly, compare the features of the dead man with those shown in the picture."

It is unclear to me what Neva Dorsa wanted: to preserve her dead husband, or to watch his decay. Her grief reminds me of kusōzu, an art form in Japan from centuries ago that depicted human corpses—most often women—in varying stages of decomposition. In the illustrations I've found, the body's degradation is graphic—skin bloating, blood leaking, animals scavenging, skeletons appearing. It is quite stark and, for the unprepared viewer, disconcerting. But the form itself draws from beliefs in Japanese Buddhism and demands that people reflect on the temporal nature of life and the physical world. In a way, that could be similar to what Dorsa had hoped. Though that might be a generous read.

X

The Memorials:

The pots of bamboo and ferns that you carefully tended to in the living room remain in their same spots. They are browned and yellowed and long dead. Cobwebs coat their stems. My father has his own plants on the kitchen windowsill that he's grown over the past decade and a half: some type of lime-green vine that coils across three pots and sits atop a bed of dried-out leaves. They stand so tall that they threaten to block out all of the light.

The holiday cards that relatives sent my father that he tapes on the family room door and leaves there for decades. Some of them are from when you were alive and are addressed to you.

Your clothes that he's left in your closet. The soiled dresses and underwear and pants still in the laundry basket. The sweaters layered with dust.

The Memorial:

In 2013, we installed a new tombstone over your grave. Caroline had been working for nearly a decade at that point. She'd saved up enough money to start the process all over.

We want to get Mommy a gravestone and I can pay for it, Caroline told our father. Steph retrieved our old designs and worked with Yi Ma to find another monument company.

OK, our father said. *Sure, whatever you gals want.* He shrugged and didn't say anything more on this topic, though when my sisters and I returned home to discuss the sketches, he hovered near us, curious.

Your tombstone was the appropriate red that you remarked that you liked. India red, the color of brick. We showed restraint when we designed it this time. The English words were carved in a respectable serif font. We included at the bottom of the stone, barely visible, as if to keep this phrase close to your physical remains and between just us: *We love you as high as the sky and as deep as the ocean.* The marker had your name in Chinese, as well as Daddy's; his was painted red to indicate that he had not yet passed. Jonathan's name sat in the middle—Jonathan Love—with his dates of birth and death. We had not yet transferred his ashes to your grave, and they remained by our father's fireplace. But none of us mentioned Jonathan as we gathered from our separate lives and stood before your new stone for the first time, brimming with self-congratulations, relieved that we'd done this for you.

×   ×   ×

Was it that my family didn't think we had to carry out your last request, or had we forgotten about it altogether? Our rationale is lost on me now, but I remember thinking that with the installation of your tombstone, we'd finally done all we could to appease your spirit. All our debts had been paid, as if that were possible.

PART FOUR

1.

Daddy, you told me recently about a dream you had of your mother the night she died.

This was nearly fifty years ago. You had just started graduate school. You say you don't know if it was a dream, feeling, or vision.

You felt a strange wave settle over your body. You kept repeating that word. *Strange. So strange.* Maybe a pang of familiarity. *Strange.*

My mommy was there, you said. In English, you still refer to parents as someone's "mommy" or "daddy," leftover vocabulary from when my sisters and I were little. Your mommy was trying to tell you something.

In retrospect, you think she was saying goodbye. But you didn't learn of your mother's death until months later and long after her funeral.

When you relay this story, I realize I hadn't known that you'd believed in spirits all this time. *When it's dead, it's dead*, you said previously about your son, which could have easily applied to your wife or your mother or your father. The way you talk about death makes it sound inevitable. I notice how your hair has thinned more each time I see you; how you hardly speak in groups or at restaurants because, you have admitted, you can't hear what anyone says; how, as you eat, you chew carefully, afraid your teeth might break.

In this same conversation, you speak of how you still dream of my mother. Your wife. This shouldn't have surprised me.

Oh, wow. What do you dream of when you dream about Mommy?

Just how your mommy used to be nice, you say. But how? Nice how? Once, I asked you what you liked about her, and you said you liked that she took care of you. She sliced you fruit for dessert. You missed that. When you told me this, I was offended. I thought this meant you believed that the women in your life owed you this type of care. That it was our duty. But look at me, so suspicious of intentions. Almost anyone with a Chinese mother knows this small gesture usually means love.

But trying to remember the contours of the dream, you couldn't say, didn't want to say, what it was about. A wall had sprung between us again.

Just, I dream of her.

X

All of these years later, when I am an adult living on my own and I don't see or speak to you much, you never feel far. You surface in my thoughts frequently, ghostlike but not quite. Daddy, all of this time, perhaps I have been trying to preserve the memory of you, too. To hold you in my mind; to try to see all the ways light reflects off of your image. Or maybe I'm readying myself for when you move on to the next life, what I could not do for Mommy. (Mommy: I have long known I'd never be able to truly *know* you. That knowledge came quick like a bolt of grief, until it just *was*.)

I'm walking the dog through Red Hook while visiting C.J. in Brooklyn. The dog—who does not like strangers, who barks until the person leaves—mistakes a man for you. Over the years, he slowly warmed to you. Probably because each Christmas, you dehydrated sweet potato for Steph and Caroline and me to give to our dogs. You saw that a pet store sold a bag of those for $9.99. *Ho gwai*, you said, horrified. *People pay that much for eight pieces?*

When visiting me, you sat on my floor and broke off bits of potato for the dog.

Sit, sit, sit, roll over, you said. You thumped a hand on the floor like a WWE referee and the word *sit* came out like *shit*. You demonstrated and dropped onto your back and rocked left and right. You repeated this for hours. I laughed each time. Didn't correct you, didn't tell you to stop feeding the dog so much fiber. The dog still refuses to roll over.

But on the sidewalk, this man has your same build, silvered hair, and tanned complexion, though he looks Hispanic. He shares your cheekbones, skin mostly taut over his face. Sun freckles. Dressed in a loose collared T-shirt and linen pants with sandals that are a couple of sizes too large. He shuffles like you.

The dog wags his tail and tries to jump on this man in greeting.

I smile apologetically and pull the dog down the block.

That's not who you think it is. I say this loudly and mostly to myself.

This must be a vision of you. Some alternate version from another world beamed into my reality. It unsettles me for days after, this potential of your future apparition. *Strange, so strange.*

In our conversation about your dream of your mother, I asked if you had any idea what you'd want for your own afterlife.

I don't know, you said. *Good people come back as people. Bad people come back as animals.*

It wasn't clear if you thought of yourself as good or bad, or if you were uncertain.

But what about ghosts? Who becomes spirits?

You didn't say anything for a while. But then you began a vague rant about how these sorts of Taoist, Buddhist beliefs were used to control people.

But what would you want *to return as?*

You found another way to hedge. You brought up *Democrats these days and their socialist agen—*

Daddy. What do you want to come back as?

You guffawed. I waited, am waiting, for your answer.

2.

One recent spring, I call my father to let him know that one of his neighbors has passed after a long sickness. This neighbor is the father of one of my childhood friends; quiet, affable, never cared if we were loud when we played inside. She texts me to share the news and mentions the memorial service. When I relay this information to my father, he says he'd like to attend.

Oh, really? I say.

Sure, sure, he says. *It would be the nice thing to do. We're neighbors. Do you want me to drive up—*

—Besides, I've never been to an American funeral.

A funeral for white people?

Yeah, he says. *This is my first time. It'll be really interesting.*

OK, I say. *But please don't treat this like some anthropological experiment.*

And then: *I'll come too.*

I have not kept in touch with this childhood friend over the years, and I have no explanation for attending, other than this seems like the polite thing to do. But in retrospect, her father was born the same year as my father, and any grief is lonely. I drive from my apartment in D.C., and on the way, I pick up ingredients to make lasagna. One for the bereaved family, and one for my father.

When I arrive at my father's house, I have to pee. I run to the second-floor bathroom. For the past decade, this has been the only toilet I've used in the house, but now one of the valves has partially disintegrated and doesn't connect right. Every time I flush, water rushes onto the floor. I never remember this will happen. I run from the bathroom and call for my father like a child.

You always forget, he says.

I know. I'm flustered and blushing and hoping my piss doesn't spring back at us. I pile towels onto the floor.

X

I worry he'll slip on one of the envelopes on his carpeted stairs and cascade down his steps, or that as he climbs onto the exercise bike in the family room to complete his morning routine, he will hurt himself, and nobody will be there to help. Just Jonathan's ashes and the photos of our dead relatives. The house will take him. I look into setting up cameras so that I can check on him, but I don't suggest this to him because that feels like admitting some sort of defeat.

He's only in his early seventies, Steph says. He's not like her high-risk geriatric patients in New York City who have Alzheimer's or dementia and are unable to live on their own.

Yeah, I say. *But he's so alone.*

You can't change how he lives, Caroline tells me.

But can't I? Can't I? Can't I?

I am cloying and trying to fight this. Is this my mother's fight, now, or mine? But maybe that was both of our mistakes.

X

The therapist in high school had told me, *The only person you can change is yourself.*

She said it so often that I would finish her sentence, not bothering to mask my exasperation.

The only person you can change—, she'd say.

—is myself, I know! I said.

For many years, I misunderstood this and thought this meant that I wasn't allowed to be angry—that I could not be mad at my father or the way he parented me, or didn't. I had thought this was meant to assign blame, and that my problems were my own.

The way you grieved was through trying to figure out how to survive, the high school therapist later tells me when I am an adult, and I visit her to recall these memories.

The way he grieved, I thought of my father, *was through trying to figure out how to survive.*

What is grief, if not the act of survival? How can it be anything else but persisting through an enormous loss? After my mother's death, I learned quickly that I would need to parent myself or find parents in others. It became easier over the years; not because my father became more nurturing, but because I'd become an adult.

It's radical acceptance, another therapist once told me. *You don't have to like a situation, but you can also accept that it's true and your reality.*

But wasn't that giving in? I kept asking, over and over.

X

After the funeral service, my father and I huddle in the kitchen to assemble trays of lasagna. We boil noodles and sauté zucchini and garlic and onions and simmer them in tomato sauce. While I wash my hands, my father dumps spices into the pan.

I stir the sauce and notice tiny dark beads scattered throughout.

Did you put sesame seeds in here?

No, he says. *Oregano.*

Oregano? These look like black sesame seeds.

I bring the spoon closer to the light. They are tiny bugs. Drugstore beetles. Dead.

Aiiiiya, these are bugs, Daddy, I say, suddenly taking on my father's mannerisms. *We can't give this to them.*

He examines the pan. *Why not? Protein.*

We just can't, I say. *Look. They're everywhere.*

Still peering at the sauce, he nods.

OK, let's just use this sauce for the lasagna you'll keep, I say. *I can make a new one for the neighbors.*

He draws his shoulders toward his ears.

Whatever you want, he says. *I'm an easy guy.*

And we're Cantonese— I let my voice trail to tee my father up for his favorite joke.

Cantonese people, he says, already laughing. *We eat everything with four legs except for tables.*

I throw out his jar of infested oregano and study the flecks in the sauce. The beetles are small as punctuation, and their spindly six legs are nearly invisible.

I crunch the lasagna. *Sesame seeds. Protein. It's fine.* When I can't continue chewing, I put my fork down. I wash my plate in the sink using the soap he's diluted with water and I return it to the dishwasher where they're stored. I swish my mouth with tap water. I'm worried he'll notice the shame I've tracked into the house like grime, that my inability to eat the bugs means I've become soft and wasteful. I can't tell which would be worse: him seeing my refusal to finish my plate as a sign that I think I'm better than him, or if he thinks it means the opposite. It is amazing how returning to this house is stepping into a warped time machine; the parent-child dynamics remain the same, the behaviors that, for much of high school, I grew to accept. Now, though, I fight against this resentment, the way neglect stings and hurts and feels, often, personal: both like a condemnation and reflection of how much love one deserves.

After, I take the other tray of lasagna—the one without the insects—to our neighbor's. I ring the doorbell just as I did decades ago. As it was then, the house remains immaculate, sparsely furnished, though the wheelchair lift they recently installed now sits unused. Our neighbor says thank you, and I offer my condolences, knowing what it feels like to be on the other side of the door.

I turn back to my childhood home and take it in from my neighbor's yard. The rhododendron bushes have grown tall enough to cover the first-floor windows and nearly the second. My father has tried to paint the garage doors to match the house. He wants to cover the rot. But instead of a soft, sandy hue, he coats the doors in an electric yellow, which only draws the eye to the splintered, disintegrated wood. He has also hacked the weeping cherry tree in the center of our front lawn into a seven-foot-tall obelisk. This was my mother's favorite type of tree, and when I was in elementary school, my family surprised her with a sapling for Mother's Day. Each spring, she led me and my sisters to coo out our front windows when the blooms emerged. Without the drape of branches, the trunk is menacing. My father had explained: *It was dead, and needed to go.* But why not get rid of the whole thing? Why leave such a tall stump there? He had shrugged. It was a lot of work. He didn't have the time.

3.

I send my sisters a selfie: I bite my bottom lip and curve my top one back to expose my teeth. My eyebrows push toward my hairline. I follow it with our favorite question, borrowing our mother's language.

ME: What doing Chow girls?

Before I transferred to my company's New York bureau, I made this face often to a friend whose desk was near mine. We threw this expression to one another when we fizzed with stress, didn't know what to say, or were sorting through some shaky opinion— usually from a man—that had been stated as indisputable fact on Twitter or in an article or in a meeting. We sat behind our monitors and flung this look at one another in lieu of words, or frustration. One summer, one of the interns noticed and lobbed it back to us. Charmed, I told her it was a face my family made, but I didn't elaborate. I didn't say that each time I made it and they returned it, or vice versa, that I felt like I'd passed my mother on to them. A virus, or a gift. I couldn't tell.

My sisters respond within the hour with their own photos, Steph at a hospital in Manhattan between seeing patients, Caroline near her office in Silicon Valley, steeped in the California sun, her hair now blond, her most recent dye washed out. Our expressions are photocopies of a photocopy of a photocopy.

X   X   X

Occasionally, my sisters and I export this roll call to our family group text.

CAROLINE: Daddy, what about you, what doing?

Days later, likely missing the previous messages, he surfaces and sends us a photo of two cherry tomatoes from his garden on a metal plate.

DADDY: This is the first harvest of my cherry tomatoes. 😃

I have never seen our father make our mother's teeth face; I have never seen him jut out his top incisors to tuck over his bottom lip, eyes bulbous. Maybe he's self-conscious about all of the dental work he needs, or maybe he feels it's not his to make.

But I can picture it: He unlocks his jaw, his gums red and swollen. Usually gnashed when around me, but now softer, fang-like, playful. The gaps in his teeth reveal his fillings and his need for dental implants. How is it that in my own pretend, my father still cannot afford to fix his teeth, and I still cannot figure out how to help him.

X

My father invites my sisters and me to Connecticut to sort through our mother's belongings. He's read an essay that I've written about a pair of my mother's old Sperrys that he gave me right after I graduated college. The leather was faded, the soles with no traction. When I slip them on, I think about the last time she might have worn them, her feet sweating, my toes and heels digging into the imprints that hers left behind. This scares me, though, being so close to her. I want to tell him about this twist of longing. I want to ask him if that's what everything in his house does to him. Instead, I write about it.

Maybe you gals want to come to the house, he says after reading the essay, *to see if you want any of your mommy's stuff?*

Yes, we agree. It has been nearly five years since we all have been home at the same time. We book our flights for August and don't ask questions. We will hang out in Connecticut, then New York, where we'll explore the city and watch the free tennis matches at the U.S. Open. This will be our family visit in lieu of seeing one another for the holidays, we agree. We're also planning a trip to Cuba in March. The U.S. government eased its sanctions on Cuba, making it possible for Americans to travel there. My father wants to look for his father, he tells us. Steph, who is still trying to get pregnant, will not join because of Zika. But Caroline and I say enthusiastically, offering to plan the trip and foot the bill: *Yes.*

Inside the house, my sisters and I rifle through our mother's closet. We work quickly and quietly as we tug our mother's dresses and shirts from their hangers, and her bras and panties from the laundry baskets and drawers. We drag them across piles of newspapers and receipts that have accumulated, my father's towering stack of *Wall Street Journals* that date back to the 1980s tucked behind his door.

Try this on. I toss a shirt to Caroline. It has navy flowers and a pale polka-dot print.

How's it look?

It fits you really well, we say. The slopes of her shoulders are like our mother's.

Steph pulls on a lilac dress with rough, wide stitches, and she passes me a matching one that is highlighter yellow. *This looks hand-sewn.* We later learn that Yi Ma made it for our mother. The fabric is stiff and tight along my back and hugs my hips.

We sort through more of her clothing. We try on dresses and create piles that we'll each take. We discover our mother's old dildo. Our father, who lingers in the bedroom in order to inspect our progress, is near Steph when she comes across it. At her reaction, he steps closer to take a look. She flinches and tosses it into the trash. Of course, all of this fazes us. But we are too mired in the dust and the day to react. We will laugh years later.

Look, Caroline says. She holds our mother's engagement ring up for Steph and me to see. It is a single diamond on a silver band. Simple, not flashy. Our father chose it. My mother once mentioned to me that Gung Gung had complained about the diamond's imperfections, and that he'd called my father cheap. Caroline has discovered it mixed with loose change on a vanity in their closet, hidden underneath our father's faded grocery store receipts.

I thought she was buried with that. I return to the image I'd always conjured of my mother in her casket, her plasticky hands clasped, the ring hugging a swollen finger.

She must have gotten too bloated and had to take it off when she was sick. Caroline looks at me. *Are you and C.J. planning on getting engaged?*

Oh. I am suddenly embarrassed.

You can have it, if you want, Caroline says. *You should take it.*

Ah, I say, shifting on my feet. *We've talked about marriage more generally and what that looks like for us, yes—*

*I'll hold on to it for now, but if anybody needs it—*Caroline wags her eyebrows—*you know where it is.*

She slides the ring onto my finger. The band is bent on one side, and this groove unnerves me. I begin to sniffle and reach for a tissue to wipe my eyes, then nose.

Allergies, I say to my sisters as I take the ring off. *All the dust.* They don't call me out.

It takes two car trips to haul all of our mother's belongings to Goodwill. We drag them to the drop-off area and are in the car when an employee begins to haul her bags inside. I run back and stop him. *Wait, I forgot something,* I say, rabid as I unknot a bag and pull out a shirt. It does not matter to me which one. Just the act of retrieving and keeping something of my mother's is enough.

X

Mommy, you linger everywhere in this house. So many of your belongings hold memories of you. You always crouched around corners, ready to jump out at us when we passed. You liked to stand very still by the coat closet while I used the bathroom next to it. When I emerged, you leapt from the shadows.

Aaahhhhhh, you shouted.

Aaaaaahhhhhhh, I screamed. I flailed and shrunk from you as you enveloped me in your arms.

X   X   X

I catch myself doing this to C.J. now. When he is about to walk into a room I am in, I inch to a spot where I think he cannot see me. I hide, not moving my body, and then, gleefully I launch myself at him and grasp for his arms.

I gotchu! I collapse into him in a fit of laughter while he yelps.

Kat. He clutches his chest and catches his breath after I've frightened him near the top of his apartment's stairs. *One of these days I'm going to accidentally elbow you in the face or something.*

I gotchu, I gotchu, I gotchu, I chant giddily, not wanting to stop.

In our childhood home, you are folded inside each of the drawers and the closets. These are your ultimate hiding spots. When we least expect it, you, as a memory, vault from them. A jack-in-the-box.

X

The next day, Steph, Caroline, my father, and I glide down the Merritt Parkway to New York. Behind the wheel, I navigate us into Brooklyn along I-278. Manhattan bursts into view across the river.

See that? I point past Caroline's lap out her window. This sight stuns me each time, the way the towers stretch upward and the sky wraps around them. It is mostly glints of sun refracting off metal, all confident show. A *look at how beautiful I am* strut onto an enormous stage. How could I look anywhere else with this sight before me? How could I not feel an opening of my self when I see this cityscape? There is also a familiarity here, the way the skyline encompasses so much, including the Mahayana Temple at the base of the Manhattan Bridge, our histories merging with a new possibility.

That trip and drive and seeing the city with my family, it gives me for the first time in years a flash of a feeling—an awe, a calmness. I'd experienced it in high school driving across the Connecticut River, and then in Seattle looking out at Portage Bay. I'd always thought it meant I was home. But it is the slow spread of radiant joy. A gentle hope.

Later, my family huddles in C.J.'s apartment. He is out of town and has offered it up to us for the weekend. I will move in with him here in just a few months, bringing me closer to Connecticut.

Steph and Caroline share the bed, and my father stretches out on an air mattress in the living room.

It's kind of weird to sleep in C.J.'s bed, don't you think? my sisters say while they help me stretch a set of clean sheets across the mattress.

Oh, it's fine, I say. *There's no other space.*

I drag the couch cushions into a closet that has been repurposed into a cramped office, and I sleep on top of them. In the middle of the night, when the cushions keep sliding apart, I crawl into the bedroom and stand over Caroline.

Move over, I say to her. I poke her shoulder until she stirs. *Hey, move over.*

Agh, Sticky, Caroline says, her eyes still closed. *It's too hot. There's no room.*

Please. Just do it?

She scoots closer to Steph, and I squeeze myself onto the edge of the bed. I try to give Caroline space, but eventually, I spoon into her and she lets me. My drool soaks into her pillow.

It occurs to me that those couple of days we spent at our childhood home might be the last time we'd be there together. Family makes a home, yes. Or maybe we make a mausoleum. I don't know. I don't know. I don't know.

4.

Caroline and I are in Havana with our father walking along Barrio Chino, a few blocks of restaurants and apartments. My father keeps remarking about this city: *This is like China thirty years ago.* And: *Everything is always rationed in Communist countries. They keep watch on their people.*

He says *This is like China thirty years ago* so many times, he must be wading in memories of his own childhood or imagining his father's life here.

We meander into the various associations' buildings. These tongs are organized by the surname of their members and the villages in China from where they came. At the start of Chinese migration to Havana, Barrio Chino and the Cuban Chinese population quickly became structured around these tongs. They provided space for the thousands of men to share meals, organize politically, send remittances to China, and find housing. Most of these tongs backed China's Nationalist leaders and raised money to fight the Communist Party.

Here, my father moves as though the more animated he becomes, the more likely people will recall his father. Frenetic forward motion, doesn't take off his backpack or introduce himself, just waves a portrait of his father and punctuates the air with his sweeping hand gestures.

Before leaving for Cuba, I took the portrait of my grandfather that my father had found in Toronto a few years earlier. He had set it on top of his TV in the kitchen, near the other photographs of our ancestors. I made copies so we wouldn't lose the original, and I tucked them into a folder to carry with us. The photo shows my grandfather in a suit with fat lapels and a striped tie. He is ageless, and could be anywhere between twenty and fifty. His thick hair is slicked back and it glistens on top of his head. Full, well-groomed eyebrows. Full, wide lips. Cheekbones so prominent they cast shadows. When I saw this photo for the first time, I texted my sisters. *How come his eyebrows are so nice? How come we don't have his cheekbones, geez.* He has the same eyes as my father. Undeniably a handsome man.

We meet up with a documentary photographer named Pok Chi Lau, a former professor at the University of Kansas whose work focuses on the Chinese diaspora. I'd heard from various people during my research that Pok Chi would be here helping another American woman who, in a previous visit to Havana, found her grandfather's remains. Pok Chi and I had corresponded for months about my family's own search, and once we arrive in Havana, he introduces my family to Mitzi Espinosa Luis, whose grandfather immigrated to Cuba in 1918 from Guangdong Province.[7] She works at Min Chih Tang, one of the tongs that provides lunch to the elderly in Barrio Chino, and she patiently listens to my father run through the brief list of what he knows about his father.

Mitzi studies the photo of my grandfather. She does not recognize his face from the records, but then, there are many men and many faces. She invites us to look through Min Chih Tang's logs later in the week.

My father continues his boisterous approach with anyone he meets, on the street, at restaurants, in the fluorescent lobbies of other tongs. He turns strangers into hesitant confidants, and Caroline and I trail him, offering to hold his backpack or papers. He asks things such as, *Did this person know anything about his father? Could he look in their record books? Could they help us to look in their associations' crypts in the cemetery?* He relays the story that I've only recently learned—how a man he had met many years ago in Toronto's Chinatown claimed he knew my grandfather. When my grandfather died, the man said, he had a mistress who was pregnant.

So I might have a brother or sister, my father says, his eyes wide in excitement when he gets to this part of his speech. He shares all this in a mix of Taishanese and English, and he drops in a couple of Spanish words for effect.

Excelente, excelente, he repeats, whenever somebody agrees to help. *Gracias, gracias.*

Many people provide my father with the same fact—that Cuba had only an estimated two hundred Chinese people remaining, this number shrinking each day. When Fidel Castro came into power, he restricted immigration from China, and many already there married Cubans.[8] We spent the morning sitting in air-conditioned offices of association leaders hearing details like this, fans sucking the perspiration off our arms and thighs.

X

Casino Chung Wah is one of the largest tongs. From the street, it is nondescript; inside, it has an expansive ballroom with a stage flanked by teal doors. The lights are off, and we introduce ourselves to Guillermo Chu, who is in his eighties and works at the association.

We pore over registry books nearly a century old in search of my grandfather's name: 周開傑. Guillermo tells us that at the start of the revolution, he hid these records from the Communists. They destroyed any property they could find, he says in Taishanese, my father translating for me and Caroline. Inside the book, there are pasted photos of young men in their twenties and thirties, and inscribed next to the pictures are their names in Chinese and Spanish, their village in China, and the date they enrolled in the association.

Caroline and I bend over these pages and compare these faces to our grandfather's. We examine the cheekbones, the side parts, and the grim smiles. We study their names.

Maybe your father used a different name here, Guillermo says to my father. *Maybe he was a paper son.*

Maybe, our father agrees. *Maybe he had a different name.* He looks at the spread with a renewed energy.

He asks Guillermo to retrieve more books. Guillermo is frail, and shuffles slowly down the hall to the small closet where they're stored.

Excelente, excelente, my father says as he tries to follow him, but is politely waved away.

We discover a name that is partially like my grandfather's, with my grandmother's surname: Kwan Hoy Kit. My father leans closer, volume increasing, gestures widening. He keeps repeating what Guillermo has just told us, about my grandfather potentially being a paper son, how this could mean my grandfather could have become *anybody.* He is hopeful, whereas I find this information overwhelming and devastating in its inconclusiveness. A woman emerges from another room and observes us for a few minutes.

He has to go, she says eventually. *He has a meeting.* She escorts Guillermo by the elbow from the room.

OK, my father says. He sees Caroline and me, our eyebrows raised. *What? He's busy.*

No, I say.

No, Caroline says. *You were yelling, Daddy.*

Yeah, I say, unhelpfully. *You kept asking him to walk back and forth to that room to get more of those books. That lady probably thought you were going to give Guillermo a heart attack.*

Bo-o-ooy, my father says. *No, that's not what happened.*

Yes it is, I say.

Ai, you girls are just exaggerating.

No, I say, my own voice rising. *You were yelling. You're always yelling.*

✕

For my own recollection, I document some of this week with an audio recorder, and in one of the sound files, we are at a restaurant. My father is chatty and animated by the possibilities this trip might bring. He mentions Steph and how she wished she could have joined us.

Is Steph your favorite daughter? I tease.

No, I don't have favorites, he says. *All of you have different personalities.*

Am I your third favorite daughter?

He pauses, and then falls into a cavernous laughter.

Bo-o-ooy. 'Am I your third favorite daughter.'

✕

The myth I told myself was that we were in Cuba because of the easing of sanctions and Caroline and I finally had money to pay for our father's travel. Never mind that we could have cut up to Canada and circumvented those rules years before if we'd really tried, or that our father could have scraped together money himself. In truth, we were there because he was old. He wanted to see the place where his father lived and passed before he died.

These tongs also took care of the funeral services of their members, who were buried in a cemetery about five kilometers from Barrio Chino in tombs special to their association. After a few years, the association would clean the bones and send them to the Tung Wah Group of Hospitals in Hong Kong, which coordinated the return of the remains to the deceased's home village.

But because of the Japanese occupation of China and the country's civil war, as well as Cuba's own Communist uprising, bone repatriation became difficult. My grandfather, despite his intentions, remained in Cuba indefinitely.

When I call Evelyn Hu-DeHart, a scholar of the Chinese Cuban diaspora and a professor at Brown University, in search of more context about my grandfather's life, she invokes this proverb: 落地生根落葉歸根. Or, lok dei sang gun, lok yip gwai gun. It translates to, she says, "Put down roots when landed, return home when leaves fall."

X

A few of the cemetery's caretakers lug a wooden plank to the first crypt. Havana's Chinese cemetery contains a mix of aboveground tombs and underground vaults. Following the funeral, the deceased's body remains in one of the tombs above ground for two years, after which their bones are transferred to a box and stored in one of the vaults.

Pok Chi has helped us arrange with a few of the association leaders to unlock their burial vaults. The cemetery itself is a sliver of the Vedado, modest compared to the nearby Necrópolis de Cristóbal Colón. Still, I feel overwhelmed as we prepare to enter the crypts, which some of the tong leaders have allowed us to search.

The caretakers joke with me and Caroline.

Married? They wink. Caroline says yes. I tell them no because I'm not sure how to say in Spanish that I'd just gotten engaged.

They slide the plank beneath the rectangular stone that sits on the mouth of the vault. They heave and pry it upward. This reveals crumbling stairs that lead to a damp and dark underground space.

My father flips up his sunglasses, but still, I cannot read his expression. He's waited seven decades for this. I hand him a flashlight and hold his backpack while he lowers himself into the crypt. Caroline and I follow, constricting our limbs so that we won't scrape the walls and the stacks of concrete boxes that surround us. They are the size of milk crates, in varying conditions, some of them more than a century old. Painted on their sides are numbers or names in Chinese or Spanish—all part of a system we haven't deciphered. That is, if they are labeled at all. They extend rows deep, and accessing the furthest ones would require a game of life-size, high-stakes Tetris in order to bring the hidden ones forward. I can't tell how large this space is; I can't see past the boxes to determine the boundaries. I can only squeeze myself into the narrow aisles between the rows, trying not to knock over the remains of the men who had been conscripted into indentured servitude, the laborers after, and their descendants. Some of the boxes gape open and greet us with exposed skulls and bones.

Before we boarded the plane to Havana, I tried to prime my father's expectations. I thought that this was smart and dutiful. I had spent months reaching out to professors or anyone who might have contacts in Barrio Chino, and quickly understood we might be disappointed.

What are you expecting to find? I'd asked my father at the airport.

I don't know, he'd said. *We might not find anything. I just want to take a look.* Resignation crept into his voice.

Someone at the cemetery tells us that some Cubans believed the remains of Chinese immigrants held magic—so they smashed the tombs and snatched these remains to procure their power. If this is true, I wonder if that desecration was worth it, and if they felt any such luck. Or if they were haunted by what they did.

My father disappears into a chamber of another tong, this one, an aboveground mausoleum. Its floor is chaotically tiled with a mound of femurs, skulls, and tibias—all stained ivory shards—protruding from one another. I follow him, confused that I am not shrinking back from this, like I did from the sea bass, like I did from the image of you stuffed in my living room. Now I am inured, though my feet are heavy and my limbs press closer to my sides. How many humans are in this pile? How, and when, did these people die? My father strains to read the names on some boxes across the room. I see him hesitate before the heap of bones, but finally, he sidesteps over the heap. One of his sneakers knocks into them and creates a skeletal wind chime.

I don't want to breathe next to those bones and their fragments and their dust. I'm afraid that if I inhale, I'll suck in the particles of the dead. Their spirits, too. But I do exhale, then inhale: a gentle must, sweet hay. This is the scent of decay and bones. And maybe, somewhere, my grandfather.

We repeat our search through new vaults half a dozen more times, whatever ones we can get unlocked. The opening of the crypts, the descent into a permanent hell, the furtive browsing of bones.

Dazed, my legs carry me around the cemetery grounds. I can't walk into any more tombs. I can't step over any more cracked skulls. A stray dog I've been watching all morning trots along the perimeter and toward me. A splinter of bone hangs from its mouth.

Jesus Christ. I back from the dog and look for my sister.

At some point, we have to stop searching. We have been at this for hours; we are becoming dehydrated and hungry. But neither Caroline nor I want to tell our father to stop looking, so we wait by the cemetery's front gate. Fifteen minutes later, he emerges. We watch him weave between the memorials.

I cannot tell what he is thinking. The way his head swivels, his lips pursed and his expression strained, he looks like a lost child. Appropriate, since he is looking for his father. It is humid and sticky, and he pants a little. There are too many unlabeled boxes; too many piles of loose, clattering remains.

This might have been easier if I'd planned our timing better. We had tried to schedule our travel to Cuba to coincide with Barrio Chino's Ching Ming celebrations. I'd heard from Pok Chi that the Chinese cemetery would be open for the public to observe the grave-sweeping holiday, and that many of the tongs' members would be around. This made it a convenient time for us to look into the tombs and ask any questions. But I had miscalculated my family's flight schedule, and we missed the festivities—and in my father's eyes, an opportunity to meet all of the associations' leaders and members. My father cites this misstep whenever he becomes discouraged or agitated. *You tell me that professor say to get here for Ching Ming*, he had said earlier, will say a few more times. *If we had gotten here earlier, we would have had an easier time getting people to open the tombs.*

I want to take a picture, he says, *and then we can go.*

He digs into his backpack to retrieve his digital SLR and attaches an enormous lens. It is the only lens he ever uses, and it requires him to stand a dozen feet back to take close-up portraits, which feels fitting, a distance required for his version of intimacy. He hoists it to his face. The twist on his mouth deepens, and I wish I could take a photo of him right here, this way, in this dusty cemetery. His camera clicks, still audible when he walks to the street to take in the cemetery's front gate and sign.

Afterward, we return to Barrio Chino.

I want to come back here, our father tells Caroline and me. She offers him water from her bottle and patiently waits as he downs most of it. His conviction has grown in the past half hour since we've left the cemetery: If he tries hard enough, if he works hard enough, if he pushes himself enough, he can find his father. He wants to sift through more records. He wants to convince more of the leaders to unlock their tong's vaults. There are so many people whom we haven't been able to meet in this short week. I can see the calculations flickering, as he tallies time and money and his own endurance.

OK, Caroline says.

OK, I say.

There is not much else to say.

x   x   x

Later, I sit with Caroline and my father in a plaza near our hostel. We purchase Wi-Fi cards to check our email or text people back home. I open a new rendering of the engagement ring that C.J. and I are designing using my mother's diamond. We were engaged less than a month earlier, and though I'd worn my mother's ring for a few days, it was too uncanny to feel the indent of her finger and to wear a symbol of my parents' marriage. There was too much weight I could not carry; I worried that my mother's ring would only remind me of what I feared our relationship would become—mortgaging each other's well-beings, as well as our own, in service of an emotional debt we could not afford. So it seems healthier, wiser, gentler, for C.J. and me to instead create a symbol of hope. It strikes me also that we are here in Cuba because my father's parents were only physically together for *two years, eight months*. My grandmother had wanted to join her husband in Havana, but he needed her to stay in China to care for his mother. The thought of this burns. All of that longing. What is a marriage, if it is not a partnership born out of affection, respect, and a closeness that makes life more navigable? Anything else feels lonely.

At dinner, we each order a mojito because, we figure, rum is made here and a cocktail is about the same price as a bottle of water. My father, who is not much of a drinker—who likes to tell the story of the single time he got drunk, on a rare business trip when he guzzled a complimentary bottle of wine in his motel room—downs his in a few minutes. His cheeks redden, and he shifts in his seat.

It's so hot, he says. He swishes the ice from his glass and sips the last dregs. *We should have gone somewhere with air-conditioning.*

Drink some water. I push my bottle toward him.

No.

You need to drink water. You're dehydrated.

No. He glares this time.

Here, put this against your wrist, I say. I slide his glass, dewy with condensation, toward him. *It'll help you cool down.*

Stop telling me what to do, he says. He stands abruptly and pushes back his chair, its legs squeaking, his voice loud and ringing. *You're always trying to tell me what to do.* The restaurant falls silent. Someone at another table says the word *Chino* and follows it with laughter.

You're drunk, I say.

He rushes from the restaurant to pace outside.

You're always so bossy, Caroline says. I'm amused and grinning because I am also dehydrated and a little drunk, and I want to provoke her and say, *I've always been a bossy asshole, which is a Chow thing.* But I shut my mouth. We finish our dinner, ignoring one another.

From our table inside, we watch our father stand under a street lamp. His arms cross his chest. He's waiting for us because he cannot remember the way back to our hostel. I point this out to Caroline, and she rolls her eyes at me and pays our tab.

As we walk, our father remains a few steps in front of us, not making eye contact or acknowledging us. Every few blocks—our voices purposefully light so as not to sound pushy—Caroline or I say, *The map says straight,* or *I think we have to turn right here.*

Caroline, also flushed with rum, records a short video on her phone and occasionally breaks into a giggle. In the video, the two of us sheepishly follow our father in the dark, the edges of smiles cracking onto our faces, all the while trying to guide him down the street.

x   x   x

The next day we hire a cab for the thirty-minute trip to Playas del Este. It is a vintage car from the 1940s or 1950s, and we are briefly thrilled by the novelty. But every time we drive over a bump, we lurch toward the roof. We spend the entire ride tense and quiet as we brace ourselves against one another.

We arrive at the beach in the early evening just as other tourists fold their lounge chairs and return to Havana.

Wooow, my father says, still thinking about the drive. He whistles. *That was really something. I thought we were going to die.*

He draws out the word *die,* and the three of us make the same laugh.

He walks along the edge of the water in his swimsuit, his two jade necklaces swinging against his chest—new ones, from another day spent in Chinatown with Steph—his arms folded. He watches the waves lick his feet with the same scowl he used in the crypts. Nearby, small children splash, and a couple embraces.

Look at Daddy frowning at the water, Caroline says. She takes a photo of him on her phone.

I'm wearing a dress I've borrowed from her, but I wade into the ocean. Warm as a bath, the sand doughy underneath my feet.

Do you like this? I ask my father. *This is nice.*

The water has good buoyancy, he says. He is suspended on his back and looking at the sky. He remains still while the waves prod him along. When I was little, he taught me to swim in a pond not far from our house. Facedown in the water, he helped me kick up my legs and blow bubbles, gamely ignoring the duck poop as it floated by our heads. He showed how if I let myself stay still, if I trusted that water could be forgiving, it would catch and hold me. *Stretch your arms out wide. Your legs, too. Close your eyes and hold your breath so you don't inhale the water.* In that moment, it was like there was nothing he couldn't do. *It's called dead man's float,* he'd said. *You don't need to do anything. You just float.*

I didn't understand then where the name originated. Suspended in the ocean, I do now. In a flash, I picture the country taking him like it took his father, those waves sweeping him out to the depths of the sea, swallowing him whole, his parents and my mother watching from high above in the sky.

I grab on to one of his ankles to keep him from bobbing further from shore.

Then I let go, and I allow the waves to cradle me.

5.

My father and I are in a hospital in New York, in the same neighborhood where my mother died fourteen years earlier, waiting for Steph to give birth.

Steph texts updates to me and Caroline, who is in California. The surgery is delayed because Steph has sent nurses scouring the floor for another cesarean drape; she wants the curtain that will separate her from the doctors to be translucent plastic so that she can watch her baby's birth.

Caroline and I text Steph back in our group chat: *Wow. Hardcore.*

And then, to one another, Caroline and I message: *OMG.* 👀

X

Days before Steph gives birth, I dream I'm on a road trip with her, our father, and Caroline.

We wind through a mountain road toward a place that feels like home.

I gotta pee, my dream-self calls from the back seat. Real-life me must have drunk too much water before bed.

Can we stop soon?

We pull into a gravel lot where a dozen other cars are already parked. Signs for restrooms point to a narrow path in the woods, which dips into gullies on each side. One by one, we make our way carefully down the trail. Steph brings up the rear. She takes wide, deliberate steps and holds her enormous belly.

Just a few more days, I think in the dream while I rush along and leap over tree roots.

In the next flash of dream: I wait with my father and Caroline by the van for Steph to return from the restrooms. Families emerge from the trees to their cars. Suddenly, someone shouts.

Bear! A man yells. *Bear!*

A guttural roar—perfectly engineered in a studio for some feature film—sounds in the woods.

And then a voice: *Run!*

Steph is in the middle of a group of tourists. She looks around, bewildered.

Hurry, a teenager tells her.

I'm hurrying.

But this isn't a dream—no, a nightmare—unless the obvious, terrible thing happens. As Steph runs to us, she trips and tumbles down the ravine. The bear bounds after her.

X

In my earliest memory of my mother, she has recently returned from the hospital and reclines on the couch. I'm around four years old. I climb onto the cushions and throw myself at her in want of an embrace. She winces, but does not say anything.

Careful, Chinchilla, Steph and Caroline say as they pull me back. *Be careful with her stomach. It has all those stitches.*

They gesture to our mother's belly, though they mean her uterus. In retrospect, this must have been when my mother had her hysterectomy. As a child, I assumed that she was still recovering from when she had given birth to me, all those years earlier. I was not quite wrong.

Steph had mentioned many times when she was trying to get pregnant that she wished she could ask our mother questions about her own births, how her body had changed, how it might have resisted.

I want to fill your silence in this early memory with what I know now. I want to ask you if all of your deliveries felt like reclamation— both of your body and of your mother's. She was afraid to have you; she was told that your birth might coincide with her death. You must have feared having your children, but you weren't scared to mother. It strikes me now that you wanted to inhabit your own negative spaces with a fierce, unfiltered attention and affection. In defense of your history; in reaction to your history; in honor of your history.

And your history is part of mine.

She always say, you are her heartstrings, Yi Ma tells me in a recent conversation. *You girls are her heartstrings.* I imagine your heart as still able to be plucked and played, that the three of us daughters have inhabited it and are helping it pitter-patter into a beat, the same as you have for ours.

X

From her hospital room, Steph's husband, whom I will refer to as Stephen King in honor of my mother, sends the family group chat photos of their baby. Their son is swaddled on Steph's chest, the two new parents smiling.

He also includes a photo of Steph seeing her baby for the first time. The doctor or nurse's gloved hand, still bloody, gently holds her son against the surgery drape, close to Steph's face. The baby is red and screaming and healthy. Steph sobs in relief, her chin wrinkled and eyes pressed closed.

6.

I trace the lines on my palms with my pointer fingers.

When I was little, my father told me that I had hands like his and my mother's.

So unusual, he said at the time, showing me the lines on my hand as though he could read my future. *You're part Daddy and you're part Mommy,* he said as though this was something he and my mother had worked very hard to make happen.

One of my palms has two lines that meet in a hooked flag between my thumb and pointer finger. The other has three lines that do not run into one another.

I can't recall which is like my father's, and which is like my mother's. My sieve brain leaks all of the important details. I have to check and double-check facts I should easily remember, and still, I am afraid of getting it all wrong.

I tilt each hand to the right, then to the left, trying to discern more of what these creases might symbolize. The gold from the ring that C.J. and I had made glints. Do my sisters have palm lines like this? What about Jonathan's little hands?

I take a photo of my right palm, the one with a flag that stretches toward the crease between my thumb and pointer finger. I tap out a text to my father.

ME: I always forget—I have two different lines in my palms. One hand is like yours, the other like Mommy's

ME: What do your palms look like? Do they make a flag?

I include the photo. My father responds the next day, after I've forgotten I've sent the message.

DADDY: The other one. All my three lines are not connected. Your left hand is like mine 😄

Your left hand is like mine. The one with the lines that do not touch. Did he know that from the image? Or did he always remember?

I take a screenshot of the exchange. When I can't remember again—in just a few weeks, and then again in a few months, and then in a year—which hand is like my mother's, and which is like his, I pull up the screenshot and stare at my palms.

7.

On an early April afternoon, my father sends the family group chat a text from Havana. He's been there for a few days, and it is the first we've heard from him since his arrival. So much has happened in the two years since Caroline and I last visited Cuba with him. C.J. and I have gotten married and we have moved from New York and back to D.C. Caroline has taken to planning elaborate family trips for us. Steph has had her baby.

DADDY: We find the bone box. Will carry back the ash with me 😃

He includes a photo of a lone box that the cemetery's attendants helped him haul from a crypt. His father's name is painted on it. 周開傑.

He follows this message with a photo of his nephew Denny and a man from Barrio Chino they'd befriended, both of them standing by the vault's mouth, their hands clasped behind their backs in patient wait.

ME: This is really great Daddy. How do you feel?

DADDY: Good.

Silence until he returns to the U.S.

X

Here is what happened, as he tells me a few weeks later—complete with some of his best digressions—when I am passing through Connecticut for work.

When he arrives in Cuba, my father is held up at the José Martí airport because security wants to scan his camera. It takes so long that he misses the Ching Ming festival at the cemetery.

The next day, with his nephew Denny—his brother's eldest son—he resumes the familiar process of walking all over Barrio Chino from association to association. The pair sits for hours at various restaurants or Casino Chung Wah or Min Chih Tang, chatting with strangers. They meet up with Mitzi, whom my father has been corresponding sporadically with over the past couple of years.

(An interlude about a restaurant: *They said the seafood is good, so we order fish and curry chicken. And rice, wow, the rice is so bad. Probably two or three days old. It's very hard. And the curry, probably they don't have the spices, so it's not spicy at all, it's just so-so, the fish is so-so, not really that fresh, although they claim it's fresh...*)

Early in the week, my father and Denny are at Min Chih Tang sifting through donation records. Denny had recalled seeing one with his grandfather's name many years ago when he was in Havana on vacation, but he couldn't remember where he'd seen it. My father keeps returning to this fact. Mitzi helps them flip through booklets until they discover a war bond indicating that my grandfather had sent $20 to China to help fight the Japanese. It did not list what association he belonged to, though, and for this reason, my father only allows marginal excitement.

We still didn't know what tong he belongs to, which we need to know what crypt to go to.

Still, the record has the address of a dormitory listed, which my father and Denny walk to in order to see where my grandfather once lived. The building is not far from Barrio Chino and, if I have the correct address, appears from my research to be a hostel.

(On the topic of a restaurant in Barrio Chino that my father went to on his first night in Havana, as part of a Ching Ming celebration with some members of the various Chinese associations: *We find out this pizza in Viejo Amigo is very good, the price is very good. They have cheese pizza, a combo pizza, and ham pizza or whatever pizza, it's really good. And the price is not too bad. I think cheese pizza is only $7, $6.50. Chicken pizza is only $5. And the soup—chicken soup! It's only $2.50 and very big chunks of chicken.*)

The next day, Denny and my father meet with the president of Chi Tack Tong, who my father says is a *very powerful* person in Barrio Chino. María Elena Hung has agreed to meet with them at the association's building and accompany them to the cemetery, where she'll unlock the tong's crypt. Denny and my father flip through an album and discover a leaflet that shows Hoy Kit donated $300 to help construct Chi Tack Tong's building, which cost $24,574.39. Ecstatic, my father poses afterward for a photo. He sits in the association's president's chair—a throne—looking thrilled and wearing his nephew's hat.

X   X   X

(An interruption to discuss feelings: *Wait, when you were looking through the book, were you anxious that you'd find it?*

Yeah, when I found it, I say, '*Oh, geez! It's here.*'

Were you excited?

Some people donate $500. See? Two Chows donate $500. And also, Ng and Choi donate $500. And my father also donate $300.

When you saw this for the first time, what did you feel?

Oh, I find him. He actually exists in Cuba. And then he donate $300.

Were you happy?

Well, at that time, I'm happy that I find him, that he exists in Havana. In Cuba. Because that time before that I cannot find his name.

Did you think he didn't live in Cuba?

I know he live in Cuba, but I thought maybe he used a different name or that the Communists take over and they destroyed the record. But I know that the record exists because Denny said he saw it.)

With this new information—a confirmation, really—the next day, they visit the Chinese cemetery with María Elena.

There, inside Chi Tack Tong's crypt, my father walks along the rows, taking in the names and the bones. Denny notices boxes that are wedged in the back, and he can see that one of them, partly obscured, has characters that resembles his grandfather's name painted on its side: 開傑. Could this be his grandfather's box?

He shouts to my father. Hastily, they kick into action.

The cemetery crew methodically shuffles the boxes so they can extract the one that Denny has spotted. My grandfather's full name in Chinese: 周開傑.

That's it, my father says. He and Denny yowl euphorically. My father bursts up the crypt stairs and into the afternoon light.

x x x

Inside were the bones of my grandfather, Chow Hoy Kit, ivory and browned at the edges, accompanied by a faded photo. The photograph was possibly there for posterity; something practical, another form of identification. It makes me think of Neva Dorsa and the photo she left of her dead husband next to his decaying remains.

My grandfather's photo is torn slightly at the bottom, though remarkably preserved considering its age and that it was stored among human remains. He is dressed in a light-colored suit, maybe linen, with a striped tie. His pants are baggy, though pressed sharply down the middle of each leg. He stands next to a pillar and his hand rests on it, his expression soft. My father had never seen this photo before, and this full-length image of my grandfather is a remarkable discovery on its own.

X X X

(On the unfortunate reality of a broken bone box: *When [the cemetery worker] was moving those boxes, one flimsy one, a more recent one— I think it's metal—and that metal thing fell apart. And all the bones fall on the floor and after they start moving the boxes, some guy bring another metal box to put all those bones back in again. But I think after they put it in, I don't think they put any names on it. So whoever comes for that thing, they won't know who that is.*)

My father arranges for the bones to be cremated. He picks up the ashes from Chi Tack Tong, along with an urn.

You should fill out some paperwork to transport the remains back with you, someone tells him.

But that would take time that my father lacks. He decides it is less risky to bring the ashes home on the plane without letting anyone know.

You should take the remains, his nephew tells him. He is concerned about transporting them without the right records.

How did you get them on the plane? I ask. On a recent family trip, I watched my father froth with indignation, arguing with airport security as they scanned his camera bag while my sisters and I tried to calm him. He kept getting pulled aside for additional screenings and he worried he would miss his flight, his agitation growing.

I carried them, he says of his father's ashes. *See, they're right there.*

We are in the family room, and he gestures in the direction of a dusty rattan couch that's covered with piles of discarded mail, magazines, and empty cardboard boxes. At its base sits a backpack and a pair of blue jeans that's been rolled into a ball.

Where? I say, standing to scan the room.

He picks up the jeans and unfurls them to reveal a mass of toilet paper. He unravels the toilet paper to show me a trash bag.

Here, see? He points at the bag, which I understand to be make-shift nesting dolls containing my grandfather. *Denny had an extra bag for garbage, so I put ash in it.*

He laughs, and tells me that he used all the toilet paper from the inn to wrap around the trash bag of his father's ashes. When he went through customs at the airport, the officer made him unroll the wad.

Did they care about the ashes?

No, they care more about the urn, he says. *They thought it was a vase! They want to scan the urn but not the ash. Ha-ha, boo-ooy. It was really something.*

My father, always so scrappy and thinking he's pragmatic. I don't want to assign sentiment that isn't there, but I wonder if my father did not want to risk being parted, again, from his father before he had the chance to reunite his parents. A twinge of pride surfaces; this is a better reaction than recoiling.

Do you want to put them in the urn? I ask. It is about a foot and a half tall with a pointed lid, coated with a thick, black glaze with a gentle yellow-brown splatter across its top curves. I could already picture us standing in the kitchen by the sink, trying to use a funnel to pour his father into the urn.

No, he says. *Why should I? We're going to bury it soon, and it's easier to transport like this.* He gestures again to the bag.

Eventually, he says, he'll bring his father's remains to Toronto to bury with his mother. His nephew Denny has already called the cemetery in order to figure out potential dates. At the mention of these plans, I glance at the metal container filled with Jonathan's remains. My father has moved it to rest on his fireplace mantel. The tin box sits between a portrait of my mother and the photographs of my father's parents. I can't look away.

X

When I return to D.C., I walk circles in my apartment with frazzled, distracted energy. I keep finding myself in the bedroom or kitchen, certain I am there to retrieve something, only to forget what I needed. Compulsively, as if this is what I've meant to do all morning, I pull three joss sticks from a drawer. I'd bought them a few months earlier for Lunar New Year, when C.J. and I cooked a spread for friends, lighting incense and joss paper before the meal.

I do not have a permanent altar set up for my mother or our other relatives, but then, neither did my parents, all of us making do. While the incense smolders, I sink to the floor and remain seated on my heels. I had always thought that my family did not pray. For much of my childhood, I considered the burning and bowing a gesture rather than an act of communication. But I see now, watching the smoke spill out the screened door, that this as an invocation of the dead's spirits, of my mother, my father's parents, and Jonathan.

They are here with me, if I allow myself to feel their presence.

Before my mother died more than a decade and a half ago, she asked to be buried with Jonathan.

Sure, sure, sure, we said. After we laid my mother to rest, we had Jonathan's remains turned to ash. But we balked when it came to the burial.

Now my father had done something my sisters and I considered impossible: fulfill his mother's unspoken request and reunite his parents in the afterlife. There is a sting that accompanies his loyalty to his mother after all these years. "You know what the Chinese think is the saddest feeling in the world?" a mother writes in a letter to her young son in Ken Liu's short story "The Paper Menagerie." "It's for a child to finally grow the desire to take care of his parents, only to realize that they were long gone." This hurts. It is true, though. *The saddest.* But then, I take a small comfort in my family's belief that the dead become spirits, and that after their passing, we tend to our loved ones to provide them the comforts we never could in life. And yet, here we are, my mother's last wish evaded.

For years, I mistakenly thought that bringing Jonathan to rest in Fairfield meant scattering his ashes. I feared what it would mean to hold his fragments, and I worried what unknown feelings this might provoke inside of me. I did not realize that the cemetery required that ashes be buried—that I would not have to feel his dust between my fingers—though my sisters and I accumulated other excuses, anyway: We couldn't gather the family in one place; a reburial of a small box is still relatively expensive; we had other family matters. When really, we were afraid to face our mother.

After the incense finishes burning, I lie on the living room floor for another hour. Eventually, I pull out my phone and look up the cemetery where my mother's remains rest, certain that the time has finally arrived.

8.

The week we open your grave to reunite you with Jonathan, July is July. It thunders up and down the East Coast, like God or the gods or goddesses or whoever—it could have been you, Mommy, for all I know—tromp on the floors of their apartments to make our sky rattle.

Steph and I pick up Caroline and Yi Ma on our way to the cemetery in Fairfield, and we arrive at the same time as our father, a downpour stilting our movements. Our father gives Caroline, whom he hasn't seen in a while, a pat on her arm. I clutch pots of sunflowers that we'll plant later, and I raise them at him in greeting. We'd chosen the sunflowers because they were bright and cheerful, and we thought you might like them; we did not consider how tall these flowers grow and that if they thrive, they will dwarf your grave.

Steph distributes umbrellas from her home. Mine has a large logo from a wildlife nonprofit, along with photos of a polar bear, a cougar, an otter, and a wolf on its panels. Steph holds a frilled one that is lime green with tiny cockatiels, blue jays, toucans, and macaws, its handle a tropical bird. My father clutches one with red maple leaves. Caroline shares with Yi Ma, and theirs is outfitted with a panda.

Nice umbrellas, huh. Caroline gestures at the kitschy collection to break the somberness.

We laugh.

For much of the hour-long drive here, Steph and I were quiet as she steered us down the highway and through the rain. Her son was asleep in the back seat. Suddenly, Steph began to talk about how after having a baby of her own, she didn't understand how our mother could do so much. How tired she must have been. Steph started to cry, trying to keep her voice soft and low so she wouldn't wake her baby. She said she thought of our mother this way every day.

That is what it means to lose someone, understanding how, after all these years, memories shift and shape us. How we cannot exorcise someone as much as we try; we must learn the ways in which we preserve parts of them in ourselves.

$$X$$

On top of your grave, a cemetery employee has left a small table for an altar.

I take out my joss sticks and I dump a bag of rice into the tin holder to keep the incense upright. My family forms half of a circle in front of your grave as Steph soothes her toddler on her hip, one of us holding an umbrella over her. I hand out three sticks to each person and thumb a lighter.

There is something communal about the rain. It forces us to pass our umbrellas to one another, my family crowding around whoever lights their incense in order to shield them from the downpour.

There is an easy way we slide into this without speaking, all of us in anticipation of one other's movements.

This reminds me of your funeral. A storm whipped through the cemetery and soaked our family as we lowered you into your grave. At thirteen, I thought that the volatile drama of the weather fit our moods, and that it was punishment. Now, I see the symmetry in the storm that appeared at your funeral and the one here at Jonathan's second burial. The sky splitting open has heralded your presence.

X

A few months after burying Jonathan, our entire family will travel to Toronto. Steph, Caroline, and I will rent a house in the city, forming our own unit. Our father stays with Denny and they hustle around the suburbs, meeting with old friends from Hong Kong whom my father hasn't seen in years.

The second day there, we convene at Mount Pleasant Cemetery and we bury my grandfather.

My father's relatives arrive with a whole poached chicken, steamed buns, oranges, and wine, which we lay out as offerings. There are so many Chinese graves in this cemetery; our cousins tell me that multiple times a year, they visit the graves like this, and I listen with envy. The snow is heavy and wet, the temperature dropping as morning stretches to afternoon. We take turns tucking a cousin's Chihuahua into our jackets, which confuses Steph's son, who repeatedly chirps *gau gau, gau gau*, throughout the ceremony. His soft toddler voice is ambient noise. We huddle together in the snow. Steph, Caroline, and I notice that our father has been attempting to give a speech, but people are caught in their own conversations.

We notice Denny asking the cemetery manager to begin the burial, since we have other graves and other relatives to visit.

Our father would like to say a few words, Steph interrupts.

Daddy, would you like to say thank you? I address him.

He looks around, his expression more indeterminate than usual behind his sunglasses. He opens his mouth. Closes it. Opens it again. Snow catches on his hat, a brown and orange one he's worn since the eighties. His relatives continue talking among themselves.

Yeah, thank you for coming, he begins. Caroline hushes everyone and gestures at our father.

It's been a long time since my father passed away and then my mother passed away. It's always my mother's desire to be with her husband a final time, and we have this opportunity to bring him back here so that they can be together…It's been a long journey. His voice warbles. *I finally bring his ashes back so that they will have a chance to be together forever. So, I hope that they will be rest in peace. Thank you.*

For the first time, I see my father cry.

Steph steps forward to comfort him. She pats his shoulders gingerly, tentatively. Caroline approaches them, uncertain, though stops a couple of feet away. I stand back and make noises of sympathy. I tell myself that having all of his daughters crowd him might embarrass or overwhelm him. But this could be another one of my excuses. I cannot bring myself to comfort my father, and I do not know how to close the distance between us as I witness this wave of grief work its way through him. For more than seven decades, he has shouldered his and his mother's longings. Though I see within him now a bittersweet relief.

The next day, my family gathers for breakfast at a cousin's house. She is Denny's daughter, and she's made a pot of congee and bought dozens of logs of yau char kwai that I help her reheat in the oven. We are finishing our last bowls when our fathers try to rush out the door. Neither of them say goodbye.

Hey, my sisters and I call after our father.

Hey, my cousins say to Denny.

You're trying to leave without saying bye? I am entertained by my father and his nephew's likeness.

Oh, they both say, stepping back inside, momentarily chastened. My father waves a hand, which I take as a gesture that means goodbye or that he can't be bothered.

I'll see you gals later, OK? His other nephew has more angelfish to give him, my father explains, and he needs to get them now, since he only has another day left in Toronto.

Don't you want to bring some food back home? a cousin asks my father, piling leftovers into a takeout container.

No, he says. He is baffled that someone would suggest that. *I can't bring food across the border. That's illegal.*

What about the angelfish? Another cousin calls after him. *Isn't that illegal?*

My father laughs instead of answering, and gives the room another flick of his wrist before leaving. In a couple of days, he will drive across the U.S.-Canada border with a small cooler in his trunk, the fish sloshing around in plastic bags.

X

In Connecticut, my family stands before your grave, about to bury your only son.

X   X   X

Your husband speaks first. I can barely hear him and can only translate part of what he tells Jonathan.

You grow up to be big up there, I think he says. I hear the word *Ah Ma* and I wonder if he's asking his mother to help take care of his son.

It's Steph's turn now. She shifts her baby in her arms. We arrange ourselves to light her incense and position her under an umbrella.

All the thunderstorms this week made me think of how, when it thundered when we were little, Mommy used to make us play hide-and-seek, Steph says. *We never wanted to because we were scared, but she thought it was so funny. And she always could find us. Mommy always knew how to find her kids. I like to think that Jonathan and Mommy were always together.*

Hearing this last part, I envision a new image of you shortly after your death: You stand in a brightly lit space with a white background, some corny movie depiction of heaven, complete with cotton-ball clouds. You rush through a crowd. You shove a few other freshly dead people aside.

Watch it! They give you a perplexed look, as if to say *How did this lady get into here?*

Where's my son, you demand. Someone brings Jonathan to you. When the two of you are reunited in body, or whatever spirit-form resembles *the body*, you finally soften. Your limbs no longer have the stiff, arthritic movements of the Ginger Ghost and the plastination has vanished. Jonathan is a newborn, never growing from what we knew. And though that might not be how the afterlife works, I like this image anyway, because it gives you the chance to mother him like you'd always wanted. Fifteen years later, you can finally listen to his coos. You snuggle your face into his.

x   x   x

I'm sorry it took us this long, Caroline says after she lights her incense.

I address Jonathan. *Our parents loved you very much,* I say. *Thank you for being a big brother to me, even as a baby, even as someone who only passed through this world for a few hours. Even though I didn't get to spend time with you, you were, and are, loved.*

After the incense burns, and after we dig into the wet earth with our fingers to plant the flowers, not caring anymore that we are soaked, we sprint to the cars.

Yi Ma suggests we take a circuitous route home so that your spirit and Jonathan's won't follow, and so that you understand you have to stay at the cemetery.

If you pull into this parking lot and then turn around, that'll work. Yi Ma points us to a nearby pharmacy across the street. *It's good to go inside.*

We can buy candy here, too, she adds. The candy will not be wrapped in white paper with nickels, like they were at your funeral, but they'll work.

I dash into the store, my dress drenched, and the air-conditioner wicks goosebumps onto my arms. At the cash register, my sisters and I study a row of sweets and debate which to purchase. Skittles? M&M's? Mentos?

Mentos, Caroline says. *She always liked Mentos.*

In the car, I slide the pink and yellow discs from their sleeve and distribute them among my family. Sometimes, when you picked me up from daycare, you'd toss me a package of Mentos that you bought from the gas station. While I sat in the back, slowly letting them dissolve on my tongue, you glanced at the rearview mirror.

Ho ng ho sik ah? you asked.

Ho sik. I smacked my lips and offered to feed you one.

Now, with a couple of Mentos melting in my mouth, I imagine you standing by Steph's car. I can just about see you clasping one of her umbrellas. You wave from beneath a flash of blue and green with painted zoo animals on the canopy. Your face is clear, and your lips pull up at their corners and your eyes blink in your mischievous way. You are trying to wink.

For a moment, I want to call out, *Hey, don't go.*

But during thunderstorms when it was your turn to hide, you ignored Steph, Caroline, and me as we cried for you to end the game.

Come get me, you whooped while you ran through our house. Although we were frightened, we gripped one another and followed the crackle of your laughter. We knew that if we looked long enough, we would find you.

Your eyes meet mine in the side mirror. You study me, as though you are saving the contours of my face and locking them into the vault of your own memory. I cannot tell how long this goes on, if in some alternate universe, it is still happening. Memory is capital. It is love and survival. And hope. It is all we have. You wink again. To return the gesture, I shut my eyes, slow and long. When I open them, you are gone.

AUTHOR'S NOTE

Language—reaching for it, exploring it, trying to understand it—has always been how I've made sense of myself and the world around me. Language provides a connection to *something* or *someone*; language is a shield against loneliness. Improving my Cantonese will always be a present tense effort, both because I tend to take my time with picking up languages, and because I don't believe one ever stops learning how to *speak*. My understanding of this dialect reflects my family's migration from Hong Kong to the United States, and the choices my parents made when raising my sisters and me; it reflects that my mother was only able to find Chinese schools in our suburban Connecticut that taught Mandarin, instead of Cantonese; it reflects our isolation from family and the distance between our little unit and a larger community. And with what has unfolded in Hong Kong in recent years, in many ways, this desire to learn Cantonese and its contexts seems especially urgent. It is an expansive act that brings me closer to my family and the many ways in which we engaged—it gives me another way of being open to our past and future.

I enlisted the help of Jaime Chu, an editor and translator, who patiently guided the Cantonese in these pages. We opted for common Cantonese romanization, then Jyutping if there was no common colloquial spelling. There are some exceptions. For example, according to some Cantonese speakers, my name and my sisters' names in Chinese, should be Ka Lee, Ka Lin, and Wan Lee, but my family always spelled them Gah Lee, and Gah Leen, and Wun Lee, and I wanted to reflect this detail in the text, since that seemed most true to my family's experiences. Also, when romanizing the Chinese, I chose not to indicate tones. This means that any homographs are not easily differentiated for the English reader.

X

In order to write *Seeing Ghosts,* I leaned on the scholarship and work of many others.

Chinese Cubans: A Transnational History by Kathleen López, *Diaspora and Trust* by Adrian H. Hearn, *Racial Politics in Post-Revolutionary Cuba* by Mark Q. Sawyer, *The Chinese in Cuba, 1847-NOW* by Mauro García Triana and Pedro Eng Herrera, and all of Evelyn Hu-Dehart's work, were instrumental in helping me understand Cuba's history with the Chinese diaspora. Thanks especially to Evelyn for the hours spent over the years answering my many questions. Madeline Hsu's and Lisa Yun's scholarship was also incredibly helpful.

The concept of racial melancholia and the trailblazing scholars who have written about it—Anne Anlin Cheng (*The Melancholy of Race: Psychoanalysis, Assimilation and Hidden Grief*) and David L. Eng and Shinhee Han (*Racial Melancholia, Racial Dissociation: On the Social and Psychic Lives of Asian Americans*)—gave me a vocabulary for something I had observed for years but was unable to put to words.

The following guided my research: Ellen D. Wu (*The Color of Success: Asian Americans and the Origins of the Model Minority*), Patricia Chu (*Assimilating Asians: Gendered Strategies of Authorship in Asian America* and *Where I Have Never Been: Migration, Melancholia, and Memory in Asian American Narratives of Return*), Russell Jeung (*Sustaining Faith Traditions: Race, Ethnicity and Religion Among the Latino and Asian American Second Generation*), Erika Lee (*The Making of Asian America*), Priscilla Wegars and Sue Fawn Chung (*Chinese American Death Rituals: Respecting the Ancestors*), Monica Chiu (*Asian Americans in New England: Culture and Community*), Rachel Poliquin (*The Breathless Zoo: Taxidermy and the Cultures of Longing*), and David Barton Smith (*The Power to Heal: Civil Rights, Medicare, and the Struggle to Transform America's Health Care System*). Yung Wing's autobiography (*My Life in China and America*), as well as the staff at the Connecticut Historical Society, were crucial. The work of Karthick Ramakrishnan, Janelle Wong, and Jennifer Lee of AAPI Data helped inform so much of my earlier reporting.

NOTES

1 **Part 2, Chapter 3:** This carving of young Cynthia Talcott was perhaps created with the help of a death mask, a sculpting technique that used casts of the deceased's corpse and was common in the Middle Ages until the nineteenth century. I learned about death masks when reading about Gustave Flaubert, whose story "Un coeur simple" (A simple heart) features a woman who so loved her parrot that she had it preserved and died clutching its taxidermic form. Also of note: Flaubert famously had a death mask made of his sister after she passed.

2 **Part 2, Chapter 4:** David Eng, a professor at the University of Pennsylvania, and Shinhee Han, a psychotherapist in New York City, wrote the book *Racial Melancholia, Racial Disassociation*. They argue that melancholia can facilitate resilience and hope. In one of their earlier papers, they write, "It is the melancholic who helps us come face-to-face with this social truth. It is the melancholic who teaches us that 'in the last resort we must begin to love in order not to fall ill' (Freud, 1914, p. 85)."

3 **Part 2, Chapter 19:** My father has similar views decades later, when the demonstrations in Hong Kong that demanded inquiry into the police, as well as full democracy and independence from China, were met with violence and tightening of laws from the Communist government.

4 **Part 2, Chapter 19:** My father did not know then—might refuse to acknowledge—that Wisconsin, the very state where he'd chosen his

college, would later have one of the highest rates of incarceration of Black men in the country. Or that in Detroit in 1982, a draftsman named Vincent Chin would be brutally beaten to death by two white men on the evening of his bachelor party. Witnesses testified that Chin's killers, who had worked in Detroit's auto industry, had said that it was "because of you little motherfuckers that we're out of work." Though Chin was Chinese American and had been mistaken for being Japanese, the outcome of that racism was the same—Chin's death. His killers would not serve any prison time. This case would become one of the most notable hate crimes in Asian American—*American*—history and is often cited in textbooks, just one of many examples of the insidious, xenophobic violence woven into the fabric of this country.

5   **Part 2, Chapter 22:** These days, I can't think about my father's restaurant and the one I worked in high school without recalling a conversation I'd once had with a law professor named Gabriel "Jack" Chin. I'd interviewed him because he had studied the ways in which lawmakers and union members had during Chinese exclusion, as he put it, waged a "war" on Chinese restaurants. There was a violence within his vocabulary that pointed to the direness of America in the late 1800s and early 1900s, how so many people had rallied to create a methodical and systemic attack on Chinese immigrants. These restaurants were considered by many white Americans in that era to be "dens of vice"—where white women were susceptible to moral corruption via booze, opium, and sex. The restaurants had become stand-ins for how society regarded the people who operated them.

6   **Part 2, Chapter 23:** Asians in the U.S.—and in particular those from East Asian countries—only ascended the so-called societal ladder when it became politically convenient or discrimination against them lessened, not because of some innate cultural work ethic or strong family values, as some conservative idealogues argue when trying to generalize Asians in the U.S. One example: The Magnuson Act of 1943, which allowed 105 Chinese immigrants into the U.S. each year, was signed into law during the backdrop of World War II, when

politicians in the U.S. worried that the Chinese Exclusion Act of 1882 would damage an allyship with China against imperial Japan.

7 **Part 4, Chapter 4:** Mitzi Espinosa Luis's story appears in *Chinese Cubans: A Transnational History*, an informative bank of research from Kathleen López, an assistant professor at Rutgers, the State University of New Jersey. Mitzi's grandfather, Francisco Luis—who had previously been known as Lui Fan—emigrated from China and lived in Cuba. He had two families—one in Havana, and one in Guangdong Province—and his older children in China referred to his daughters in Cuba as sanmei and simei, or third and fourth sisters. Mitzi, not long ago, traveled to China to visit the village where her grandfather had grown up, and was able to meet her cousins. I read about this transnational reunion with a longing.

8 **Part 4, Chapter 4:** Though the Cuban Revolution, writes Kathleen López in *Chinese Cubans*, "held the promise of better treatment for ethnic minorities . . . state revolutionary ideology and the loss of small businesses made it difficult, if not impossible, for Chinese and their descendants to actively engage in ethnic practices. On the other hand, unlike the situation in the United States, Chinese were not excluded from cultural citizenship in Cuba. The Chinese who remained on the island are simply never asked by fellow Cubans, 'Where are you from?'"

ACKNOWLEDGMENTS

Ancestors guided each iteration of this story, including the many versions that my younger self attempted. It feels miraculous to be here now after stumbling along such a circuitous path, similar to the one that I took to honor my family's ghosts. I finished writing and editing this book during the pandemic, amidst the protests against the police killings of Black people and the surge in hate crimes against Asian Americans. So much gratitude for the people who were endlessly buoyant and carried me through this.

Thank you to my mother, Florence Yu Chow, for teaching me both resolve and tenderness, and for propelling me to tell this story and so many more.

Thank you to my family for sharing their memories and becoming such an integral part of this process—especially when it felt hard or ma fan. Daddy, thank you for all those hours on the phone and FaceTime recounting family stories and helping me understand your history, and therefore, you—that time was a gift, and I will try to remember that I don't need an excuse to call you. Steph and Caroline, thank you for your unfiltered love and thoughtfulness, for reading early drafts of this book, and for mothering me always. I have immense gratitude for my mother's family, my yi ma, Kevin, Garrick, Garvin, Ivy, and many others, for their generosity in helping me understand my mother and her history. I have only love for my kau fu, who passed suddenly in the spring of 2020, and who taught me about the fierceness of caring so deeply.

Maddie Caldwell shepherded this book with wit, humor, and empathy, and understood from the beginning what this book could become. The rest of the Grand Central crew—Jacqueline Young, Matthew Ballast, Ivy Cheng, Morgan Swift, Tree Abraham, Albert Tang, Luria Rittenberg, Marie Mundaca, Lori Paximadis, Helen Chin, and so many more—gave this book a home and treated this story with care and respect. Jin Auh came on board at a crucial time and brought new life and energy to this project—thanks to Jin for the sharp insight and the tireless advocacy of this book. Thanks also to Elizabeth Pratt and the rest of the Wylie Agency, for the support during this process.

Many of my earlier personal essays would not have existed without Keith Woods's encouragement and the ways he challenged me to interrogate my writing. Our conversations about *Seeing Ghosts*'s many drafts at that little spot in Mount Pleasant were defining, and his feedback helped this ghost *haunt*. Thanks to Keith, especially, for leading me to one of this book's defining questions about what it is that we owe.

I am so thankful for Mariya Karimjee, our friendship, her rigorous feedback on countless drafts, and our daily check-ins about writing. Thanks to Mariya for telling me that writing a book was like a series of trust falls—advice I have returned to every day. Whew.

Thank you to LeiLani Nishime and Shawn Wong, who in my formative years at the University of Washington, took hours each week to chat with me about immigrant narratives and Asian American literature—and, crucially, to read my writing. LeiLani's guidance and friendship over all these years have meant so much, and Shawn's stories have remained with me.

ACKNOWLEDGMENTS

Thank you to my writing teachers: Blakeslee Lloyd and Tim Sanderson in Glastonbury, for reading the many handwritten poems and stories, freshly torn from notebooks, that my teenaged-self left on their desks with hopes for a critique; and Danielle Lazarin and Tony Tulathimutte, for leading classes at Catapult and through CRIT that gave me space to play with my fiction.

I have so much gratitude for Claire Tran, whose meticulous research helped me write the sections about Hartford. Thank you also to Jack Dougherty of Trinity College and Beverly Lucas, director of Cedar Hill Cemetery Foundation, for answering my various questions. Jaime Chu's keen eye and help with my Cantonese were crucial. Thank you to Mary Glendenning for pointing me toward archival material. Jay Venables, at many points, provided invaluable notes and guidance.

Thank you to my amazing crew of readers, whose encouragement and feedback shaped what *Seeing Ghosts* has become. Many of my favorite parts can be traced to your comments, and I am both so sorry and grateful for the friends who read a billion drafts of this book, including the pages that will not be published: Alison Grubbs, Stephanie Foo, Camila Domonoske, Leah Donnella, Lillian Li, Tobin Low, Caitlin Dewey, Tanvi Misra, Cathy Linh Che, Enkay Iguh, Ruth Tam. Thank you to Ariel Zambelich, Kiah Wagner, and Emily Bogle, for their visual expertise.

My sieve brain is surely leaking names, but so many people sustained me throughout this process through their words or advice or friendship: Nicole Chung, Rahawa Haile, Diana Khoi Nguyen, Ocean Vuong, Jacqueline Woodson, Reese Kwon, Elise Hu, Eyder Peralta, Nadine Ajaka, Lenika Cruz, Tuyen Nguyen, Lexie Krell, Joanna Nolasco, Kyle Kim, Tracie Hunte, Masuma Ahuja, and Kathy Tu. Each one of you lent a listening ear at a crucial time. Thank you to those who helped me recount memories—Lucas Anderson, Colin Gorenstein, Kristen Steenbeeke, Meg Dagon, and Peggy O'Neill, to name some—and to my friends and former colleagues at NPR who encouraged me to write this book, especially Shereen Marisol Meraji, Karen Grigsby Bates, Matt Thompson, and Alicia Montgomery.

Seeing Ghosts took shape at the magical Jack Jones Literary Arts Retreat in Taos, New Mexico, where I found strength and community—and so many incredible ghost stories—in Kima Jones, LaToya Watkins, Larissa Pham, Robin Beck, Nichole Perkins, Yalitza Ferreras, Lise Ragbir, Branden Janese, Morgan Mann Willis, Jenna Wortham, Meredith Talusan, Mona Chalabi, Conley Lyons, Destiny Birdsong, Yvonne McBride, and Hope Olaide. Thank you to Alexander Chee for creating the Yi Dae Up fellowship, and for being so generous with your words over the years. My gratitude also goes to Calliope Nicholas and Monika Burczyk for providing a gorgeous space for me to write at The Millay Colony.

An enormous thanks to Mitzi Espinosa Luis, Pok Chi Lau, Graciela Lau, María Elena Hung, and many others, whose help in Havana made the discovery of my grandfather's remains in Cuba possible. My family is eternally grateful.

Thank you to C.J., for being my best friend and creating a home within yourself for me, and for allowing me to make a home for you, too. I am so incredibly charmed by all of the new ways you make me laugh. I have so much gratitude to your family for welcoming me, and it means so much that you love my family as your own. Your love makes anything feel possible.

ABOUT THE AUTHOR

KAT CHOW is a writer and a journalist. She was a reporter at NPR, where she was a founding member of the Code Switch team. Her work has appeared in *The New York Times Magazine*, *The Atlantic*, and on RadioLab, among others. She's one of Pop Culture Happy Hour's fourth chairs. She's received residency fellowships from the Millay Colony and the Jack Jones Literary Arts Retreat.